The Red Pelican
Life on Africa's Last Frontier

Jon Arensen

ISBN# 978-9966-757-07-4

Published by Old Africa Books
A division of Kifaru Educational and Editorial Consultants LTD
PO Box 2338, Naivasha, Kenya 20117

Cover photo: Brian Arensen
Cover design: Blake Arensen
Sudan Map: Paul Shaffner
Chapter drawings: Kendra Inglis
Photos courtesy of Michael Lyth

Jon Arensen, PhD Oxford University, recently retired as Professor of Cultural Anthropology at Houghton College in New York where he directed Houghton's Tanzania Semester for 16 years. Before teaching, Jon spent over 25 years working in Sudan and Kenya where he did linguistic and anthropological research. Jon presently lives with his wife Barb in Fillmore, New York. Jon and Barb's grown children live abroad and have worked in Cambodia, Sudan, Kenya, Uganda and Mozambique.

The Red Pelican is the third book in what Jon Arensen calls his 'Sudan Trilogy.' His first book was **Drinking the Wind**, a memoir tracing the author's early years in Africa and ending with his time in southern Sudan among the Murle people at Pibor Post. It was here that the author first encountered stories about Kemerbong, the Murle name for Dick Lyth.

Chasing the Rain is the second book in Arensen's trilogy. It follows the life of a Murle man named Lado and his unquenchable thirst to know more about Tammu, the name for God among the Murle. Lado became a translator for the British military where he met Dick Lyth in 1941. It was Dick who answered Lado's questions about God. *Chasing the Rain* is based on an old manuscript Dick Lyth had written about the life of Lado.

Drinking the Wind, Chasing the Rain and *The Red Pelican* are all available from Old Africa books at www.oldafricamagazine.com, Amazon.com and other leading book sellers world wide.

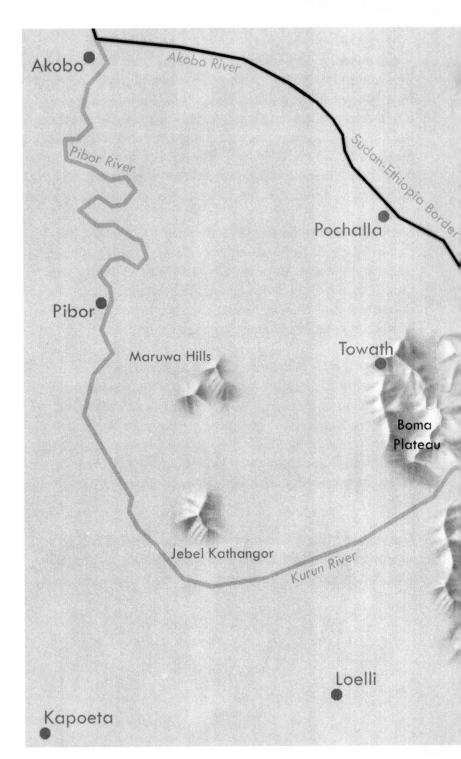

Akobo

Akobo River

Pibor River

Sudan-Ethiopia Border

Pochalla

Pibor

Maruwa Hills

Towath

Boma
Plateau

Jebel Kathangor

Kurun River

Loelli

Kapoeta

4

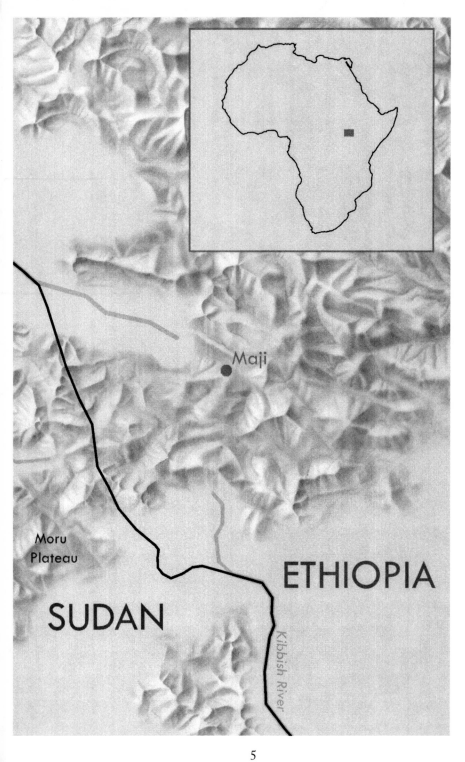

Maji

Moru
Plateau

SUDAN

ETHIOPIA

Kibbish River

Dedicated to my parents
Ed and Esther Arensen
who by their example inspired me to love Africa

Preface

On the great continent of Africa there is one location that has barely been touched by the outside world. This is a region of 80,000 square miles located at the confluence of Sudan, Ethiopia and Kenya. Although on paper all three nations have a stake in these borderlands, they are far from the major towns and their sheer remoteness means that none of the three governments has made any serious efforts to bring this vast area under direct control.

Part of the reason for the isolation of this area is the harsh environment in and around this pristine wilderness. It is made up of a combination of floodplains, deserts, rock-strewn mountains, and cold montane forests. Up until the present time there has been no easy access to this area. Approaching from South Sudan involves crossing extensive floodplains. In the rainy season this area is underwater and the sticky black clay is bottomless. Tough grass grows up to ten feet tall, making a virtually impenetrable shield. During the dry season the floodplains become a desert. The temperatures intensify and the yellow grass is burned. The black clay shrinks and forms deep fissures in the ground.

The approach from Kenya involves crossing vast deserts made up of broken lava rock. Heat radiates off the black stones and water is almost impossible to find. In both approaches, after crossing the lowlands, it is then necessary to climb the steep ridges made up of ancient granite cliffs and volcanic plugs. Only a few narrow footpaths snake up through the steep mountain passes.

Travel from the north is restricted by tall Ethiopian mountains that reach up to 9000 feet. These are separated by deep, rugged valleys. The terrain in the higher elevations is covered by thick forests. On the high plateaus the days are often cloudy and the land is frequently covered with dense fog. Temperatures can remain uncomfortably cold and damp for days at a time.

Wildlife flourishes in this vast region. The floodplains of the eastern Sudan contain two of the largest animal herds in the entire world. The white-eared kob, *kobus leocitis*, are a beautiful water-loving antelope that follow the receding rivers, making a circular migration every year of approximately 800 kilometers. The total number in this herd of kob is well over one million animals. In contrast, the tiang hartebeest, *damaliscus korrigum tiang*, stay on drier ground and migrate east and west, with the total herd numbering about 400,000. Other animals that thrive in these floodplains include buffalo, giraffe, Mongalla gazelle, Lelwell's hartebeest, eland, Roan antelope, and warthogs. All of these animals are preyed upon by the ubiquitous carnivores, including lions, leopards, cheetahs and hyenas.

These floodplains once held some of the biggest elephants in all of Africa. As far back as 1905 a British hunter named William Bell trekked into the area in search of gigantic tusks. He was successful in finding large bulls and took out scores of tusks averaging over 100 pounds apiece. In the desert regions to the south the wildlife species change to those that can live with a minimum of drinking water. These include Beisa oryx, Rainey's gazelle, lesser kudu, and dik dik. The overall region is one of the last natural reserves for wildlife on the African continent.

Tribal people also live in this region. They have managed to find a way to eke out a living in these harsh environments and have been dwelling here for hundreds of years. They continue to practice their traditional customs with little interference from the outside world. On the Sudan side are the Anuak, Murle, Toposa, and Didinga people. These people focus their economic system on keeping cattle and they migrate frequently in their constant search for pasture and water. In the Kenya desert are found the Turkana and Dassanech people, relying on pastoralism to survive in this arid climate. The Ethiopian peoples are broken down into a number of smaller tribes, including the Mursi, Bodi, Suri, Tirma, Kara, Chai, and Nyangatom. Most of these people live in valleys and along rivers where they grow sorghum and keep cattle.

All of these people are fiercely independent. The men carry spears (and now rifles) and feel free to use them. Cattle raiding is still a way of life since cattle are necessary for paying bridewealth. Even though national boundaries are demarcated on maps, they hold no significance for the people living in the region. None of the three governments that claim this region have done much to bring these peoples under their governance.

Few outsiders ever visit the region. The first European explorers went through the area at the turn of the past century. They described the region as inhospitable and left as quickly as possible. In 1900 Major Austin put together a caravan and made plans go through this region on an exploratory trek from Khartoum to Mombasa. It was a large expedition with 62 men and over 100 donkeys and camels to carry the food and gear. As they entered the floodplains north of Pibor, they suffered from the severe heat, long grass, and mosquitoes. The dry clay had formed deep cracks and many of the heavily-laden donkeys caught their hooves in these fissures and injured their legs. When the expedition finally got to the base of the rocky cliffs near Boma, the men were plagued by tsetse flies: vectors of trypanosomiasis. Many of the men died as well as their donkeys. Austin reported seeing very few tribesmen during this long trek. They simply slipped away and hid in the long grass and rocks, occasionally appearing with spears to kill anyone lagging behind the caravan. Therefore the expedition was unable to trade for fresh food and soon all of the men were suffering from severe cases of scurvy. Food became short and men began to starve. Their primary food was the meat they procured by slaughtering the remaining donkeys, but this did not provide the balanced nutrition they needed. By the time the men climbed up and over the mountains and crossed the deserts into Kenya, the expedition was in shambles. Most of the men died and out of the original 62, only 17 made it to Mombasa alive. The region had enhanced its reputation as a hard land. After that ill-fated expedition, explorers (and governments) largely stayed away from the area.

A 21-year-old British officer named Dick Lyth entered this region in 1939. He came as a military officer assigned to fight against the Italians. He ended up as District Commissioner for the Sudanese government and stayed in the region until 1954. He fell in love with the region and its peoples. He lived with the Murle people and learned their culture and language. Dick walked thousands of miles to fulfill his administrative duties and over time he brought peace to the region. In this remote, harsh land he flourished where others had perished. He is still revered by those who remember him as Kemerbong: The Red Pelican.

This book tells his story.

1

Stuck in the Sudd

The deep throbbing rhythm of the steam engine awakened Dick from a fretful sleep. He had tossed and turned all night in the humid heat. Under his closely tucked mosquito net the air hardly moved, but the net was absolutely essential to keep out the clouds of voracious mosquitoes. Dick pulled up the edge of the net and stepped out into the pre-dawn air. The air actually felt cool and raised goose bumps on his arms and legs. He opened the small door to his cabin and moved out onto the deck. Placing his elbows on the wooden railing, he looked out on the green mass of papyrus. In every direction the tall green stems lifted their tasseled heads up into the light blue morning sky.

The great paddle-wheel steamer splashed, creaked, and gurgled as it pushed the wooden blades through the brown waters of the White Nile – thrusting the steamer south against the northern flow of the longest river in the world. Dick looked back at the wake of the steamer and watched the three barges being towed at the rear of the steamer. The barges carried cement, grain, and mercantile products from Khartoum. Rusty metal sheets bolted tightly to the sides of the barges protected the cargo. On top of the metal sheets sat hundreds of third class passengers – fully exposed to the rising sun. People camped in family groups and smoke curled up from small charcoal braziers. As Dick watched, a brightly clothed woman dipped an empty tin can into the Nile and brought up the brown water. She mixed the water with red sorghum flour. Then she set this mixture over the hot charcoal fire and stirred until it set into a thick paste. Breakfast for the day.

A steward, dressed in a white robe and wearing a red fez, walked up to Dick and greeted him politely in Arabic. "Salaam aleikum?"

Dick responded with the same words, but in reverse order, "Aleikum salaam."

After the obligatory greetings the steward handed Dick a white china cup and saucer filled with strong tea. It was obvious to Dick that first class passengers were much better treated than those in third class who had to care for their own needs. Dick sipped his tea and looked over the primordial scene in front of him. Below the walls of papyrus were mats of floating water cabbage and flotillas of water hyacinth with their pink and blue flowering spires. Here and there among the profuse plant life stood long-legged water birds. Dick saw various egrets, herons and storks: all perfectly adapted to life in this gigantic swamp.

The Sudd was the largest swamp in the world, expanding up to 60,000 square miles when the Nile River and its tributaries were in full flood. It was all so different and unfamiliar. Dick thought back a few weeks to his final days at Oxford University. He had spent four pleasant years in that famous place of learning. Under the tutelage of his mentors he had studied logic and military history. He had filled his days reading books and wandering through the quads of the colleges, admiring the ancient architecture and the manicured lawns and gardens. He had played squash for his college team and chased cricket balls on the green lawns. But now he was in a world that differed dramatically from the city of Oxford with its sleeping spires.

It was 1939 and Dick Lyth was heading into the southern Sudan – one of the most remote corners of Africa. From what little he had read he expected to find tribal people continuing to live out their traditional lives as they had for many centuries. Much of the Sudan was still untouched by the powerful influences of the modern world. As if to reinforce this opinion, he noticed they were passing an island that rose just a few inches above the flow of the water. On this slip of land was a small tower made out of papyrus stems, tied together at the top to provide a strip of shade. Next to the tower was a simple rounded hut, also made out of papyrus stems. Standing in front of the tower was a tall, dark human figure. He stood on one leg with the other foot resting on his knee, and he leaned on a long fishing spear. He was extremely tall and angular, and his frizzy hair was dyed rust red. All he wore were triangular white beads, one string at his neck and the other string around his waist. He watched impassively as the steamer edged by his little island in the middle of the vast swamp. At one point he looked at Dick and casually raised one hand in greeting. Dick noticed deep V-shaped scars that had been cut into his forehead. These raised keloids marked him as a member of the Dinka people, recognized as the tallest people in the world. Sitting in front of the hut was a woman holding a small child. She too ignored the noise of the steamer as the great paddle-wheeler splashed by. Instead she focused her attention on her nursing child. Dick wondered how anybody could survive in such a remote and hostile part of the world.

Half an hour later a small bell rang to indicate that breakfast was being served. Dick drew on a pair of khaki shorts and a light shirt and headed for the small dining room. Three other first class passengers were already there and Dick nodded briefly to each of them. Then he tucked into a delicious slice of ripe papaya sprinkled with lemon juice. The rest of the breakfast was not as good. It was made up of a rubbery fried egg and a slab of hard toast smothered in bitter orange marmalade.

Dick had met his fellow passengers earlier. One was an Italian priest with a long uncombed beard. He was heading back to his parish among the Bari people. His English was limited to a few greetings and he usually sat quietly, staring down at the table. The second passenger was a government medical officer. He was returning to his assignment among the Azande people where he was trying to eradicate sleeping sickness by moving people out of the forests and into large open villages. The third was a Scottish prospector who told long rambling stories about the gold that could be found in the sand rivers near the Sudan/

Kenya border. All three of them had spent many years in the southern Sudan. Dick Lyth was the new boy on his first visit to this remote hidden country. He was only 21 years old with little life experience, but for much of his life he had been intrigued by Africa. Adventure was in his blood. He had Viking ancestry and could trace his family history as far back as 1100. His last name meant "Man on the Hill" and his forbears had a reputation for being tough adventurers. Upon graduating from Oxford University, Dick had been accepted by the Anglican Church to serve with the Church Missionary Society in the southern Sudan. His primary assignment was to teach at a school in the little town of Yambio, which was near the Congo border. His secondary assignment was to trek out into the countryside and oversee small village schools.

Dick had struck up a friendship with the Scottish prospector. His name was Alex Duncan and he had spent many years wandering around the remote corners of southern Sudan, hoping for that one big strike that would let him retire a wealthy man. After chewing on his rubbery egg, Dick turned to Duncan and asked, "Who was that tall, dark man I just saw standing on a little island? How can he possibly survive in this steaming swamp?"

Duncan grunted and then explained, "That man is a member of the Dinka tribe. The Dinka are famous for their large herds of long-horned cattle that they herd around the edge of the Sudd. When the swamp water rises in the rainy season, the herd boys move the cattle south to higher ground. However, the older Dinka men and their families continue to camp in the swamp. They use this time to trap and spear fish." He went on to point out that the man might seem isolated, but for much of the year he would be living in a village with his cows and extended family.

This made sense to Dick and as he stood at the railing over the next few hours, he noticed more little clay islands inhabited by small Dinka families. He also saw narrow dugout canoes moored to the islands and he realized they used these canoes to move from one island to another.

Dick also noticed the channel was getting narrower. As the day progressed the walls of papyrus pressed in from both sides of the channel until the tall green stems actually touched the steamer on both sides. Suddenly the steamer shuddered and came to an abrupt stop. With the lack of movement there was no breeze, causing Dick to quickly break out in a sweat. Dick looked up to the wheelhouse and saw the Arab helmsman gesturing to his assistants. Looking forward, Dick saw a thick wall of papyrus and no channel whatsoever. Then the engine stopped and an eerie silence settled over the swamp. All Dick could hear were the raucous calls of herons.

Dick went and found Duncan and asked him what was wrong. Duncan shrugged his shoulders in resignation and told him, "The channel is blocked. The papyrus plants we have been passing are only loosely rooted to the mud. When the river rises, great mats of papyrus are ripped from their base and start floating downstream. Some of these floating islands can be half a mile across and weigh thousands of tons. In the early days steamers were sometimes trapped in the Sudd for weeks and even months. In one case several hundred people died from a deadly combination of heat, malaria, and lack of food."

Dick thought about what he was hearing. "Why does the

government do nothing to remove these floating islands of papyrus and keep the channel clear for boats?"

Duncan shrugged again. "They tried," he said. "In the old days workers were assigned to ride the steamers. Their job was to attack the floating islands with machetes. But they could make little headway against the tangle of stems and roots, so eventually they gave up." He pointed out that their steamer would simply have to wait until the papyrus island shifted and the captain could find a clear channel. Hopefully the steamer would only be stuck for a few days.

Dick noticed that nobody seemed overly upset. Being stuck in the Sudd was part of travel to the southern Sudan. Since he had time on his hands he decided to do something useful. He sat down and took out a small handbook on pidgin Arabic: time to learn the trade language of the southern Sudan. Meanwhile the captain and his crew dropped a large anchor to try and keep the steamer in position with the prow facing upstream. The anchor embedded in the black alluvial mud, but it could not hold the boat in place against the rising stream. However, the resistance from the dragging anchor did keep the steamer facing upstream and kept the following barges from getting tangled in the tow ropes.

As the steamer and barges slowly drifted backwards, Dick sat on the deck and watched the papyrus slowly glide by. The situation had the potential for being intensely monotonous, but Dick always took an interest in his surroundings. Among the green stalks he saw hundreds of yellow weaverbirds. Many of the male weavers had woven pendulous nests and were displaying in front of them, fluttering their wings and trying to entice the female birds to inspect their nests. On another occasion he caught a glimpse of a tall grey bird with large yellow eyes and grotesque looking beak – the rarely seen shoebill stork. By evening the steamer had floated back to the place where he had first seen the tiny islands inhabited by the Dinka fishermen.

Dick slept fitfully that night. He spent the sleepless hours thinking about the young lady he had left behind in England. Nora had been raised in Rwanda by missionary parents. She was working on her nursing credentials so she could return to her beloved Africa. A few months earlier they had taken a long hike together to the summit of Ben Nevis, the highest mountain in Scotland. At this beautiful location he had asked Nora for her hand in marriage and she had agreed, remarking, "That would be lovely." He wished she were here with him so they could share the experience of being stuck in the great papyrus swamp. But his assignment with the Church Missionary Society was to last two years. Sending letters by slow post would be the only way he could communicate with her until he returned to England and took her hand in marriage.

When Dick got up in the morning, the steamer was still enmeshed in the great floating island of papyrus. He wondered what he could do to fill time for the whole sweltering day ahead. He noticed that the current was getting slower and he could see small open channels going in different directions. A long dugout canoe came down one of the channels, poled by two tall Dinka men. They came alongside the steamer and one of them shouted something in his local language. One of the stewards heard him and went to the railing and began talking to them.

Dick saw Duncan watching the verbal exchange. He walked

over to him and asked, "How does the steward know the language? What are they talking about?"

Duncan laughed and pointed out that the steward was himself a Dinka. "They are probably sharing the news and talking about their shared relatives," he commented. Duncan called to the steward and talked to him in pidgin Arabic. After he listened to the reply, he smiled, turned to Dick and stated that he was correct. "The steward comes from this part of the Sudd and the men know each other," he explained. He went on to say that the men in the canoe were hungry. They were short of meat and were on their way to harpoon a hippo.

Dick was intrigued. "How can two men in a fragile dugout canoe kill a gigantic hippo? Wouldn't it be suicidal?"

Duncan again talked to the steward who answered at great length and with many excited gestures. Duncan listened carefully and then turned back to Dick. "I once heard about a small group of Dinka warriors who harpooned hippos," he explained. "The steward has assured me that these men are part of that specialized group. They have developed unique hunting techniques and they're going out to kill a hippo right now."

Dick being naturally impetuous, asked Duncan, "Can I go with them? I want to see how they kill a hippo."

Duncan laughed. "That's not something I would ever try. Sitting in a canoe and being attacked by a maddened hippo is not my idea of a good time." But he spoke to the steward and he in turn talked to the Dinka in the canoe. One of the Dinka men stared at Dick for a moment and then nodded his head and gestured for Dick to get into the canoe.

For a moment Dick hesitated. Then he grabbed his hat,

swung over the railing and let himself into the canoe. It was fortunate that he was a thin man, for his hips barely fit into the narrow dugout. He yelled at Duncan and asked, "Is there anything I need to know?"

Again Duncan talked through the interpreter. After a long exchange he grinned and replied, "If a hippo charges and tries to bite the canoe, jump into the water and dive as deep as possible. The Dinka believe a hippo can't open its mouth and bite underwater."

As the two Dinka warriors poled the canoe into a narrow waterway, Dick wondered what he had gotten himself into. Would they really get that close to an adult hippo? Why couldn't a hippo bite a person underwater? Perhaps if they opened their mouths, water would go down their throats and they would drown. But that did not make any sense since a person could open his mouth underwater without any problem. As Dick contemplated this issue, he enjoyed the beauty of the quiet channel.

The two sinewy Dinka men in turn pushed their long poles into the mud and then effortlessly leaned their weight into the poles, making the canoe glide gracefully through the calm water. Dick enjoyed being down at the level of the river. Red dragonflies, with black spots on their transparent wings, perched on the leaves of the hyacinth plants. Little green bee-eaters clung to bent stems of papyrus, occasionally darting off to grab bees out of the air. Each bird then returned to its original perch, bashed its bee against the stem until it was dead and then swallowed it.

The channel started getting wider and lily pads began to dominate the scene. Their lovely pink and purple flowers opened widely to the hot sun and gave off a sweet fragrance in the humid air. Dick looked ahead and saw open water. He saw another dugout canoe being poled by Dinka men – then another and another. He quickly realized a hippo hunt was not a solitary activity, but highly organized and taking a number of hunters. Dick's canoe soon joined the others. For a few minutes conversation filled the air as the hunters greeted each other and made plans for the upcoming hunt.

Several of the Dinka looked dubiously at Dick and some tried to engage him in conversation. However, Dick could not understand a word they said and just shrugged helplessly. After making their plans, the men stopped talking and they all started poling the canoes in the same direction. Dick sensed they knew exactly where they were going. The canoes all kept close to the wall of papyrus and eventually they rounded a corner and entered a small lake covered with lily pads. Suddenly Dick heard a loud hissing snort like a railroad engine letting off steam. The Dinka hunters ducked low in their wobbly canoes and pointed in the direction of the sound. Dick realized they had made contact with a herd of hippo.

Meanwhile Dick had been looking at their equipment. Most of the men rode in dugout canoes, each carved laboriously out of a single tree. All of the warriors carried long spears with wide sharp blades. Dick also observed two ungainly craft. They looked like square rafts made of small poles lashed together to form a floating grid. He found out later that they were constructed from ambatch trees, wood that was as light as balsa and impossible to sink. On each of the rafts was a large coil of rope made out of twisted papyrus stems. One end of each rope was tied to the base of a large harpoon, a heavy metal spear with two sharp barbs. The opposite end of each rope was tied to a raft. Dick realized these ungainly rafts, with their coils of rope, were key to the attack on the hippos.

All the men readied their weapons and quietly poled their crafts toward the sound of the hippos. Dick heard a loud honking sound as an irritated hippo pushed against his neighbor. Hissing sounds erupted from the water occasionally and soon Dick saw plumes of vapor rising into the cool air from the nostrils of the hippos. Dick saw large dark heads in the water ahead. The hippos were relaxed and they twirled their ears to rid them of water. Their heads were uniquely shaped so that only the ears, eyes, and nostrils were above the water while the great bulks of the animals remained hidden under the surface. Beside the large hippos Dick observed smaller heads. These had a pinkish color – baby hippos swimming next to their mothers. He realized he was looking at a matriarchal herd with their young. Suddenly to the left a gigantic hippo burst to the surface. It raised its head and shoulders entirely out of the water and opened its mouth in a great yawn, exposing two foot-long ivory tusks. Dick learned later that this gesture was not a yawn from a tired hippo, but a threat display by dominant male hippo. He was showing to all observers that this was his private territory. He was sending a strong message: Keep away!

By now the hippos were wary and watching. As the Dinka warriors piloted their crafts closer to the hippos, one of the hippos suddenly honked a warning. Immediately all the hippos dove underwater and disappeared, leaving only widening circles of ripples. These ripples soon calmed. For the next ten minutes the water was smooth, with no indication whatsoever that there were mammoth animals just under the surface. Meanwhile the Dinka men poling the two rafts maneuvered their bulky craft into the area of water between the female herd and the big male. There they waited. Suddenly a female hippo stuck up her nose, opened the sphincter muscles in her nostrils and took a deep breath of air. Then she dove again. Within minutes all the hippos in the female herd had taken a breath of air and returned to their hiding places under water.

The last hippo to surface was the dominant male. He came up, took a breath, and looked around. He saw the two rafts now located between himself and his female herd. He let out a great roar and dove. The men could see ripples coming in their direction and they prepared for the enraged hippo to attack. On each raft a warrior stood up holding his harpoon and poised to throw. For several seconds there was no sound, but the surge of oncoming ripples moved faster and faster. Abruptly the great hippo erupted out of the water with mouth wide open and its chest hurtling through the air. He was only a few feet away from the first raft when the waiting warrior threw the harpoon into the open mouth of the charging hippo. Then the man leapt to one side of the attacking hippo and dove deep into the swirling water. The hippo came down on the raft with both front feet, savaging the poles with his long sharp tusks. The harpooner in the other raft stood up and hurled his weapon with all his strength. The point went into the chest of the hippo and the sharp barbs caught in the thick skin. With his initial attack foiled, the hippo dove under water and tried to flee. But the two rafts were attached to the wounded hippo by the harpoons and the braided ropes. One raft was badly broken, but it still floated. The other raft was intact and the harpooner was still sitting on it. He held on tight and was pulled through the water at great speed.

Now that the hippo was attached to the two rafts, the other Dinka men followed the wounded hippo in their canoes. They pushed hard on their poles, trying to catch up with the moving rafts. The wounded hippo quickly tired and could only go so far underwater without coming up for air. Each time he came up for a breath, the surrounding Dinka threw their spears at the surfacing animal. Soon the hippo had several spears sticking out of his back. There was blood in the water and the hippo quickly lost strength. The dugouts moved in cautiously for the kill. Dick's canoe was moving in from the right when the hippo made one last desperate move. The enraged animal reversed direction and burst out of the water with mouth wide open and teeth slashing. The wave of water almost swamped Dick's canoe. The hippo came down on the dugout next to Dick's. He seized the canoe with his teeth and snapped it in half. Both of the warriors flung themselves into the water and dove to the bottom. As he savaged the canoe, the hippo was exposed for several seconds and the warriors threw another barrage of spears into his body. He sank back into the water and after a time the rafts stopped moving. The hippo was dead.

The Dinka warriors regarded it as a successful hunt. They had lost only one raft and one dugout canoe. Three men had dived into the water to save themselves, but they were all retrieved unharmed. The men poled their canoes to the nearest shore and drew their boats up into the papyrus. Here everyone rested for the next several hours and waited. Then Dick heard a yell from a nearby warrior and looking up he saw a foot of the dead hippo rise above the surface of the lake. The grass in the dead hippo's gut had created methane, causing the hippo to float to the surface. The men in one canoe poled out to the hippo and tied a rope around its leg. Then the men on the shore heaved on the rope and gradually pulled the great carcass into shallow water. Here they butchered the hippo, loading large pieces of red meat into the canoes.

In late afternoon the hunting party broke up and the men started to disburse. Dick wondered how anybody knew where to go when the channels kept opening and closing. He had no choice but to stay in his canoe and trust his hosts knew where they were going. The weight of the meat caused the canoe to rest low in the water and blood sloshed around the bottom of the boat. The men poled the dugout from one channel to another, all totally bewildering to Dick. But the Dinka warriors were denizens of the swamp and they knew where they were going. Suddenly in front of him Dick saw the dirty, white side of the steamer rising above the papyrus stems. Dick climbed aboard, accepted a piece of hippo meat and waved goodbye to his intrepid companions.

Duncan greeted Dick as he got on deck. "You look a filthy mess," he said chuckling. "We were beginning to wonder if a hippo had got you."

Dick just grinned. He was well aware he had observed something quite special – a primordial duel between man and beast. He was thirsty, dirty and very tired. He went and took a long drink and headed for the shower to wash up.

That night at supper he gave a detailed account of the hunt. Even the bearded priest picked up his head and listened carefully.

Then there was a full debate on whether a hippo could open his mouth and bite a person underwater.

Exhausted, Dick slept heavily that night, but he still woke up briefly to the deep throb of the steamer's great engine. The great papyrus island had finally broken up and the channel was open again. They were heading south.

2

King of the Jungle

Within two days the steamer and its row of barges emerged out of the Sudd. There were still islands of papyrus and mats of water hyacinth floating by, but these were small and caused no problem for the mighty paddle-wheeler. The Nile River was now contained between high banks and the water flowed at a faster pace. The river was 200 paces wide and occasionally Dick saw hippos diving to avoid the oncoming steamer. On mud islands near the banks were hundreds of black and white skimmers: birds with elongated lower beaks. Periodically these birds flew low over the river with their red beaks skimming the water as they attempted to snatch fish from the smooth surface.

Lying near the birds, Dick occasionally saw large Nile

crocodiles basking in the sun with their mouths open to absorb heat. Their open mouths exposed their orange membranes and long conical teeth. Dick was intrigued to see an Egyptian plover hop into a crocodile's open mouth and run around energetically, pulling out bits of food from between the great reptile's teeth. This partnership between crocodile and plover had been noted in Pliny's book written 2000 years ago.

But the most beautiful sight of all was the flocks of carmine bee-eaters that had nesting colonies in the steep banks of the river. They had dug holes into these banks and laid their eggs at the end of the four-foot tunnels. Periodically several hundred birds would vacate their holes at the same time and sweep out across the river. Their bright red and blue feathers were in striking contrast and their ability to maneuver in the air captivated Dick who watched them for hours.

Twice a day the steamer pulled up to the bank to take on firewood to stoke the boilers. Piles of wood were stacked and waiting and a stream of strong sweaty men hurried to load the dry firewood on to the steamer. Dick wondered where the wood came from. He had seen virtually no trees for a number of days. Duncan pointed out that the trees near the river had all been cut and now the workers had to walk many miles away from the river to find adequate trees. After being cut and dried, this firewood had to be carried to the loading point. The steamers used a lot of firewood and as a result, trees were becoming more and more scarce. The time was soon coming when there would be no more firewood available to run the steamers. Then the great paddle-wheelers would have to be adapted to run on a different type of fuel, such as diesel.

A big hill appeared on the right side of the river. This was the first bit of elevation that Dick had seen in over two weeks. Duncan pointed at it and said, "That hill is named Lado. That is where the famous Emin Pasha once built his capital to administer Equatoria." He went on with his history lesson telling how Lado had been abandoned when Emin Pasha fled to Uganda to escape the ravages of the Mahdi and his fighting dervishes. Later the British had moved the capital south to higher ground and named the new town Juba. Duncan ended his lesson by stating that they were close to Juba and should arrive in about two hours.

Dick knew that Juba was the end of the steamer ride. Beyond Juba there were rapids that prevented the paddle-wheeler from going any further south. This small town was now the capital of the entire southern Sudan. It was from government headquarters in Juba that the British government administered the three southern states of the Sudan – Equatoria, Bahr el Ghazal and Upper Nile. From the town of Juba, dirt roads led out into the distant provinces. Trade goods were brought by barge from Khartoum to Juba and then lorries moved these goods into the remote towns and villages.

Dick went to his cabin and packed his few items of clothing into a small leather suitcase. Then he stood on deck and watched the scenery. They were passing large villages located on the riverbanks. Most of the villages had kraals holding hundreds of long-horned cattle. Duncan explained that these were the Bari people, a tribe closely related to the Dinka. Eventually Dick saw the buildings of Juba and then the pier at the river's edge. As the steamer edged into the cement dock, large hemp ropes were thrown to the dock workers and made fast. At once there was pandemonium. Arab merchants waited on the dock to collect their trade goods. They wore spotless white *jalabiyas* and white turbans. They had brought strong-backed stevedores to unload the merchandise. As soon as the barges were tied up, they rushed aboard. At the same time the hundreds of passengers tried to disembark. For several minutes there was a mass of humanity pushing in opposite directions. Children wailed and men cursed, but eventually everyone got to where they were going. The metal tops of the barges were opened and the stevedores started their heavy lifting, bending and sweating in the hot sun. Soon there were strings of men marching in line like ants, carrying the heavy goods on their shoulders and dumping them on the cement dock.

Disembarking from first class was more dignified. A wooden gangplank was set in place. A porter grabbed Dick's suitcase and headed down the gangplank. Dick hastened after him, calling back his thanks to the boat's captain. As he stepped on to the soil of southern Sudan he heard his name called. He looked around the crowd and saw a tall Englishman wearing a pith helmet. He heard his name called again and worked his way through to the man calling his name. Upon meeting him Dick received a firm handshake.

The man introduced himself as the Right Reverend Carey, the leader of the C.M.S. work in southern Sudan. He asked Dick about his trip. "You were expected three days ago," he commented. "What happened?"

Dick explained, "A great mat of papyrus choked the channel and our steamer got stuck. We could do nothing but wait it out."

Reverend Carey nodded. "It happens all the time," he said. "It is just part of traveling in Sudan." He then led Dick to a battered grey Commer pickup. The porter placed Dick's suitcase in the back and the two men got into the cab. As the experienced missionary drove through the little town of Juba, he pointed out the prominent features. There was an open market with hundreds of people sitting on the ground in the open sunshine. They were selling mangoes, pineapples, guavas, sugar cane, sweet potatoes, cassava and dried fish. At the other end of the market were the butchers, stripped to the waist and cutting up cow meat with axes. They made sure every piece of meat sold had a mixture of meat and shattered bone. Then Reverend Carey drove down a quiet street with small general shops owned by Arab and Greek merchants. Here could be found a wide variety of canned food and all the practical equipment needed for survival in the bush.

The climate was hot, well over 100 degrees Fahrenheit. Even with the vehicle windows open Dick was already sweating. Moisture ran down his chest and the back of his shirt stuck to the seat of the vehicle. His guide continued driving down the main road, pointing out government offices and cement houses used as residences for the British administrators. The main road was well lined with shade trees, the green leaves standing out in contrast to the whitewashed trunks. Reverend Carey pointed at the trees and stated, "The shade provided by those trees makes all the difference here in Juba. They're called *neem* trees and they are a hardy plant introduced from India. They are able to thrive in the most inhospitable soil and provide welcome shade throughout the year. They are also called the medicine tree because the bitter leaves are believed to cure many types of diseases, including malaria."

They passed by a two-story white house placed back from the road. Reverend Carey indicated that this was the governor's mansion. Then he turned the pickup to the left and entered a hedged compound with several houses and a large cathedral. They had arrived at the headquarters of the Anglican Church. The pickup was parked under a tree and several people came out of their offices to greet Dick and welcome him to the southern Sudan.

Dick was shown into a small guesthouse and Reverend Carey advised him to have a wash and then take a rest. That evening they would all eat together so Dick could meet the rest of the team. Reverend Carey explained the house rules: "Don't drink the water out of the tap, tuck in your mosquito net at night and shake the scorpions out of your shoes in the morning." And with these kind words of advice, he left.

There was a ceiling fan in the room and it spun lazily providing a slight breeze. After a cold shower Dick had a long sleep. He had arrived. He was content.

That evening Dick met other members of the Church Missionary Society. Some were based at the headquarters in Juba and others had come in for supplies from outlying stations in the provinces. In talking to them Dick learned that the British government in Sudan did not want missionaries from different denominations competing with each other for converts. The colonial officers felt it would confuse the local people to be introduced to several types of Christianity at the same time. Therefore southern Sudan was divided into eight areas and each denomination was given an exclusive region in which to work. The Anglican Church was given Equatoria to the west of the

Nile River. This area extended along the borders of Uganda, Congo and Central African Republic: a region 500 miles long and 300 miles wide. It included local ethnic groups speaking over twenty different languages. Dick enjoyed getting to know these new companions and hearing about their work.

Returning to his guest room he saw a ladder extending up to the flat roof. Being a curious person he climbed the ladder and found a bed on top of the roof. Overhanging the bed was a large square mosquito net. Dick decided it was much better than sleeping in a stuffy room. He climbed under the net and made himself comfortable. Looking up at the bright stars and feeling a faint cooling breeze was a great way to end a busy day.

The next morning he met with the Reverend Carey and learned more about his assignment. He was to go to the little town of Yambio, located far to the west and situated among the Azande people. The Reverend went on to tell him, "You will start by teaching in the church school. The British government has neither the time nor the inclination to build schools. Therefore missions like the C.M.S. have the permission and blessing of the government to set up educational centers."

Dick hesitated for a moment and then spoke up. "I have a college degree from Oxford University, but I do not have the formal qualifications to be a teacher."

Reverend Carey smiled. "It is not an issue at this point in time. The schools are operated at a very basic level and the government is not concerned about the formal qualifications of the teachers. I suggest that you spend time getting to know the boys and then teach a basic English class. More importantly, get to know the Azande people and learn some of their culture. You can start by learning a few Azande phrases and then walking out to the villages and making friends." He went on to point out that the Azande had a long, complicated history. They were also known to be good hunters. They lived largely in a rain forest, quite different from the rest of Sudan.

After the briefing Reverend Carey stated that there was a mission car going to Yambio the following day. "Spend the day getting your kit together," he advised Dick. "Hassan will drive you down to the Greek shops. How is your proficiency in pidgin Arabic? I am assuming you can make the necessary purchases."

Dick was a bit embarrassed and admitted his pidgin Arabic was not very good. He had only studied it for a few days while he rode on the steamer. The Reverend Carey shrugged and said, "It doesn't really matter. The Greek merchants know a little English and Hassan could help translate if necessary. You probably won't need pidgin Arabic in Azande country. They're so far from Juba that most people there actually don't understand pidgin."

Dick spent the rest of the day buying and packing, trying to figure out what he would need in Yambio. The following morning Hassan pulled up in the old Commer pickup. The back was full of gear, two barrels of petrol and various boxes of food and equipment. On top of the load perched eight people, all hooking a ride to Yambio. Dick wondered where to put his gear and the canned food he had bought at the Greek shops. But nobody seemed to worry about it. They simply handed up Dick's gear to the passengers and made the load another tier higher. Then they all settled down for the long ride.

Hassan drove the pickup out of the mission compound and picked up the main street heading west. They quickly left the town of Juba and started down a dirt road. Dick sat in the front seat next to Hassan. The road had a surface of small rocks held together by murram clay. Technically it was an all-weather road, but it was very rough. In most places the road was severely corrugated like a washboard. Going very slowly up and down the corrugations made the ride somewhat comfortable, but one could not go more than ten miles per hour. Hassan used the other method: driving fast and letting the tires just touch the tops of each ridge. This was actually more comfortable, but it led to a lack of control. The car often slid sideways on the corners and Hassan had to do some fancy steering to keep the vehicle on the road. The weather was dry so the pickup put up a trail of red dust. Soon everyone in the back of the vehicle was covered red, with only their eyes and teeth showing white.

They drove through flat savannahs covered with long yellow grass and some stunted acacia trees. Occasionally large granite hills stuck up out of the plains. At midday they stopped at Loka, a great granite inselberg. Here they ate a few bananas and Dick walked a few hundred feet up the granite rocks to get a view of the surrounding area. Then the road headed south toward the little town of Maridi near the Uganda border. Before entering the town they drove through a plantation of large-leafed trees that had been planted in long straight rows. Hassan explained, "They are teak trees planted by the British forestry department for use as house beams and fence posts. They are valuable because they grow straight and are impervious to white ants."

In Maridi they went to the C.M.S. compound, where Dick was welcomed for the night. He met the missionaries working there and after supper they talked about the war in Europe. The missionaries had been listening to the BBC broadcast and were concerned that Hitler and his troops were taking over great parts of Europe. There were even rumors that the Italians would attack Sudan. To Dick it all seemed so strange. The civilized world was tearing itself apart and here he was sitting in a quiet remote corner of the world, completely detached from the life he had formerly known. He felt a bit guilty. There were thousands of young men his age out there risking their lives in the battlefields. He believed God had called him to work in southern Sudan. But was this the time? He was 21 years old and in excellent shape. He had taken a little military training at Oxford University. Should he not offer his services to the great cause?

But right now he was heading to Yambio. He decided to stay with his spiritual calling. The following day a new driver took over the driving. His name was Kilpa. He had been born in Yambio and spoke excellent English. His father was the paramount chief of the Azande people. As they drove, the vegetation near the road grew denser and Kilpa pointed out colobus monkeys as they leaped through the trees, their bushy white tails trailing behind them. Soon the trees met overhead and they drove through heavy shade. Many of the trees had shiny green leaves and Kilpa identified them as mango trees. Usually mango trees were full stately trees planted near villages and each tree had an owner who picked its delicious fruit. But the soil and climate here was so perfect for mangoes that the trees had gone wild. People and monkeys ate the mangoes and threw away the seeds. The seeds then sprouted and now there were mango trees growing everywhere.

Dick asked how far the wild mango forest extended. "It goes

for many miles in every direction," Kilpa replied. "During the harvest season millions of mangoes fall to the ground and rot. They give off a strong smell that attracts monkeys, antelope, bush pigs – and especially elephants. Thousands of elephants cross the border from Congo, migrating north to eat the rotten mangoes lying on the ground. These mangoes ferment and the elephants eat so many they actually get drunk. Then they stagger around, pulling down trees and feeling happy."

Kilpa laughed at his own story and Dick laughed with him. The idea of drunk elephants amused both of them. Dick changed the subject and asked Kilpa about the origins of the Azande people.

Kilpa explained that they were once a small tribe of hunters who lived in central Congo, but over time they formed a hierarchical society with the Avongara chiefs at the top. Under their leadership young men were trained to be warriors. They used spears and poison arrows and developed new military maneuvers. Using their new military prowess they attacked neighboring tribes, killing the men, marrying the women captives and adopting the children. In this way they quickly expanded their numbers and their territory. Over a period of 200 years they conquered 30 different ethnic groups. Everyone in the region now spoke the Azande language and practiced the Azande culture. The Avongara chiefs held great riches and power, once ruling over one of the greatest kingdoms in central Africa.

Dick was surprised. "Do the chiefs still maintain their power?" he asked Kilpa.

Kilpa shook his head sadly. "The countries of France and Britain conquered the Azande and then made colonies. In the process they drew up strange borders. The Azande kingdom was split into thirds and they ended up in three countries: Congo, the Ubangi-Shari region of French Equatorial Africa and Sudan. Chief Yambio was the most powerful chief in Sudan. The town where we're going was named after him."

"How unfair!" Dick said to Kilpa. "What right did the countries of Europe have to divide this tribal kingdom?"

The driver just nodded, but after a period of silence he spoke aloud. "There have been some benefits. The Azande people now live in peace and do not fight with their neighbors. The British government has also introduced strong medicine, especially useful for curing people with malaria and sleeping sickness. Most importantly, the missionaries have brought the message of Christ and have translated the Bible into the Azande language. These are good things. Many Azande now attend church. But most of them still turn to witchcraft as the explanation for evil."

As they continued the drive through the mango forest, Dick contemplated what Kilpa had said about Christianity and witchcraft. How would he as a Christian missionary approach such an issue?

Late that afternoon they pulled into the town of Yambio. It was well laid out, with large mahogany trees shading the road. Kilpa drove to the Anglican Church and then turned down a shady lane with three houses. He parked the car in front of the maintenance building. Some Azande workers immediately appeared and started unpacking the load. Dick indicated which gear was his and then he was led to one of the houses, where he was introduced to Dr. Joel White and his wife, Irma. They welcomed Dick into their house and gave him a cold glass of red hibiscus juice. The next hour was a pleasant one as they all talked and got to know one another. Dr. White was the head missionary for the Yambio area and he explained some of the projects to Dick. Then he took Dick to a neighboring house, the building that was to be his home for the next two years. It was built out of red laterite bricks with a tin roof. It was small and had only two rooms: a bedroom and a living room. The kitchen was a lean-to outside and further back was a shower facility and an outhouse. It was exactly what Dick had imagined and he knew it would feel like home once he put some personal photos on the walls. That evening he went back to the White's house for supper, where he met the other members of the C.M.S. team working in Yambio – a nurse named Rosy and a teacher named Ingrid. They were all happy to have Dick join their team and during the evening they filled him in on life in Yambio. Later the discussion moved to the topic of the war in Europe. It was like a distant cloud hanging over their heads. What was really happening? Where was fighting taking place? Were any of their relatives involved in the battles?

Dick slept well that night with the good feeling of having arrived home after a long journey. He awoke the next morning to a cup of hot tea being handed to him under his mosquito net. A cheerful face beamed at him and said something he could not understand. He assumed it was a greeting, so he replied in pidgin Arabic, "Salaam Aleikum!" The face disappeared, but Dick heard noises in the little outdoor kitchen. After getting dressed Dick went out to see what was happening. He found the "tea man" working over a charcoal brazier cooking a mess of scrambled eggs. Dick realized he had hired a cook. He learned that his name was Kuju. His initial skills were limited to making tea and scrambling eggs, but he was cheerful and eager and quickly learned to cook the foods that Dick liked.

The night before Ingrid had talked to Dick about starting at the school. He would start with teaching only one class per day. At nine o'clock a student hit a tire rim hanging from a tree. The ringing sound announced that classes were to begin. Ingrid stopped by to get Dick and together they walked down the dirt road to the classroom block. As they entered the English class all the students stood up and as one they chanted, "Good morning, teacher."

Ingrid answered, "Good morning, students. You may all sit down." With much shuffling and shifting all of the students eventually found their seats. Then Ingrid introduced Dick to the class, telling the students he was an expert in the English language and he would be their new teacher.

Dick spoke to the class, speaking slowly and enunciating carefully. Most of the students stared at him blankly and he realized they understood little of what he was saying. It quickly became obvious he would have to start at the very beginning.

Dick spent the next weeks working on basic lesson plans. He found the students to be polite and they tried hard. But Dick found going over the same simple English words every day was extremely boring. He could not connect at a deep level and the students put him on a pedestal since he was their teacher.

Increasingly Dick sought out the company of Kilpa, the Azande driver. Since Kilpa knew English fairly well, Dick was able to ask him questions about the area, the people and the wildlife. One day he saw a small party of men walk by the school.

Each of them was carrying a large pile of ropes over his left shoulder. In their right hands they held sharp spears. They were obviously Azande men since they were reddish in color and their bodies were squat and well muscled. Later in the day Dick asked Kilpa who they were and what they were doing. Kilpa smiled and explained, "They were Azande hunters. The ropes they were carrying were woven nets. The hunters you saw were going into the forest to catch antelope."

Dick was intrigued and asked Kilpa if he could one day go on a hunt with the Azande men. He remembered his experience harpooning hippos with the Dinka. Hunting with the Azande in the forest would be quite a different experience. Kilpa agreed to talk to some hunters and a few days later he brought word that there was to be a big hunt and that Dick was welcome to participate. Dick canceled class for that day and in the early morning Kilpa led him into the thick rain forest. The air was still cool and dew coated the leaves. Within minutes Dick was soaked to the skin. Kilpa led him on a faint path. Gaudy jungle butterflies fluttered in front of him. Soon they left the sounds of human habitation – no more cocks crowing, women pounding grain and babies crying. They only heard the sounds of birds singing, monkeys chattering and the distant whoop of a chimpanzee. Kilpa and Dick walked quietly and soon several Azande hunters joined them, each carrying his load of nets.

Eventually they came to a clearing in the forest. Here they met up with about forty men: each hunter with his net and spear. Dick noticed that some of the hunters were accompanied by small sturdy dogs. These dogs had long sharp ears and tails that curled tightly over their backs. They were bouncing up and down with pent-up energy, and each had a metal bell hanging from its neck. The bells made no sound in spite of the jumping of the dogs. Dick looked closely and saw that each bell was stuffed with leaves so the clapper could not hit the metal and make a sound. Dick was looking at basenji dogs: famous because they could not bark. For a while the hunters sat around a small fire smoking and chatting quietly. They smiled and laughed at Dick and offered him a seat near the fire so he could dry his wet clothing. They seemed quite happy to show the slight white man how to hunt. Dick saw two short men with hairy bodies and realized he was looking at pygmies, the real people of the rain forest. One of the pygmies started talking in a high voice and the Azande hunters became quiet and listened carefully. The pygmy hunter explained what was going to happen and pointed to a part of the forest where the hunt was to take place.

When he finished talking, all the Azande men stood up and walked single file into the forest. One of them gestured at Dick to follow him. As they left the clearing Dick noticed a group of teenage boys heading in the opposite direction. They were leading several of the voiceless dogs. The boys carried no nets, only spears. The men with Dick walked quickly and quietly, and eventually they entered a part of the forest that had tall trees but little underbrush at the ground level. Here the men spread out in a line, each man standing about ten paces apart. Then each man began unloading his net off his left shoulder, carefully taking off one layer at a time so it did not get tangled. The nets were six feet high and each hunter tied one end of his net to a tree and then stretched out the net and tied the opposite end to another tree. The end of one man's net reached to the next man's net so eventually there was one continuous net for half a mile. The extended net made a gradual U curve with the open end facing west. The bottom of each net touched the ground and was folded over and under so any animal running into the net would be entangled in the loose folds. The hunters took up their positions behind the buttresses of large trees, each holding his spear. One of the hunters gave Dick a spear and he took up an appropriate hiding place.

Soon in the distance Dick heard high yodeling sounds and an occasional thump of wood hitting wood. The teenage boys were making noise and driving animals toward the nets. Dick also heard the sound of bells. The boys had removed the leaves from around the clappers. As the dogs coursed through the forest, the ringing sounds of the bells drove the animals ahead of them. The sounds drew nearer and suddenly Dick saw a small red antelope come sprinting along the ground. It threw itself into a net thinking it was just branches and therefore an avenue of escape. Immediately the owner of the net stepped out from behind his tree and thrust his spear into the chest of the antelope. It gave a despairing cry and kicked violently. In seconds it was dead. The hunter withdrew to his hiding position behind the tree.

Then Dick saw a large antelope bounding toward the nets. It was brilliant red with vertical white stripes on its flanks. It held its head high and Dick saw that it had long twisted horns with ivory tips. Its beauty was stunning and Dick felt he was looking at the king of the forest. The antelope sensed the net at the last second and made a great bound. Its front feet cleared the net, but its back hooves clipped the upper rope. For a moment it looked as if the antelope would fall. But it kicked hard, got free of the net and raced on into the deep forest. No hunter was able to hit it with a spear as it dashed by and it escaped without a scratch.

The hunters once again hid behind the trees and waited for more game. Dick could see up and down the line of nets. Every few minutes he saw small animals race into the nets where they were quickly dispatched by the waiting spearmen: porcupines, aardvarks, chevrotains, red antelopes and cane rats. All of them would provide good meat for the Azande villagers.

Then things slowed down. The sounds of yodeling and ringing bells got closer and Dick assumed the hunt was coming to an end. Suddenly he saw a large brown shape coming at his section of the net. It was racing very fast with its head held low to the ground. Down its back was a wide stripe of long yellow hair. It hit the net at top speed and squealed loudly when it found itself entangled. Dick jumped forward and thrust his spear into the writhing animal. The animal squealed again and tried to slash Dick with its teeth, but Dick wrenched out the spear and thrust again, pinning the animal to the ground. Immediately one of the pygmy men leaped forward and put another spear into the animal, ending its life.

The hunt was over. The Azande hunters came out of their hiding places laughing and yelling. They congratulated Dick on his kill. It was a strangely shaped antelope with high back quarters and short front legs. It had two short horns on its bullet-shaped head. It weighed well over 150 pounds and the Azande were pleased with the amount of meat it provided. It was the largest animal killed on that particular hunt.

That night Dick went over to Dr. White's house and borrowed his wildlife book. He discovered that the animal he had killed was a yellow-backed duiker. This was a rare jungle antelope and the largest of the duiker family. It received its name of "duiker" from the Dutch word for "diver" - from its habit of running with its head down and diving under bushes.

Dick also discovered that the big red antelope that escaped the net was called a bongo. The book noted that it was one of the largest antelopes in the world and also one of the most secretive. Dick had been fortunate to see one in the wild. It was indeed the king of the jungle. Kipla later told Dick that the hunters were somewhat relieved that the bongo had jumped over the net and escaped. Snared bongo could be ferocious fighters. In addition the Azande did not really like its meat. They considered it to be too red and too rich.

The hunting trip into the thick rain forest made Dick eager to get out of town and see more of the countryside. Going to a classroom every day was becoming routine and boring. Dr. White was a sensitive man and soon realized Dick wanted to do more. Teaching involved only a few hours in the morning so he was given the assignment of planting a large garden down by the Yambio River. He hired a crew of men and they quickly cut down the big trees and dug out the stumps. The soil was rich and black and soon Dick had his men planting bananas, pineapples, cassava and guavas as well as many types of vegetables. The mission needed new buildings so he was also given the job of making bricks. Kilpa pointed out a good source of clay near the garden and this clay was dug up, mixed with water and molded into small bricks. These were set out to dry in the hot sun. When they were dry they were stacked in piles, eventually forming a large rectangular kiln thirty feet long. The entire structure was covered with a coating of black mud. Empty tunnels were left at the base and firewood from the garden was pushed into these holes and then lit. The logs burned hotly and the workers kept adding logs for the next six days, never letting the fire go out. The kiln was given a week to cool and then the outside mud was removed, revealing row upon row of hard red bricks. Dick's first experiment in brick making was a success.

But Dick wanted to go further afield than the town garden. Dr. White realized this and therefore asked him to supervise the bush schools. Yambio was the location of the mother church in the region and to reach the outlying areas there was a program of starting small rural schools. This involved a trained evangelist entering a village and establishing a home. He then built a small grass-roofed building that was used for a church service on Sunday and for reading classes during the week. The evangelist did both the preaching and the teaching. These evangelists were capable men, but often needed encouragement in their work. In his new role Dick would leave Yambio and go on trek every other week to these various bush schools. He planned each trip carefully, so he could visit at least two schools per day. None of these schools were located on roads and the only way to get there was to walk, following the narrow dusty footpaths through the jungle. Dick put together a camping kit with a small tent. Kuju always went with him as camp cook and several porters came along carrying the camping equipment on their heads. Dick made it a practice to wear a felt hat to keep the scorching sun off his head and he always carried his .22 rifle. It was not much good for protection against large animals, but it was useful for shooting guinea fowl for the pot.

Dick enjoyed these treks and soon made good friends with the evangelists. Some of the treks lasted up to a week and Dick visited some remote locations where people had seldom seen a white man. Many of the trips took him south into the deep jungle. The dark forest seemed mysterious and beautiful at the same time. Hanging orchids and air-breathing epiphytes festooned the tall trees. The little villages were welcoming and were small beacons of human life in the middle of the forest. At night Dick lay in his tent and listened to the distant trumpeting of elephants and the rasping cough of a roaming leopard. But the most mysterious sound was a high mournful wail. The Azande insisted it was the call of a chameleon advertising the presence of honey.

Other trips took Dick north into the open woodlands where he encountered tall mahogany trees. Long grass covered the open ground between the majestic trees and the sun was brutally hot. Villages were located on the small rivers where people had small gardens and also caught fish. Dick tried his hand at fishing with a hook and line. The fish were voracious and he caught a small catfish on every cast. The hard part was getting them off the hook. They had poisonous spines, one in each fin and one on the back. After Dick was badly stung several times, the local boys showed him how to break the spines before trying to release the hook. The woodland country was full of game and Dick frequently saw herds of Nile buffalo, Lelwell's hartebeest and Roan antelope. He once saw a herd of the rare and timid Lord Darby's eland, the tallest antelope in the world.

Dick reveled in this nomadic life. He kept a diary and after one trek he wrote, "I had often wondered what the first days on the mission field would be like. I had expected days of suffering from the climate, days of testing and temptation and perhaps backsliding. Praise God it is at every point the reverse." But life on trek was not always easy. The sharp grass scratched Dick's legs and these scratches quickly got infected in the hot humid conditions. They grew into open ulcers and became quite painful. He tried putting antibiotic powder on them, but they continued to spread. After one particularly long trek he limped back into Yambio and went to see Dr. White. The doctor was concerned and immediately ordered Dick to have absolute rest for four days with his legs elevated above his body. Dick felt like he was wasting time laying on his back day after day, but it started the healing process. After a few days his legs healed and he was able to go back on trek.

On the following trip Dick taught Kuju had to use the .22 rifle. Kuju was young and eager and he learned quickly. The next evening he came back to camp with six guinea fowl he had shot. He was quite pleased with himself and from that day onward he often procured fresh meat for his cooking pots.

Dick thrived in his role of overseeing the bush schools. He wrote in his diary, "I am loving this life, so free and so essentially positive . . . I was chosen for this work. I am out adventuring with God." However, he went on to write, "My chief complaint is that at night the baboons ate my toilet paper. This strikes me not only as bad taste, but shows distinct lack of poise."

While on these treks, Dick kept thinking about his fiancée, Nora. He wanted to share this remote corner of Africa with her. He knew she would love it. She had the perfect background for such a life. Nora had been raised in Uganda by her missionary parents, Algy and Zoe Stanley-Smith. Her father had earned his medical qualifications from Cambridge University. After spending a number of years in southern Uganda, they became the first Protestant missionaries to Rwanda, entering that country in 1935. Nora grew up in Rwanda playing with her African friends and feeling quite at home in the bush. She had later attended boarding school in Limuru, Kenya, where she was captain of the hockey team and had a reputation for climbing tall trees.

As much as Dick enjoyed the treks into the bush, he also enjoyed coming back to the mission in Yambio. Mail arrived once a week from Juba on the government lorry. The trip took two days if the roads were dry. Dick could anticipate several letters a week from his beloved Nora. In her beautiful handwriting she would tell him what was happening back in England where she was working as a nurse. She also kept him aware of how the war was spreading in Europe. Dick continued to listen to the BBC radio broadcasts and learned that the war in northern Africa was going badly for the British. The Italians controlled Libya and were putting pressure on Sudan's northwest border. Under Mussolini they had taken over Ethiopia in 1935 – driving out king Haile Selassie. Now in 1939 the Italians had entered the war on the side of the Germans. They were gathering their forces on the Sudan/Ethiopia border and there were fears they would attack Sudan and try to cut the Nile River.

One night after listening to the BBC, Dick lay in bed under his mosquito net and wondered what he should do. He felt called to Sudan to do God's work. But at this momentous time in history, teaching English to little Azande boys and trekking around the bush did not really seem to be that important. He decided to talk to the District Commissioner the following day.

After breakfast the next morning, Dick walked down to the government post and waited outside the District Commissioner's office. After half an hour of waiting he was ushered in to see Major Tiger Wylde. He was an older man with a face weathered from the hot tropical sun. He had spent much of his life in the political service of Great Britain and had a good grasp of what was happening in various African countries. Dick talked to the District Commissioner about his dilemma. The political officer was well aware of the dangerous situation on Sudan's northern borders. Egypt was also under pressure and whatever happened in Egypt would eventually have serious effects on Sudan and vice versa. The Commissioner had many memos and telegrams lying on his desk. After listening to Dick, he reached into a file and pulled out an application form to the Sudan Defence Force. The District Commissioner went on to explain, "The SDF is a small military organization and at the present time is in dire need of new officers. You could be one those new officers."

Tiger Wylde was a kindly man and he understood Dick's dilemma. He invited him to come for afternoon tea at his home. Later that day Dick presented himself at the front door of the red brick house and was met by Milka, Tiger Wylde's Russian wife. It was highly unusual for a District Commissioner to have his wife with him on assignment. However, Major Wylde had been a District Commissioner for a long time and was highly regarded by the British government. He was known to make good decisions and had an in-depth understanding of the people over whom he ruled. So there had been few protests when Wylde ensconced his beautiful wife at his base in Yambio.

Milka invited Dick into the house and took him through the living room. It was a spacious room with large windows. Tanned animal skins festooned the floor and horns of various trophies hung on the walls. Bookcases lined the walls, filled largely with books about Africa. Milka guided Dick out into the back garden. Her husband was seated at a table in the speckled shade of a flamboyant tree. Dick was enthralled by the flowering bushes and the colorful orchids hanging from the trees. He asked about the orchids and Milka answered, "Both of us enjoy gardening and we like to find new species. We spend our free time scouring the rain forest looking up into the canopy for wild orchids. If we are fortunate enough to find some, we carefully gather them and replant them in the trees of our garden." The Commissioner took Dick on a tour of the garden while Milka was setting out the tea and scones. During tea Dick asked Tiger and Milka about their life in southern Sudan.

"We both enjoy living here in Yambio," Milka replied. "Tiger is often gone on trek to inspect various outposts so I am a little lonely, but I feel quite safe living in the house and spending time in the garden." Tiger also talked about his work as District Commissioner. He pointed out that the object of his work was the welfare and contentment of the people living in the region. He took this work seriously, but he also pointed out that the position gave him the opportunity to live an adventurous and exciting life, free from many of the restrictions in Europe.

After tea Dick returned to his house. He sat on the front step and gazed into the overhanging bougainvillea bush. He watched a flap-necked chameleon as it moved slowly up a branch, moving forward an inch and then back again as if it could not make up its mind where it wanted to go. Dick saw it as an analogy of his own life. As he watched the stuttering steps of the chameleon, he knew he must make a firm decision and he prayed for wisdom. He felt strongly that he must get involved in the war. He must fight for his country. After a time of prayer his mind was made up. He walked over to Dr. White's house and told him what he was thinking. The doctor listened carefully. In the end he nodded. "If you decide to go you will be missed. There is still much work to be done here in Yambio. But I understand your desire to fight for your country. I agree that teaching English to little boys is not of primary importance when much of the world is at war." Dr. White offered to release Dick from his duties as a C.M.S. missionary and Dick accepted. As Dick stood to leave the room the doctor told him, "Go and fight for your country. Go with my blessing." As Dick left the room, the doctor said softly to himself, "If I were a few years younger, I would go with you."

3

Training Fresh Recruits

Four days later, while Dick was eating his breakfast of papaya, a soldier appeared at the front door. He saluted sharply and handed Dick a note. It was a summons from the District Commissioner to appear at his office at 9 am.

Dick appeared in the front office exactly on time and after a few minutes he was called into Tiger Wylde's office. Dick took a seat in front of the large mahogany desk. The District Commissioner picked up a sheaf of papers and drew one out: a telegram. He handed it across the desk to Dick with the words, "My congratulations."

Dick read the flimsy yellow paper. In terse words it read,

"Richard Lyth accepted into Sudan Defence Force. Report to headquarters in Khartoum for training immediately."

Dick was a little taken aback. With the words on that yellow parchment his life was going to change completely. He looked over at the elderly officer who stood and offered him his hand. The Commissioner spoke gruffly. "Go out there and fight for Sudan. There is a government car going to Juba tomorrow. Be on it." Dick gave the officer a firm handshake. Then he was out the door and into the bright sunshine. Things were happening too fast. He felt dazed. He wandered over to Dr. White's house and told him the news. The doctor congratulated him and told him to spend the day packing and closing down his personal affairs. Dick first went to the classroom and told his students that he was leaving immediately to go to war. His students cheered. They all wanted to go to war with him, but he explained that they must remain in Yambio until they were older. He then went to his house and started putting together his basic kit.

Kuju, his faithful cook, was quite upset when he heard Dick was leaving. He insisted on going with him. "I will do your cooking and washing. I will fight with you."

Dick shook his head. "It's just not possible, Kuju."

Kuju got even more upset. "People in the army need to eat! They need to have clean uniforms!"

Dick tried to explain there were other people to do that work, but Kuju would not accept Dick's arguments. He insisted over and over, "Taking care of you is my work! I am going with you!"

Dick held his position and Kuju finally walked away, grumbling and hurt. Dick put all his basic survival gear into one duffle bag. That evening the C.M.S. missionaries got together for a good meal and to give their blessing to Dick's new venture.

The next morning Dick was on the road to Juba, back-tracking the same route he had taken a few months before. Upon arriving at Juba he was put up in military barracks for the night. They told him he would not be taking the slow steamer through the Sudd. Instead he and four other recruits were to be put on a military airplane and flown straight to Khartoum. This did not please Dick since he had never flown on a plane before. There was also a story going about Juba that made him nervous. Several months earlier a contingent of Gladiators had flown from Nairobi to Juba. The chief pilot radioed ahead requesting that aviation fuel be available at the airport so the squadron could proceed north to Khartoum. The British officer in charge left the airport to go procure the necessary fuel, but he neglected to inform the police guards about the incoming aircraft. As the planes came in for a landing, the guards assumed they were being attacked by Italian warplanes and opened fire. The planes banked away to avoid the incoming bullets and flew low over the town of Juba. A prison officer hearing the shooting at the airport and seeing the low-flying planes also assumed that Juba was being attacked. He grabbed his .303 rifle and shot at one of the planes. The bullet hit a cable in the plane, causing the pilot to lose control. The plane came down on an island in the Nile, rushing through the long grass and eventually ending up upside down. The pilot was able to exit the plane unhurt, but had the ignominy to be rescued by a Dinka fisherman in a canoe who rowed him back to the town of Juba.

Dick boarded a military plane the next morning and once they were in the air, he quite enjoyed the flight. From the window of the plane Dick looked down at the White Nile as it meandered its way north. He especially enjoyed looking down at the great green Sudd, remembering the days the paddle-wheel steamer was stuck behind the floating papyrus islands.

Upon landing at the Khartoum airport, Dick and the other recruits were driven across a bridge over the White Nile and through the ancient city of Omdurman. They passed the tomb of the Mahdi and then slowed down to a crawl as the vehicle worked its way through the crowded Arab *souk*. North of the city with its thousands of single-story clay houses Dick saw the camel market with hundreds of animals for sale. The vehicle proceeded north to the training camp of the Sudan Defence Force. This was simply a windswept plain with a few concrete buildings. Stepping out of the vehicle, Dick noticed there was a great deal of activity. Previously the Sudan Defence Force had been an elite club with a few older officers. But now there was a national crisis and the Sudan Defence Force was trying to rise to the occasion. New recruits were coming in from various parts of the Sudan and the experienced officers were trying to bring some sort of order and get the new recruits trained and into the field.

Dick and his companions were ordered into the mess to get a meal and then into the fitting room. Here they were measured by a tall Dinka man who handed them various parts of their uniform – khaki shirts and shorts, black boots with puttees to protect their lower legs and a felt hat pinned up on one side. They were then shown to a long wooden barracks where Dick chose a top bunk. After making his bed he lay down and tried to get some rest in the torrid heat, wondering what he had gotten himself into.

That night after the evening meal the new recruits all met in the hall. The commander of the Sudan Defence Force, General Platt, stood up to address them. He gave a short history of the Sudan Defence Force and the purpose for its existence. He explained that this military organization had been formed in 1925. After World War 1 nationalism had flared up in Egypt and Great Britain removed all British and Egyptian troops from Sudan and sent them to Egypt to put down the rebellion. This left a vacuum in Sudan and the Sudan Defence Force was formed to fill this vacuum. It was made up largely of Sudanese troops with British officers. General Platt pointed out that men from the Nuba Hills made the best soldiers because they came from a culture that promoted wrestling and warfare. He went on to state that the express purpose of the Sudan Defence Force was to put down tribal mutinies and defend the Sudan from outside forces. All units were in a perpetual state of readiness, prepared to go to a trouble spot at a moment's notice. They were primarily infantry who marched from place to place on foot. Using riding animals was not possible in many locations in the Sudan. The ubiquitous tsetse flies carried trypanosomiasis, a disease that killed horses and camels. The units frequently went on foot patrols simply to "show the flag" and to reinforce the fact that the British were in control. In total, officers and troops, the force numbered 5000.

General Platt went on to explain what was happening in northeastern Sudan. Italy was now a member of the Axis powers and therefore a partner with Germany. Italy had attacked Ethiopia in 1935 and made it into an Italian colony. There were now 300,000 Italian troops in Ethiopia and many of them had massed on the Sudan/Ethiopia border. They had made several sorties into the Sudan and had even captured the Sudanese town of Kassala. In conclusion the General reiterated, "The Sudan Defence Force has a vital role to play in holding back the Italian troops. We must not allow them to invade Sudan and cut the Nile River. Time is of the essence. Training will be extra tough. We have only six weeks to train you as officers and get you into the field. Calisthenics will start tomorrow morning at 5 am."

The next morning Dick found himself up and running in the brightening dawn. It was July in Khartoum and the temperature would top 120 Fahrenheit at midday. The recruits ran and walked and ran again for two hours. Fortunately Dick was thin and in excellent shape, so the physical side of training was relatively easy for him. However, many of the new recruits were older men and others had held desk jobs. For many of them the physical training was brutal. During the heat of the day officers from various military units came and taught military strategy and weapon use. Dick quickly realized much of what he was learning was conventional warfare. It might be useful information for Europe, but much of it was useless in the Sudan. Therefore as his teachers gave him lectures on tank warfare, various formations and heavy weapons, Dick only listened with one ear. He wondered how warfare operated in traditional African cultures where manpower was the key, not highly mechanized armaments.

Training was intense and went on daily for six weeks. By the end of this time Dick was superbly fit and had a good mastery of small weapons. He had been a crack shot at Oxford University and this background served him well. Little did he know that his accuracy with a rifle was going to be essential when it came to shooting game to feed the soldiers under his command.

Graduation came and Dick was at the top of his class. He was awarded the military position of *Bimbashi* - an old Turkish term that was the equivalent of a major in the British military system. Dick was now 22 years of age and held the position of a major: ready to go out and lead men into battle.

The next day the newly commissioned officers were given their assignments. Most of them were given positions in northern Sudan and were being connected to various units in locations where the Sudan Defence Force was already working. But General Platt saw special abilities in Dick and summoned him to his office. The commander explained again that it was crucial to keep Egypt and the Suez Canal under the domain of the British government. Since the Italian forces were massing on the Sudan/Ethiopia border near Kassala he was sending most of the new officers of the Sudan Defence Force to beef up the active military units already in the region. Colonel Boustead was to be in charge of this major military operation. It was to involve hundreds of troops and thousands of camels to supply these units. But there was another more subtle threat. Italy had gradually taken over the outlying districts of Ethiopia. More recently they had moved into the southwest town of Maji, forcing Richard Whalley, the British consular officer, to abandon his post. The Italians were now building forts in the southern mountains along the Sudan/Ethiopia border. These forts were built in rugged country overlooking the flood plains of Sudan. From these highland forts it would only be a quick dash across open country to the all-important Nile River. If Italian troops were able to cut the Nile, it would stop all river transport from eastern Africa north to Khartoum and thence north to Egypt. If this happened, Egypt would be trapped between the German forces to the west and the Italians to the south.

General Platt explained it was absolutely essential that the Italians be held in place and not be allowed to enter Sudan. This was the reason Colonel Boustead and his troops were being assigned to hold the ground against the massed Italian troops near Kassala. But he went on to explain that the Sudan Defence Force did not have battalions of troops that could be employed to hold the border far to the south of Kassala. It was a long, porous border covering hundreds of miles of wilderness and unmapped territory. The Sudan government only had one small police unit in the entire area of 60,000 square miles.

The general then went on to offer Dick a unique and daring assignment. "I am asking you to proceed to the town of Torit in Equatoria Province. This is the headquarters of the Equatorial Corps, the southern branch of the Sudan Defence Force. Here you are to recruit local warriors and train them into a mobile militia of irregular forces. Your task is to hold back the Italians by whatever means possible."

At first Dick wondered if the general was joking, but Dick looked at his face and could see he was deadly serious. The general explained he was looking for somebody who could work closely with the local people, somebody who was flexible and yet a leader of his men. The general admitted, "This is very much an experiment, outside most military procedures." He then asked Dick, "Are you willing to consider such an assignment?"

Dick hesitated, but only for a moment. He knew there would be many challenges ahead. But what freedom he would have!

What opportunities! He nodded and said, "I would be honored to take this assignment. When do I start?"

General Platt was pleased. "Right away! Spend the next week in Khartoum looking at old maps and travel books. Then proceed south to Torit. Good luck!"

Upon being dismissed, Dick immediately went to the Khartoum archives and started reading, trying to gain an understanding of the physical terrain of southeastern Sudan and the mountainous western corner of Ethiopia. There were no roads in this vast area, only faint footpaths. As Dick pored through the limited information, he did a special study of streams and water holes. These would be absolutely essential when he was marching on foot across miles of hot, arid terrain. Dick also spent some time cramming to upgrade his knowledge of pidgin Arabic. Since there were over 80 languages spoken in the southern Sudan, this basic form of Arabic had been developed in the military to communicate to the soldiers from the various ethnic groups. Since Dick would be training and leading troops from several different language groups, it was essential that he master this military trade language so he could communicate accurately.

After a week Dick caught a military flight back to Juba, the capital of southern Sudan. From here he caught a lorry heading southeast to the town of Torit. It was nestled at the base of the Immatong Mountains, the highest peaks in all of Sudan. Since Torit was the main base of the Equatorial Corps of the Sudan Defence Force it was here that Dick formally took up his assignment. He met with the commanding officer to get more details. The officer explained that the only police post in the entire Sudan/Ethiopia border region was Towoth Post on top of the Boma plateau. This had been established by the Sudan Defence Force in 1936 to ensure that the Italians did not take over the plateau. A road had been built across the hot plains 125 miles from Kapoeta to the base of Boma. Later the road was extended up the steep escarpment, built entirely with hand labor. At the top of the cliffs a fort had been built out of stone and a police post established – named Towoth. It was presently manned by Richard Whalley, who held the position of Frontier Agent.

Dick had already heard of Richard Whalley from General Platt in Khartoum. He knew Whalley had formerly been the British consular officer at Maji in Ethiopia, but he had been forced out by the invading Italians. The commander went on to say, "Whalley asked the Khartoum government for 1000 local troops and 2000 rifles so he could go back into Ethiopia and harass the Italians. But Khartoum has refused the request, thinking Whalley is a bit of an eccentric who wants to be another Lawrence of Arabia. Therefore he is stuck holding down the small police post at Boma."

The commander went on to point out that the Sudan Defence Force was more flexible than traditional forces and the southern command of the S.D.F. thought harassing the Italians was a good idea. They had decided to do it, but on a much smaller scale than Whalley envisioned. This was Dick's assignment: march to the borderlands and harass the Italian forces so they would not invade the Sudan.

Dick's first job was to recruit and train his troops. With the help of an officer from the Sudan Defence Force, Dick sent messages to all the local chiefs in the region asking for young men who wanted to go to war. Within days hundreds of warriors showed up, eager for the chance to fight. Under the British colonial government, local fighting between the tribes had been restricted for a number of years. But there were still many young men who wanted to be warriors and this was their opportunity to prove their manhood. Around the Torit area lived eighteen ethnic groups. There were small variations in their languages and cultures, but they were all grouped under the general heading of Lotuxo. Men came in from all these groups. From further south along the Uganda border came warriors from an entirely different group called the Acholi. They too came from a warrior culture and were eager to fight.

Most of these warriors were magnificent examples of manhood. They were tall and very dark. They wore no clothing and had scars carved into their ebony skin. They had spent their lives hunting and herding and the muscles stood out on their chests and thighs. For Dick choosing who should serve was problematic. The recruits were eager, but they had never used a modern weapon like a rifle. Dick narrowed his choices by having ten warriors at a time line up and face him. Then he selected the men who looked the toughest, often based on size, musculature and bearing. Some just looked like fighters and some did not. An Arab attaché wrote down the names of the men who Dick had selected.

Then Dick asked each chosen man show his athleticism. At the blow of a whistle a warrior would sprint twenty paces, bend down and grab a stick and then reverse quickly, dashing back to the starting point. This was timed and Dick could quickly judge which men were the quickest and most agile. He then had them throw their spears, first for accuracy and then for distance. These were not weapons they would use against the Italian guns, but it did show Dick which men had trained to use their spears. The last test was a long run of several miles to gauge endurance. Most of the men were already superbly fit and sprinted the entire distance. Upon finishing the long race Dick noticed that some of them were not even breathing hard.

After several days of putting the recruits through their paces, Dick and the Arab attaché carefully studied their notes and made their selections. It was not final since some men would fail the training aspect, but it was an excellent start. Thirty men were selected for each platoon and Dick set up four platoons – a total of 120 men. These would be the men he would use to hold back the Italians. Dick had them all pledge an oath of loyalty to the British crown. He incorporated a traditional custom in which he held up a fighting spear and each of the selected recruits stepped up in turn and licked the blade of the spear. Over the months they would prove their loyalty over and over again.

The men who were not chosen as soldiers had the opportunity to sign on as porters. It was essential to have porters to carry food and ammunition. In addition to the 120 soldiers, Dick recruited 120 porters. These men carried no weapons, but if they proved themselves worthy, there was always the opportunity to move up in the ranks. Many stalwart men signed up as porters, looking forward to the day they too could carry a weapon and be a soldier fighting for the British empire.

Training for the new soldiers started at once. This involved marching and presenting arms with empty rifles. The guns were all standard issue .303 Lee-Enfield rifles. They were simple to use and, most importantly, continued to fire under harsh conditions. They did not jam even when filled with dust and mud. It did take some time for Dick to get his men proper uniforms. The first thing they needed was protection for their feet. Marching, stomping and turning sharp corners was painful in a land full of two-inch thorns. Dick procured some old truck tires and the men spent a few days cutting them up and making tire sandals. Then the men were given bayonets to attach to their rifles. They were taught how to aim the rifles and how to use the bayonets. Bayonet skills came easily since this involved similar skills as wielding a stabbing spear. In time the men were given bandoliers with live ammunition. These were hung over the left shoulder and fastened at the right waist. The soldiers still had no uniforms and Dick found it a bit incongruous to see his naked soldiers lined up at parade wearing only tire sandals, bandoliers and rifles. The order for khaki shorts finally arrived from Juba. Dick issued these shorts to his men and there were a hilarious few minutes as the men tried to put them on, often getting them backwards or with both legs in the same hole. But in the end they worked it out and stood at attention. Over the next weeks they were also issued khaki shirts and jerseys so each of them had a complete uniform.

Other than the .303 rifles, the only other weapons issued were a limited number of hand grenades. Dick held a competition to see which soldiers could throw spears the farthest. He then selected six men with exceptional throwing ability and carefully taught them how to lob grenades, releasing the locking device just before the throw. The soldiers wore these grenades on their belts and were warned never to use them unless Dick gave them a direct order.

Now Dick started taking the new soldiers out on patrol for several days at a time. Each man was issued a plastic ground sheet with a long thin stick and two pegs. At night the pegs were driven into the ground six feet apart and the long stick connected the two. The ground sheet was then laid over the stick, making a small tent 18 inches tall. Each man dug a small hole for his hips and then lay on his back for the entire night. The ground sheet kept off the rain and the mosquitoes.

On the training patrols each soldier was also issued ten pounds of sorghum flour. This could be mixed with water and boiled until it formed a thick nutritious paste that they called *asiera*. It was tasteless, but it provided the basic food for soldiers on the march.

Water was absolutely essential for survival in the heat of the southern Sudan. Each man was issued two metal canteens for drinking water, two pints carried on the left hip and two pints carried on the right. One canteen was used for the trip out and the other canteen was saved for the return trek. If the patrol found a water source while on the march they could indulge in all the water they wanted, but in dry country it was an issue of survival that every soldier keep the basic rules about drinking. Soldiers could not drink unless given permission by the sergeant in charge of his platoon. During a patrol the sergeant would order periodic rest stops during the heat of the day and then allow each soldier to drink three gulps of water. The sergeant would watch the Adam's apple of each soldier as he drank to make sure he only swallowed three gulps. After the three swallows the men were taught to keep some extra water in their mouths. They would insert a hard pebble and suck on the pebble for the next few miles. This technique helped to keep the glands salivating. One particular soldier developed the ability to swallow without moving his Adam's apple. When it was discovered that he had drank up most of his canteen, he had to be disciplined and then watched closely to make sure he did not do it again.

Gradually after many practice patrols, Dick felt his new troops were getting fit and ready to fight. His main concern was training the men how to use their rifles. At first the warriors had the misunderstanding that if one simply pointed a rifle in the general direction and pulled the trigger the loud sound would do the rest. Initially few men could hit even the largest target. But over time Dick taught the new soldiers to aim carefully and pull the trigger slowly. They also learned to break down and clean their rifles on a nightly basis. Most of the .303 rifles were well worn and had battered stocks, but even though they were ugly, the old guns were generally serviceable in the harsh conditions.

The porters also underwent some basic training. For every soldier carrying a rifle, there was a porter. Loads were carried on the porters' heads. A porter carried either fifty pounds of food (usually sorghum flour or dried meat) or fifty pounds of ammunition. A porter needed to be brave as well as tough. Occasionally during training they came to a river too deep to wade across. Most of the porters did not know how to swim. Dick would check the depth and width of the river and then taught the porters to march into the water with their loads balanced on their heads. When the water covered their mouths and noses they held their breath and kept on walking. The weight on their heads kept them from floating away and after a few steps they moved into shallower water and emerged with their loads and their lives intact. Dick quickly gained a great deal of respect for his porters and a number of them eventually moved up in rank and became some of his best soldiers.

At the end of a four-day training patrol Dick sank into his string bed in Torit and enjoyed a restful sleep. Early the next morning a broad, smiling face greeted him and handed him a cup of hot tea. It was Kuju! When Dick got up he found a hot bucket of water for washing and also discovered Kuju had cooked him a delicious breakfast of eggs, toast and marmalade. Kuju told Dick how he had spent weeks looking for him and was now very pleased he had finally found him. However, Dick explained to Kuju that he was now an officer going off to war. "You don't want to be part of this war," said Dick kindly. "There will be long marches every day in a hot land. There will be fighting. People will be killed. Go home to your family."

Kuju scowled. "I already know that!" he retorted. "But you still need to eat. Somebody needs to wash your uniform."

When Dick refused to enlist him, Kuju raised his voice and shouted, "I am an Azande! I come from a chiefly family! I too am a warrior. I want to go to war."

Dick did not have the heart to send Kuju home so he was permitted to join Dick's unit. Kuju was ecstatic and over time he became invaluable to Dick as a personal assistant, valet and cook. He developed the ability to come up with delicious meals in the most remote areas. He often looked out of place: a short muscular red man among the tall dark Nilotic soldiers. But his infectious enthusiasm was a positive force during the difficult days to come.

4

Into the Desert

After four weeks of intense training Dick felt his recruits were ready for battle. They were physically fit and eager to go. Dick still had some questions about their ability to shoot straight, but he knew their bayonet work was superb and he had no doubt about their bravery. If they got close enough for hand-to-hand combat with the Italians, they would prove themselves to be good fighters. Dick reported to his commander in the Sudan Defence Force. Upon entering his office he saluted and gave his assessment. "Sir! My four platoons are fit and ready to go to war. I am awaiting your orders."

The commander had been watching the steady progress of the 120 warriors. He knew they were not trained soldiers according to modern standards. But this was not a normal battlefield. The new soldiers were tough and they also knew how to live off the land. They knew how to fight in their own way. The commander had also been watching Dick closely and could see he was a natural leader of men. The commander did have some concerns about his youth and his lack of formal military training. But these were extraordinary circumstances. Therefore he gave Dick orders to proceed with his four platoons by foot to the small desert town of Kapoeta. The commander pulled out a worn map and rolled it out on his desk. With his finger he traced a footpath from Torit to Kapoeta, a distance of about 130 miles. The trail wound around the base of the Dongatona and Didinga hills. Beyond the town of Kapoeta the map was vague. There were virtually no place names and vast areas had no data at all. There were some curved sets of lines indicating mountains, but Dick could tell the mapmaker had drawn these in free hand and that they had little connection to reality.

The commander continued with his briefing. He pointed at the map and said, "Kapoeta is right here, located in a semi-arid area at the junction of two sand rivers. The town only exists because it is possible to dig wells in the sand and find water. The temperatures are extremely hot. Your soldiers will need to proceed from Torit to Kapoeta on foot. This will give them the experience of marching under real circumstances. They should be able to do the march in three days. Your porters should march as well, but carrying a minimum of loads. Meanwhile I'll send a lorry ahead of you to Kapoeta carrying the bulk of your food and ammunition."

The commander looked down at the map again and put his

finger on a spot to the east named Loelli. "This will be your first destination after leaving Kapoeta. Loelli is a permanent waterhole surrounded by rock. It is sometimes used by the Nyangatom tribesmen for watering their goats. There is no water between Kapoeta and Loelli and it is a distance of over 100 miles, so your men would have to make a hard two-day march and carry all their own water. Think they're up to it?"

Dick nodded and again looked closely at the old map. Beyond Loelli there was nothing, just the few vague lines that indicated mountains. The commander and Dick strategized for another ten minutes. The commander suggested Dick and his men build a base at Loelli so they would have somewhere to retreat when necessary. From the base at Loelli they could march into the mountains and engage the Italians troops – whenever and as often as possible.

Dick left the commander's office with a deep sense of excitement and also with a sense of duty. He called for his four sergeants. His master sergeant was named Musa. He was a Nuba from the northern Sudan: a tribe famous for their wrestling. Musa stood six feet and four inches tall and he still had the wide shoulders and bulging biceps that showed he had been a champion wrestler in his youth. Musa had already had training and experience fighting with the Sudan Defence Force and was the obvious choice for master sergeant. Since all the other men were new recruits, the commander of the Sudan Defence Force in Torit had insisted that at least one of Dick's men be an experienced fighter. Musa also knew some basic English, so Dick had one man in his command with whom he could communicate clearly.

The other three sergeants were chosen from the Lotuxo recruits. In the selection process they had demonstrated superior fighting skills as well as leadership qualities. Kutur was older than most of the recruits and even had a few grey hairs on his balding head. He was thin as a whippet but was still extremely fit. He carried himself with dignity and exuded authority. When he spoke, people listened.

Loro was quite the opposite, a younger man who seldom spoke. He led by example and was always the first to see work that needed to be done. He was mature and calm under pressure.

The final man that Dick had considered was named Bakit. He was an impetuous young man, full of enthusiasm and laughter. Dick had noticed him right away. When there was hilarity and loud talk around the fire at night, usually Bakit was involved. Because of his young age Dick at first hesitated to give him a position of authority. But he was liked by all and many of the younger men gravitated to him and looked to him for orders. As Dick watched him he realized that Bakit was a natural leader and that his men would follow him anywhere. So he had chosen Bakit as the fourth sergeant and put a number of the younger men under his command. With their enthusiasm they would be the first troops sent into battle. Dick knew his troops needed a strict chain of command. But he also knew instinctively that the chain of command was much more effective when men respected their leaders. Dick chose well and this was proven over and over in the tough months ahead.

Dick called his four sergeants together. He talked quietly with them and informed them of the general plan. He told each of them to have his platoon ready to march an hour before dawn on the following day.

The next morning in the gray light of the coming dawn the soldiers lined up at attention wearing full battle gear. Each platoon lined up behind its sergeant. Dick stood before them and gave a short speech. The sergeants presented arms, saluted and stomped their right feet. It was a glorious scene: young men dressed and ready for war.

Each platoon then broke ranks and the soldiers headed out, walking one behind the other in single file. Marching in formation was not an option. They were following a small footpath that curved around thorn bushes and trees and wound in and out of dry riverbeds. On this first march Dick rode a gray horse. He wanted to be able to move up and down the line of soldiers and keep an eye on how they were doing. As the sun rose over the sharp peaks of the Dongotona Hills, it shone on the long line of armed soldiers. They were a noble sight and Dick felt proud to be part of this unique fighting force. But he wondered what lay ahead. His men were barely trained and they were unseasoned. He felt like he was marching into the mouth of a lion. His orders were clear and yet vague at the same time. Stop the Italians.

Dick could see his soldiers and the porters were stepping out at a good pace. The line stretched out for about half a mile. In the cool of the morning they talked and joked among themselves. Occasionally the footpath passed a Lotuxo village with its tall-roofed houses. The women and children came out to watch the passing soldiers. The women ululated loudly, making the high trilling sound with their tongues that spoke of heroes and courage. The soldiers lifted their sandaled feet higher and took longer strides, urged on by the adulation of the women. Even Kuju picked up the pace, proudly carrying a large cooking pot on top of his head.

At midmorning the line of solders entered a grove of tamarind trees. Dick signaled to his sergeants to take a short break. They gave the appropriate orders and the men sank to the ground in the welcome shade. Upon the orders of the sergeants, each of the men took three swallows of water from their canteens. After ten minutes, before they had time to stiffen up, they were ordered to stand and start marching again. They marched for two more hours. By now the heat was getting intense and there was little talking or joking. From the back of his horse Dick watched carefully to see which men were still stepping out with vigor and which ones were plodding along with heavy feet.

At noon Dick signaled for another stop. In the heat of southern Sudan nobody walked in the middle of the day when the sun was directly overhead. Again the men were allowed three gulps of water. Then each man pulled out a cold piece of *asiera* – a chunk of paste made from sorghum flour. This was easily digestible and would give them energy for the rest of the day. Guards were set and then everyone else stretched out on the ground and slept. Dick also took advantage of the long midday break. He dismounted from his gray mare, took off her saddle and tied her to a tree. He gave her a little drink from his canteen and some sorghum grain. Then after eating some tasteless *asiera*, he stretched out on his saddle blanket and was soon fast asleep. He was awakened by the movement of men around him. It was 3 pm and the men were stretching and preparing for the last trek of the day. It was still hot, but they were hiking east and the sun was at their backs. As the afternoon went on it became a bit cooler, a welcome respite for tired bodies and legs. At 6 pm the final halt was called near a grove of trees on the edge of a sand river. The soldiers quickly scrambled to set up camp for the night. Everyone knew what to do. Some gathered firewood while others started fires and began to cook up sorghum flour into *asiera*. As the porridge bubbled away they cut up pieces of *biltong* and added them to the mixture. The pieces of dried meat added flavor to the bland porridge. Other men went to the sand river and dug shallow wells searching for clean water. Thorn branches were cut and were used to form a *zariba*, a wall of thorns around the camping place. This would give protection from marauding hyenas and lions.

Dick again unsaddled his gray mare and gave her a quick rub-down and some water. He then tied her to a tree with a 30-foot rope, giving her space to crop the yellow grass. Kuju appeared with the porter who had been carrying Dick's camping gear. The porter set up a folding table and chair while Kuju busied himself making a fire and heating water for Dick's bath. One of the men also set up the sticks and hung up Dick's groundsheet. After Dick had washed off the sweat and dust of the day, he returned to his table and found it set with a plate, cup and silver. The food that was set before him was the same *asiera* and dried meat the men were eating, but it was presented in a formal way as befitted the *Bimbashi* in charge of four platoons. At the end of the meal Dick was presented with the two halves of a juicy grapefruit. This was followed by a strong cup of tea, well sugared to give energy. It was hard for Dick to believe he was actually going to war. It felt like he was on a picnic. That night as he lay on the sand, he looked up at a brilliant milky way full of myriads of stars. He thought of Nora so far away in rainy dull England. Communication between the two of them would be virtually impossible over the coming months. He would have to rely on his memory and imagination.

The next morning they were up and walking before daylight, starting out in the cool of the morning. The sharp peaks of the Dongotonas rose above them, but they were in the flats and skirted around the northern end of the hills. They followed the same sequence of walking and resting as the previous day, a sequence that would become their pattern for the coming months. Dick continued to ride his horse up and down the line of soldiers, getting to know the strengths and abilities of each man. Occasionally he would dismount and march along with his men. He was coming to the realization that a horse would be difficult to feed in the coming days. Forage would be at a minimum in the semi-desert and it was not feasible to have porters carrying grain for the horse. Dick also knew they would be scaling some steep rocky hills where a horse would be a liability.

On the afternoon of the third day the men reached the small dusty town of Kapoeta. They set up camp under some straggly acacia trees on the bank of a dry sand river. Immediately some of the soldiers started digging and they found cool clear water under the coarse yellow sand. Meanwhile Dick rode into town and checked in with Geoffrey King, the District Commissioner for the southeast region of Sudan. He was an officer working under the Sudan Political Service while Dick was serving as an officer in the Sudan Defence Force. However, there was usually excellent cooperation between officers of the two organizations.

They had different jobs to do, but both needed the other. Dick talked about logistical issues for an hour and received a generous offer of help. As Dick left the office he was invited to come back for dinner at the District Commissioner's home. That evening they shared an excellent meal of roasted kudu steak and rice. There were no vegetables and fruit, such delicacies being a rarity in the hot, arid climate. Dick spent several hours questioning Geoffrey King about the Toposa people who lived in the surrounding area. He learned the Toposa were a warrior people that belonged to the Karamajong cluster. They had immigrated into this region from northeast Uganda several hundred years before. They were hard to govern since they were constantly raiding cattle from the neighboring people like the Didinga, Boya and Turkana. The District Commissioner said he had his hands full trying to keep the peace. He told Dick many stories of raids and counter raids. He also pointed out that Dick and his four platoons were heading into the harshest area in the district. Even the Toposa avoided it. Only a highly mobile tribe called the Nyangatom used this region and then only in the rainy season. He also confirmed that in the dry season Loelli held the only permanent water in the area.

Then the District Commissioner changed the topic. He leaned across the table and insisted, "You must take a guide who knows the area. I recommend a Didinga man from the nearby hills. He has a reputation as a famous elephant tracker. His name is Logoto. He has formerly guided ivory hunters into the mountains of Ethiopia and knows the location of the ancient trails. He can also speak the language of the mountain Murle who live in the Boma region."

Dick agreed he needed such a man. Logoto was called in and Dick spoke to him for a few minutes. He was an older man who carried himself with dignity. Dick questioned him through an interpreter and he answered the queries quietly but with authority. The short interview revealed that Logoto knew the region well and would be invaluable for the coming military campaign. Dick, impressed by his knowledge and bearing, enlisted him on the spot.

The next morning was the real thing. No more practice. The loads for the porters had been laid out the night before. At Dick's command the porters rushed to pick up the loads, each struggling to find the heaviest load and wanting to show off his strength and endurance. The four platoons presented arms in the cool gray dawn. Dick gave them an inspection and then ordered them to start marching. They were guided by Logoto, the Didinga tracker. Only he knew the faint path that led toward Loelli. He was followed by three of the platoons. Then came the 120 porters with the loads on their heads. At the rear walked the fourth platoon protecting the rear of the long caravan.

Dick had decided to abandon his gray mare and left her in Kapoeta with Geoffrey King. Eventually somebody would ride her back to Torit and she would re-enter the military stable. Dick walked near the front of the long caravan. It felt good to be stretching his legs and he liked being on the same level as his men, not on a horse looking down on them. He also enjoyed hiking near the front of the caravan because he could look ahead and enjoy the birds and wildlife before they were frightened by the line of soldiers.

For the first few hours they marched along the bank of a large sand river. They walked in the dappled shade of large acacia trees and passed a number of Toposa villages with their graduated grass roofs. Dick noted that every village was surrounded by a high thorn fence with a stout gate that could be closed against night-time marauders, both animal and human. Toposa warriors came out of their villages and watched them curiously as they marched by. The men wore blue mudpacks woven into their hair, often with several ostrich feathers rising like a plume above their foreheads. All of the warriors kept their sharp spears near at hand – just in case they were needed.

The four sergeants monitored the water situation carefully. Water was going to be a problem once they left the sand river. During the midday break some soldiers were assigned to dig wells in the sand river and everyone drank their fill and topped off their canteens. This would be the last source of water until they reached the pool at Loelli.

That afternoon Logoto turned east away from the sand river and the caravan entered a dense acacia thicket. It seemed to Dick that every bush had two-inch thorns and these tugged at his arms and legs. The footpath led through this scrub for several hours and then they suddenly came to a semi-desert with red gravel underfoot. Now Dick could see for a long distance and he spotted animals on the horizon. Using his binoculars he identified them as Beisa oryx, beautiful desert antelope with long straight horns. Later on in the day Dick also spotted a flock of ostriches and some Rainey's gazelles. All of these animals were adapted to desert life and could live for long periods without water. The scrub forest they had left seemed to be perfect habitat for black rhino and Dick asked Logoto about the absence of rhino sign.

He said that in the past there were many rhinos in the area, but that the *shifta* from Ethiopia had come into the region and shot most of them, taking their horns to sell in Addis Ababa.

That night the caravan bivouacked out in the open under the stars. The soldiers and porters cut thorn bushes and made a tight *zariba*. Guards were set and changed every four hours. Dick had been impressed by how Logoto was able to find and follow even the faintest trail. That night he wrote in his diary, "A path is a long thin ribbon of certainty and destination in the trackless wastes of wild country." Later, as Dick lay under his ground sheet, he could hear the rising whoop of a spotted hyena in the distance and he was glad he was safely inside a thorn enclosure.

The following day was a long, hard march. The drinking of water was tightly controlled and by late afternoon Dick estimated they had trekked over forty miles. Again the terrain changed. Now they were walking on black gravel with large rocks everywhere. These radiated heat in the afternoon sun and burned the soldiers' feet even through their thick tire sandals. Logoto led them to an area of large basalt rocks and suddenly they arrived at a large depression. Here Dick saw a pool of water covered with a green scum of algae. They had arrived at Loelli. Logoto assured him that water was always to be found in the pool even in the height of the dry season. Many of the men were foot-sore and limping, but they had all made the long trek successfully. The porters threw their loads to the ground and rushed to the pool where they waded in and took long drinks of the green water. Then they waded in deeper and washed off the dust from the long trek. The soldiers from the rear of the caravan were particularly dirty from the dust and Dick made a mental note to himself to keep walking at the head of the long procession.

That night the troops and porters slept the sleep of the exhausted. But again sentries were set to watch out for wild animals and hostile tribesmen. The next morning Dick rose to a pink dawn and the whir of many wings as thousands of birds came to drink at the pool. Most of them were ring-necked doves, but there were also flocks of sand grouse and spurfowl. Right on schedule Kuju showed up with a hot cup of tea. Dick realized he was drinking tea prepared from the water of the green scummy pond. But Kuju had boiled it well. It tasted fine and Dick did not get ill. A few minutes later Kuju served up an excellent breakfast that included toast and eggs. Dick wondered where Kuju procured the fresh eggs. He later discovered Kuju had buried eggs in the loads of sorghum flour that were carried by the porters. The flour kept the eggs fresh and also kept them from breaking.

After breakfast Dick wandered around the local area looking at the lay of the land and the various rock formations. The original plan was to build a simple fortified enclosure in the area that they could use as a bolt-hole if they needed to retreat from the borderlands. After looking around Dick decided Loelli itself was an ideal location to fortify because of the many loose rocks and the presence of permanent water. Dick made some rough plans on paper and marked out the area with sticks driven into the ground. Then both soldiers and porters were assigned the job of picking up large stones and bringing them to the markers. Other soldiers were given the job of placing these stones to form rough walls. No mortar was used, just stones fitted on top of one another. The finished walls were about four feet high and two feet thick. They were high enough to hide behind and thick enough to stop any incoming bullets. The men spent the next three days building and extending the walls. In some locations inner walls were also built so there was a secondary line of retreat. The resulting walls faced north, east and south. On the west side and almost enclosed by the walls was the pool, so drinking water was always accessible. When the project was finished, Dick made a final inspection and was convinced the simple fort was defensible if it ever came under siege by the enemy.

5

Living off the Land

Now Dick had to think about the next phase of the operation – engaging the enemy. Looking at his simple map full of blank space he estimated it was 50 miles east to the base of the mountains. The tops of the nearer mountains were part of Sudan territory. But the further mountain range was inside Ethiopia and Dick suspected this was where the Italians had built their forts. He conferred with his Didinga guide and Logoto assured him there was an ancient footpath that led up to the top of the first range of mountains. Logoto said he had once been there with a white man who was hunting elephants for their ivory. He described a wide valley between the two ranges of mountains – a valley that contained thick forest and many elephant and buffalo.

Dick decided to give his men two days rest before making a forced march into the mountains. They had all worked hard building the fort and deserved a short break. They also needed protein. The dried meat was coming to an end. The next morning after breakfast Dick loaded his rifle and taking several soldiers with him he headed south to a small rocky knoll. At the top of the knoll he sat under a small whistling thorn and glassed the area to the south. The shimmering heat waves made it difficult to focus, but eventually he spotted a small herd of oryx. They were feeding slowly to the east, their long black horns glinting in the bright sunshine. Dick decided to make a try for them. After studying the terrain he and his men set off at a lope, moving southeast so as to intercept the oryx at a small *wadi* in the distance. Dick and his men made good time and reached the *wadi* before the oxyx spotted them. Once in the shallow ravine they bent low and moved forward to the location where they thought the oryx would cross. When they arrived at that point, Logoto carefully raised his head and looked over the bank. He immediately ducked back down and nodded to Dick indicating that the oryx were nearby. Dick removed the safety catch from his rifle and carefully raised his head so he could see over the bank. The oryx were walking steadily towards him, only about 100 paces away. Dick aimed carefully at the chest of the lead oryx and slowly squeezed the trigger. The oryx staggered, caught itself and started to run. But then it stumbled and fell. Upon hearing the shot the rest of the herd took off running, heading for the far horizon. However, one oryx realized its companion was not coming. It stopped for a moment and looked back over its shoulder. Dick had already reloaded and was able to get off a quick shot. The second oryx dropped immediately with a shot to the spine. One of Dick's men sprinted out to the second oryx and cut its throat with a bayonet. This made the meat *halal* so it could be eaten by the Muslims who were part of the caravan.

The soldiers immediately started to skin the two oryx and to cut up the meat. Dick admired the long horns and the beautiful patterned faces of the dead oryx. In a way he regretted what he had done, but he had shot well and the oryx experienced little suffering. More importantly the caravan had to live off the land. The two oryx provided over 500 pounds of good meat, more than the hunting party could carry. One of the soldiers ran back to the fortifications at Loelli and soon a string of porters headed for the location of the dead oryx. They were pleased to see the fresh meat and walked back across the hot plains, each with a large piece of meat balanced on his head.

That night the rich smell of roasting meat permeated the camp. The men sat in small groups laughing, talking and singing. After eating their fill of meat, a soldier started drumming. The rhythm throbbed through the dark evening and the men stood up and started to dance. They abandoned themselves to the sound of the drum and beat out steps as ancient as the African continent itself. Dick sat at his table alone eating oryx cutlets and rice and thinking it was one of the tastiest meals he had ever eaten. The sound of the men dancing was a beautiful backdrop to his meal in the wilderness.

The next morning the sergeants had their men up before dawn. The porters picked up their loads with the extra weight of meat balanced on top. With the guide leading the way they headed straight east. The path was very faint and there were no landmarks, just rocks and the occasional thorn bush. They knew they had a long trek ahead of them and no guarantee of finding water. Dick informed his sergeants to monitor the men carefully and to make sure they did not drink their water too soon. Everyone was given orders only to drink water upon command and then only to drink three gulps.

By the end of the first day everyone was exhausted. Camp that night was simple, but even in his exhaustion Dick was careful to set sentries at the four corners of the makeshift camp. The next morning they were up again early and walking before dawn, trying to get as far as possible before the heat of the sun burned down on them. By midmorning Dick looked ahead and saw the faint blue outline of a large mountain on the eastern horizon. As they kept marching, the lines of the mountain became more distinct. It rose up thousands of feet out of the hot plains and the cliffs were sheer granite. Dick realized from his map he was looking at Moru Agippi, one of the largest plateaus in the region. This mountain was part of Sudan. Dick wondered how they would ever climb to the top of such steep cliffs. He conferred with Logoto. He smiled and pointed south of the cliffs, indicating through gestures that there was a more gradual route around the south end of the plateau.

By late afternoon the men were getting very tired. They were also thirsty and many of them were sucking on small pebbles to keep their saliva flowing. As they neared the base of the cliffs, they gained elevation and the terrain started changing. The ground changed from black clay to brown soil and soon they saw small groves of deciduous trees. The grass got longer and in the low spots it rose over their heads. This long grass made walking miserable. The sharp edges of the grass leaves were like saw blades and made minute scratches on the soldiers' arms and legs. The heads of the grass also contained pointed seeds and these fell and embedded themselves in the uniforms of the hot, sweaty solders. There was also a total lack of breeze when marching through the tall grass. It tended to make the men feel claustrophobic. It was a relief for everyone when they came out on some higher ridges and got a little fresh air. At the front of the caravan Dick now spotted animals: not desert animals, but giraffe, warthog, reedbuck and Lelwell's hartebeest. In the far distance he saw a line of black. It was a large herd of Nile buffalo, the great wild bovines of Africa.

Gradually the temperatures got cooler and coming around a corner of the mountain they encountered a small gallery forest. Such a forest meant water. Dick indicated to his men that they could break rank. They set down their equipment and loads and ran into the forest, finding a small clear stream. Here they drank deeply and washed the dust from their tired bodies. The cool water felt especially good as it soothed the minute scratches left by the sharp grass. Then the sergeants called for order and the men quickly cut thorn branches and made a protective *zariba* for the night. Dick went to sleep that night with a real sense of accomplishment. They had successfully traveled over 230 miles of country and the last 100 miles were really rough. All of his men had made it and were still in good shape. Now it was time to tackle the mountains and move into enemy territory.

6

The Great Buffalo Hunt

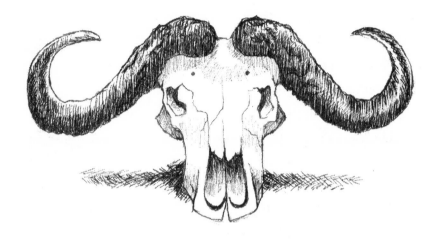

Dick woke the next morning to the soft rhythmic cooing of a tambourine dove, a clear indication they were camped in a gallery forest. He heard the quiet voices of his men as they finished their morning breakfast and started organizing their equipment and their loads.

At first light they stepped out with Logoto once again leading the way. He led them straight up a gap to the south of the granite cliffs. At first the faint path was fairly smooth and the grade was gradual, but it soon grew steeper and after a short time the men were having to scramble over large rocks. Here they were exposed to the fierceness of the scorching sun. By late morning the rocks were radiating heat and burned their feet right through their tire sandals. Most of the soldiers were people of the plains and not used to climbing mountains. The backs of their calves ached from the constant climbing and their breaths came in hoarse gasps. It was even harder on the porters who had to carry heavy loads on their heads and keep them balanced as they scrambled over the rocks. Being from the Didinga tribe, Logoto was a hill man used to walking up steep trails. He sprang from rock to rock like a klipspringer. Dick followed closely behind him, but he eventually came to a stop and stood gasping for air. He signaled for the following men to take a long break and catch their breaths. For the rest of the day they took regular breaks – then short climbs – then more rest stops. Gradually they gained elevation and the air became somewhat cooler. During his many breaks Dick turned and looked back over the hot plains they had navigated the previous days. He also looked down on the men climbing below him. By now they were spread out over a mile and were blowing hard. Some were scrambling on all fours and others were grabbing branches and using them to pull themselves upward. Trees were now infrequent and only stunted bushes and tufts of mountain grass grew on the rocky escarpment. Dick looked ahead and saw Logoto standing on the summit. Dick made one final effort and finally stood at the top, exhausted but triumphant. The view to the west was magnificent. It was vast, open country shimmering in the heat. He turned and looked east toward the Ethiopian border. In front of him he saw many hills and ridges and in the far distance he saw the faint hazy line of large mountains. Ethiopia! Those were the mountains controlled by the Italians. The hills and valleys in front of him was Sudanese territory. It was his assignment to clear this zone of Italian troops and push them back into Ethiopia.

Over the next hour the soldiers reached the crest of Moru Agippa, followed by the tired porters. It was getting late in the afternoon and Dick did not want his men in the open overnight. He conferred with Logoto who led them down the gradual slope heading east. They entered a wooded valley and found a small stream of flowing water. Logoto led them to a grove of strangler fig trees. Underneath the large trees the ground was open. There were piles of ashes, indicating this spot had been used by travelers in former times. The men threw down their loads and sank to the ground exhausted. Dick gave them a few minutes of rest and then told the sergeants to have the men gather firewood and start cooking. Since they were in a valley the fires would be hidden and the smoke dissipated by the heavy foliage covering the camp. After the meal of *asiera* and dried oryx meat, sentries were set on the large boulders surrounding the camp. That night there was little sound as the soldiers and porters slept like dead men.

The next morning, after Kuju delivered his cup of tea, Dick walked around the area and did a recce. The location was well hidden and had a constant source of clean water. Dick decided to make this spot his base camp for sorties into the eastern valleys. The first order of business was to send the porters back to Kapoeta. Much of what the porters had carried was sorghum flour and half of this food was being used to feed the porters themselves. With the porters gone there would be twice as much food available for the soldiers. Dick decided he would cache the surplus food at his new base camp. His troops could carry their own food for short treks and then return to base to rest up. Then they could pick up more food and ammunition for the next sortie.

Dick informed the porters they would be returning to Kapoeta. He gave them two days to rest up and on the third day they were given four days worth of flour and sent back down the mountain. They were also given a small escort of four soldiers. Since they were traveling light, Dick figured they could get back to Loelli in two days and then two more days on to Kapoeta. Dick wrote a note to the military attaché based in Kapoeta with a request that the porters be given a rest and then be issued with more sorghum flour and basic food supplies. The porters would then carry these supplies back to Dick's base camp at the crest of Moru Akippi.

With the porters gone, the camp became quiet and Dick started making plans for the first attack on the Italians. The location where they were camped was uninhabited, but 70 miles to the north lived the highland Murle. These people were located on the plateau called Boma and behind the plateau was an enormous volcanic plug rising hundreds of feet into the sky. The Murle people called this spire Towath. It was a landmark that could be seen from many miles away. On future treks this spire of rock helped Dick keep his bearings as he moved through the area. Eventually Dick would get to Boma, but for now he was located far south of the police post located there and would not meet the officers for another year. But he did need information from the Murle people who lived in the area, so he sent Logoto to contact them. In the Khartoum archives he had read that the Murle had originally migrated from Ethiopia to Sudan hundreds of years earlier and their language was from the Surmic language family. Logoto's mother tongue was Didinga and this language was also from the Surmic language family, so Logoto could communicate at a basic level with Murle speakers.

Logoto was gone for several days. Dick occupied himself by climbing the ridge behind the camp and glassing the area with his binoculars. He tried to get familiar with the lay of the land so he could make decisions quickly when needed. On the third day he saw large dark bodies moving down a valley. Buffalo! His men needed meat and these large herbivores would provide a great amount of protein. However, Dick did not want to give away his position by shooting with rifles. He went back to the base camp and talked to his sergeants. Upon hearing about the buffalo, they got very excited. Kutur explained to Dick that the Lotuxo soldiers were experienced buffalo hunters and they could kill the buffalo quietly, using spears instead of bullets. This met with Dick's approval and two of the sergeants, Kutur and Bakir, climbed back up the ridge with Dick and studied the location of the buffalo. Dick told Bakir that he and his men could be the hunters. Dick knew Bakir and his young men were eager to show their valor. Bakir raced back to the base camp and quickly chose twenty of his men. Ten of them carried their traditional Lotuxo spears, having refused to give them up even though they were now armed with rifles. The other ten men carried their rifles, unloaded but with bayonets at the ready. All of them took off running toward the buffalo herd with Bakir in the lead. Dick sat on the ridge with Kutur and watched their progress through his binoculars. When the hunters neared the herd of feeding buffalo, most of the men veered off and entered a rocky valley below the herd. Here each of them took up positions behind large rocks and trees. The three remaining men ran up the slope and got behind the feeding buffalo. When they were in the right position, they showed themselves and ran at the buffalo, yelling and screaming. The startled buffalo took one look at the charging warriors, turned and fled. They headed down the slope into the wooded valley, seeking the closest cover. As they raced past the hidden soldiers, each of them stepped out from his hiding place and thrust his spear or bayonet into the chest or gut of a passing buffalo. Within minutes it was over. There were eight dead buffalo lying on the ground. Dick sent Kutur down to the base to get more soldiers to help with the butchering. Several wounded buffalo had escaped, but the warriors followed the blood spoor and later found four more buffalo lying dead in the bush. Twelve buffalo proved to be a lot of meat. The butchering was done quickly because Dick did not want to attract attention by having vultures circling over the site of the kill. As the meat was cut into small pieces, it was picked up and carried back to base. Here it was cut into strips. Drying racks were built. The strips of raw meat were dipped in a salt solution and then placed on these racks. Small smoky fires were lit under the racks and kept going for several days. By this time the meat had lost its moisture and had shriveled to thin black sticks. These weighed almost nothing, but still had good protein value and would keep for months. Now Dick had the needed provisions and could move freely around the area.

The next day Logoto showed up with two Murle men. They were wearing decorated bark cloth and had elaborate upswept mudpacks worked into their hair. Both men were middle aged.

They had slight builds, but had sharply defined muscles. Logoto said he could communicate well with these two men. Dick, speaking through Logoto as interpreter, began asking the men about the movements and locations of the Italians. He quickly learned what he had already surmised. The Italians had dug in and made forts along the ridges which marked the border between Ethiopia and Sudan. These forts were made of stone. Each fort was manned by Italian officers together with Ethiopian soldiers. Some of the forts had big guns and these were mounted facing the Sudan. The Murle men said the tribal people in the area did not like the Ethiopian soldiers who were fighting with the Italians. They frequently went out into neighboring villages and demanded corn and manioc from the local farmers. This food was taken back to the forts to feed the soldiers manning the ramparts. Although the region had the potential to produce good crops, the local tribesmen were now half starved and were only surviving by eating wild grasses, insects and mushrooms.

Dick liked the demeanor of the two Murle men. They seemed forthright and honest in their answers. Dick asked if they would like to work for him as scouts. They both readily agreed, seeing the young British officer and his men as a much better option than the Italians. Dick entered their names in his little pay book: Korok and Kireer. Then they were escorted to the nearest fire where they were given roasted buffalo meat. They gorged themselves and were quickly convinced they had made the right decision. Both of them carried old worn .303 rifles, the same caliber that Dick's men were using. Dick offered them bullets and gun oil and they promptly sat down and started cleaning the rust off their guns.

Dick sat with them and continued to ask questions. Korok explained that the little town of Maji was the Italian headquarters for the region. But in recent months the activity had shifted from Maji to the Sudan border where the stone forts had been built. Mules had been used to bring in the big guns and there were many soldiers assigned to man the forts. Both Italian officers and their Ethiopian troops were now moving around the area in large numbers.

Dick knew a little about the town of Maji from his studies in Khartoum. This small town was located 120 miles to the east at the top of a rugged escarpment, well inside Ethiopia. It was situated at the edge of steep cliffs and faced south toward the distant Kenya border. For many years it had been the hideout for *shifta* bandits who used it as a base for raiding into Kenya and Sudan. These raiders went out on horseback and came back heavily laden with ivory, rhino horn and slaves. From 1903-1935, the emperors of Ethiopia had various governors based at Maji where they maintained a small administrative compound surrounded by giant eucalyptus trees. Being located at 9,000 feet, the climate at Maji was often cold and damp and could become depressing to those living there on a long-term basis. But the coolness was much appreciated by those who trekked in from the hot arid lands to the south.

Slaving had been a way of life in Maji for centuries. The Ethiopian governors were supposed to suppress the slave trade, but more often they were involved in it. Whenever an emperor died in Addis Ababa, all governors automatically lost their jobs. They would seize as many local people as possible before leaving the area, selling them as slaves and using the money as retirement pay. Dick had read a book written by Major Darley who visited Maji in 1905. While Major Darley was in Maji the governorship changed and the area fell into chaos. Darley was arrested and imprisoned in a small hut. Over a two-day period he had watched 20,000 people walking by his hut in chains, all heading for the slave markets near Addis Ababa.

Dick also knew about Captain Whalley who had been assigned to Maji as British Consul in 1931. His job had been to establish firm borders between Ethiopia, Kenya and Sudan. He had traveled extensively around the area trying to curtail the illegal raids of the *shifta* and to stop slaves being taken from Kenya and Sudan. He had been evacuated from Maji in 1936 when the town was invaded by Italian forces.

Now the Italians were obviously making a big push east from Maji to the Sudanese border. Building the forts along the border had taken a lot of work and effort, so clearly the Italians were doing this with a goal in mind. Kireer entered the conversation and pointed out that in recent months the Italian troops were making frequent forays out from the forts and into the valleys of the Sudan. Some of these units were made up of ethnic Eritreans from the far north. They had a reputation for being good fighters. The rest of the units were made up of Somalis, an ethnic group from the eastern deserts of Ethiopia. These units were always led by Italian officers, dressed in blue uniforms and riding white mules. On their sorties into Sudan they would camp for a few days and do some hunting. Then they would return to their forts in the mountains. Kireer pointed out that these forays were happening much more frequently and each time the units were going further west into the Sudan. In fact one small group was presently camping at the base of the mountains near a small spring.

Dick listened carefully. What he heard confirmed the fears of the officers of the Sudan Defence Force. The Italians were making plans to invade the Sudan and cut the Nile River, thus isolating Egypt. That night, after conferring with his four sergeants, Dick decided they should make the first attack against the hunting party camped in the Sudan. He needed to establish the fact that the British military had arrived and would not tolerate the Italian military entering the Sudan.

Dick had been doing some serious thinking about his military strategy. He had only four platoons, a total of 120 fighting men. He was up against a number of established forts built on high ground. These forts were well manned and some of them had big guns. There was no way that Dick and his soldiers could go up against the larger numbers and win. He and his soldiers would have to harass the enemy, but not get locked in combat. This meant that in each case there must be a brief skirmish and then a quick line of retreat. He would have to be careful not to get his men in a position from which they could not escape.

The next day they marched out, fully loaded and ready to fight. Dick left only a handful of men to guard their camp and supplies. They walked all that day, led by Korok and Kireer. For most of the day they stayed near valley bottoms or on slopes facing west, so they did not reveal their presence to the Italians based in the east. The country they were traversing was fairly rough with large stones and clumps of coarse grass. Only in the valley bottoms were there large trees. Fortunately finding water was not a problem. Every valley had a small stream or a low spot where the men could dig for water. In the late afternoon they climbed a steep ridge. The Murle guides indicated they were getting near to the Italian camp so Dick signaled for his men to drop and take cover. Dick followed the Murle men as they quietly crept on hands and knees to the top of the ridge. Here they peered over. Half a mile below them Dick could see the Italian hunting camp. There were three large white tents made of canvas and in front of the tents sat several Italian officers in camp chairs. On a table in front of them were two empty wine bottles. Using his binoculars, Dick could also see a number of small green tents with Ethiopian soldiers relaxing in the vicinity. Dick did not notice any sentries on duty. The Italians were obviously a small hunting party and Dick could see several hartebeest carcasses hanging from a tree. He shifted his binoculars so he could see the lay of the land. The ridge they were on ran down toward the camp and there were large boulders that could be used as cover. Dick devised a plan of attack and retreat and then he signaled for the guides to step back from the ridge.

Upon reaching his troops Dick explained the plan to his sergeants. They then rested, staying right where they were. That night the men kept a cold camp. They lit no fires, talked in whispers, and ate only cold balls of *asiera* for supper. They slept on the hard, stony ground and were awakened at 4 am by their sergeants. The morning was cold in the mountains and the men could see their breath in the cold air. For most of the men this was a new experience, something that had never occurred in the heat of the Sudan lowlands. The men were given orders to climb quietly up to the ridge. At the top of the ridge Kutur and his platoon broke left and started creeping down the hill, moving silently from boulder to boulder. Bakir and his platoon of young eager warriors moved to the right and also made their way silently down the slope. Dick gave orders to Musa for his platoon to stay at the top of the ridge to give covering fire. Dick then led Loro and the members of the fourth platoon straight down the slope toward the camp. All of the men were experienced hunters and knew how to cover ground silently, placing one foot carefully in front of another. It was still dark, but the men had sharp eyes and were able to negotiate the rough terrain. Within an hour everyone was in place, hunkered down behind rocks and trees with guns aimed at the camp. They all had strict orders not to shoot until Dick gave the opening shot. Gradually the gray dawn came filtering down the eastern slopes. In the silence Dick heard a boubou shrike and its mate singing a beautiful duet. It seemed surreal that he was going into battle on such a pristine morning. There was movement around the green tents as some of the Ethiopian soldiers awoke and added fuel to the cooking fires. Then the door of a white tent opened and an Italian officer stepped out into the dim light. He casually looked around and then placed his hands on his hips and stretched out his back. Dick was only 100 paces away. He placed the foresight of his rifle on the officer's bare chest. A squeeze of the trigger and the officer would be dead. But Dick hesitated. He had never shot a man before. This man was not threatening him. He was only on a hunting trip. Dick lowered his rifle slightly and pulled the trigger. Dirt shot up between the man's legs and the sound of the shot reverberated in the quiet of the morning. The officer leaped back and bolted for his tent. Immediately, upon hearing the shot, all of Dick's men started shooting into the camp. Some aimed at definite targets, but most of the Italians and their troops were still sleeping in their tents. Many of Dick's men just shot at the tents. There were screams and yells from the tents as men were hit by the flying bullets. Within seconds men came barreling out of the tents like a swarm of bees, guns in hand. Now the Sudanese troops had live targets to aim at and they sent a withering hail of lead into the encampment. Some of the Ethiopian troops were badly hit, but others took cover behind rocks and started firing back. For the next half hour bullets flew in both directions. The Sudanese were on higher ground and were definitely getting the better of the battle. Two of the Italian officers went down, but the third officer managed to get behind a large boulder and began reorganizing his men. The Italian-led troops had bigger and better guns and they knew how to use them. Dick gave a loud whistle and signaled to his sergeants to retreat and this message was passed on to the three platoons. A bullet hit the rock near Dick's head and several rock splinters hit him in the cheek and forehead. Dick ducked low and started crawling up the slope, moving carefully from rock to rock, trying not to expose himself. The soldiers around him were doing the same. When they had cleared the lower area Dick signaled Musa who was waiting at the top of the ridge. Immediately Musa and his men started shooting bullets into the camp. They were too far away to do much damage, but it made the Ethiopian troops take cover and this gave time for Dick and his men to get to the top of the ridge safely.

At this point Dick ordered everyone to retreat. They all stopped shooting and took off down the western slope at a sprint. After several miles they stopped in a valley and Dick and the sergeants evaluated the battle. The two Murle scouts had not taken part in the battle, but they had watched carefully and were able to report what they had seen. They confirmed that two of the Italian officers and twenty Ethiopian soldiers were dead. They also estimated that another fifteen Ethiopian soldiers were badly wounded. The sergeants were confident the Italian party had been badly beaten and that they would return to their fort in the mountains. They were sure that they were too badly shot up to try to follow and avenge the battle. Dick agreed, but he was still cautious. He gave the order for the platoons to march at a fast pace for the next three hours. Then they took refuge in a large copse of trees where they could look back over their trail. Sentries were set and everyone lay down on the ground and slept.

Dick was awakened by a twig hitting him in the face. Looking up he saw a gentle movement in the trees over his head. Soon he saw grivet monkeys shyly looking down at him. Their long white whiskers quivered and made Dick smile. He thought back over the day. It had been a successful battle. Only three of his men had bullet wounds and none of them were serious. But now he was in a real war. The remaining Italian officer would report back to headquarters and all the forts would go on heightened alert. There would be no more sneaking up on sleeping hunting camps.

7

Retreat to Loelli

Dick was right. His attack on the small hunting party enraged the Italians high in their forts on the Ethiopian escarpment. They promptly sent out several well-armed units to track down and attack the Sudanese troops. Fortunately, Korok and Kireer had contact with the Surma people who lived in the area of the Italian forts. These Surma hated the Italians and were more than willing to have the Italians leave the area, so they sent messages to the Murle with information about the movements of the Italian units. This information was quickly forwarded on to Korok and Kireer and then on to Dick. He learned there were now three separate units moving around in Sudanese territory, all of them looking for an opportunity to engage and fight. The largest of these was in the north and they were moving quickly, using mules as pack animals. The other two groups were in the south and were moving more slowly on foot, given the rough terrain.

After conferring with his four sergeants, Dick decided his troops should try to attack both of the smaller Italian units at the same time. He knew this was dangerous, splitting his small number of soldiers into even smaller units. But he wanted to give the impression of having many more soldiers than he actually had. Korok and Kireer were called in and asked to find accurate information on exactly where the Italian units were located. The following day they returned with the information that they were camped in two separate valleys about ten miles apart. Dick put master sergeant Musa in charge of two platoons and made plans to send them to the further valley. Musa was a proven fighter and over the previous weeks had gained the respect of the Lotuxo and Acholi warriors. Musa was given strict orders to wait and attack the Italian camp an hour after dark. The Sudanese troops were told to locate themselves on higher ground and then fire into the Italian camp for only half an hour. Then they were to retreat. Musa was firmly instructed not to allow his men to get into hand-to-hand combat. Instead they were to fire from a distance.

At first Musa protested these orders. "No, *Bimbashi*! My men want a real fight! They don't want to run away like cowards!"

Dick, however, insisted on his original plan. "I promise you Musa, in time there will be some tough battles with a chance for your men to use their bayonets. Just tell them to be patient."

Dick then took the other two platoons led by Loro and Bakir.

Guided by Kireer they headed for the closer valley. They hid on the ridge until well after darkness had fallen. Then they crept down the valley until they had the Italian camp surrounded. The Italians had placed guards around their camp, but the Sudanese troops were very quiet and managed to get close. At 9 pm Dick took a position behind a large tree and fired into the camp. Immediately all of his men opened fire as well. In the dark it was hard to find specific targets and Dick knew they would not be able to kill many enemy soldiers. But the main idea was to create chaos and fear.

The Italian officers and their Ethiopian troops fired back with superior firepower. But in the dark they had no targets other than the red streaks coming out of the barrels of the Sudanese guns. After half an hour of firing, the Sudanese troops glided away into the darkness, leaving the Ethiopian troops shooting at shadows. For the rest of the night Dick and his men moved at a fast lope, heading for a rendezvous with sergeant Musa and his men. He found them at dawn. They had made a successful attack on the second Italian camp and escaped with no injuries. Dick saw both missions as a complete success. The Sudanese were creating an impression that they had many troops that were well armed and on the attack. Surprise was Dick's main offensive weapon. He decided that vigorous patrolling along the border and making occasional attacks would keep the Italians on the defensive. If he moved fast enough it would also cause the Italians to overestimate his small number of troops.

Dick gave his men two days rest in a copse of tall trees. By then they were out of food so they headed back to their cache in the valley of the fig trees. They were on the alert but casually so, knowing they had done some serious damage to the two Italian units. As they walked into the glade of fig trees, Dick suddenly became aware they were not being hailed by the sentries he had left in charge of guarding the food. He had a sudden premonition of disaster and leaped behind a large boulder. Immediately a volley of shots rang out from a well-prepared ambush. The men walking behind Dick fell to the ground, dead or severely wounded. The men at the back of the line dove into cover and soon bullets were flying in all directions. It was very close quarters and some of Dick's soldiers were forced to use their bayonets to defend themselves. Two Somali soldiers raced around the boulder with their weapons at the ready. Dick shot the leading man in the chest. By then the second Somali was upon him with a raised knife. Dick seized his arm and tried to hold him off, but the soldier was tough and wiry and broke out of his grasp. As the man leaped at him again Dick raised his bayonet and stabbed it into the man's belly with all his strength. The Somali let out a gasp and the knife fell from his nerveless hand. Then he sank to the ground. Dick looked around and saw many of his men involved in hand-to-hand combat, giving as good as they received. But Dick quickly realized that they were seriously outnumbered. He blew the whistle that signaled retreat. The Sudanese soldiers who were still on their feet stood side by side, continuing to fight as they edged backwards. The troops from the rear platoon led by Musa kept shooting at the Eritrean and Somali troops and many of them dashed for cover. This gave an opportunity for the Sudanese fighters at the front to withdraw. As soon as they had made a little space they turned and ran, pursued by the Italian-led troops. In the background Dick could see an Italian officer in his blue uniform shouting orders to his troops. But there was no opportunity to fire at him. Instead Dick turned and ran with his men, all of them heading out of the valley and toward the track that led down the mountain toward Loelli. Fear was a good motivator. The Sudanese troops were able to outrun the enemy and eventually the pursuers slowed up and let them go.

Dick was deeply troubled by what had happened. Many of his troops were badly wounded and they were bleeding and limping. He rightly assumed they had been ambushed by the larger Italian unit that had been moving around the northern valleys. He surmised that his sentries had been killed and the food stores had been pillaged. The Italians must have had a local guide who led them to their base under the fig trees. The Sudanese troops continued to make their way down the mountain trail until they reached the spring at the bottom. Here they drank and tried to wash their wounds. One of the Lotuxo soldiers had a little training as a medic and he carried a bag with basic bandages and medical supplies. He did his best and tried to wrap up the more serious wounds. Dick called in the four sergeants and asked each of them for a report on their platoon. At least 20 men were missing and presumed dead. Another 28 had been wounded, some of them seriously. Loro himself had a bayonet wound in his abdomen and could hardly stand up.

But there was no time to rest. Dick had to assume the Italian officers together with their Eritrean and Somali troops would be hard on their trail. He ordered everyone to their feet and Logoto led them back to the trail heading for the makeshift fort at Loelli. It was a sad looking caravan that set off across the scorching plains, so different from the high stepping warriors of a few weeks earlier. Many were limping badly and others wore blood soaked bandages. The wind was searing hot and the burning sun beamed down on the exhausted men. Each man had been ordered to fill his two canteens at the pool, but those with serious wounds were soon desperately in need of additional water. As the day wore on some of the men started to fail and collapsed to the ground. But Dick forced them to their feet and pushed them forward. He occasionally stopped and looked back at Moru Akippi with his binoculars. He was able to spot the Ethiopian forces working their way down the mountain toward the water hole. Dick knew their only chance of survival was to keep moving. There was no way his beaten troops could stand and fight against the larger force of Italian-led troops. They had to outrun them.

The setting sun gave them some relief as the air became slightly cooler. Dick decided they must keep walking through the night. Otherwise he knew the scorching sun would kill some of his wounded men the following day. Therefore he pushed the men and kept them moving. Dick stayed near the end of the line where the slowest men were limping along. He talked to them and encouraged them to keep walking, taking one step at a time. One of the last men in the line was his young sergeant Loro. The bayonet wound in his abdomen was serious and he struggled to keep up the pace. Finally he sank to the ground, unable to take another step. Dick knelt beside him and quickly realized Loro was finished. There was no way he could be carried. It would only mean death to those who tried to carry him. Even if they got him to Loelli there were no medical facilities to care for him. Dick spoke a few words of encouragement to his loyal sergeant. He put his hand on Loro's shoulder and gave a short prayer, asking God to take Loro into his kingdom. Then he took a single bullet, inserted it into his pistol and gave it to his brave sergeant. Loro nodded. He understood he was to use it on himself: a better death than being torn to pieces by hyenas. Dick stood up with tears in his eyes and then did a fast march to catch up with the rest of his troops. For Dick this was one of the greatest trials of guerilla warfare – lack of medical care and no chance of evacuation to a hospital facility. This was a fact known and accepted by the soldiers, but it still caused Dick great stress to have to leave wounded soldiers behind on the battlefield.

That night was hell for the wounded troops. Their bodies ached and their tongues were dry from the shortage of drinking water. But they kept shuffling along. Those that were fit shared their limited water with the wounded. Morning found them only ten miles from Loelli. As the sun rose and shone its hot rays on the weary soldiers, it sucked out the last of their energy. Knowing that they were close, however, they kept putting one foot in front of the other, driven by their desperate need for water. By mid-morning the leaders arrived at the green pool at Loelli. They waded into the pool and sucked up the water as if it was the nectar of the gods. Then they filled up their canteens and went back into the desert to share the water with the incoming wounded. Dick was still bringing up the rear and he eagerly drank the dirty water his soldiers brought to him, not caring about future stomach problems.

By noon the last stragglers had made it to the pool at Loelli. The porters were already camped there, having arrived from Kapoeta a few days earlier. There was plenty of food available.

Dick talked to the headman of the porters and soon there were pots of *asiera* boiling on the cooking fires. Dick and his three sergeants quickly set up sentries and then did a head count of their platoons. They also made plans for defending their fortification if it became necessary. For the next two days they stayed on high alert, but the Italian-led forces never appeared. Dick concluded that the enemy was not prepared at that time to face the hardships of the desert. He and his men were in a safe location where they could heal their wounded, build up their strength and prepare for the next phase of the war.

8

Rest on the Kibbish

Loelli was the land of scorpions. Every time a soldier turned over a rock, the scorpions would scramble for cover. The hard ground was filled with their oval-shaped holes, dug in such a way that the scorpions could back down their holes and have their lobster-shaped pinchers at the ready to fight off intruders. At night the men had to be careful not to sit too near the fires. The heat of the crackling fires drove the scorpions out of the cracks in the firewood, and in their desperation they would attack the nearest target they could find. Some of the scorpions were large and black with huge claws. They looked frightening, but their sting was not as bad as those of the small red scorpions. Sleeping on the sand with a ground-sheet created a potentially dangerous situation. On many nights Dick heard one of his men yell with pain. It normally took about a day for the pain to subside and Dick would give the suffering soldier a day off from duty.

Having lost twenty men, Dick needed to build up his numbers. He asked the porters for volunteers and without hesitation they all asked to be considered. Dick put them through their paces and selected twenty of the men that seemed to be the most eager and the most fit. For the next ten days he gave them military training. However, he did not have enough ammunition to teach them how to shoot with rifles, so most of the training was in hand-to-hand combat using bayonets and spears.

The wounded men used these ten days to heal from their wounds. Loelli was not an ideal camp. It was very hot and lacked good shade. But it was the best Dick could do. Most importantly they had water. There were also many animals in the vicinity and Dick went out with his rifle daily and shot hartebeest and oryx to feed his men. The Sudanese troops loved to eat fresh meat and the abundance of good food buoyed their spirits.

Since Dick did not have a wireless radio with battery power, he did not have direct contact with headquarters in Torit. He could only communicate by sending a runner carrying a hand-written message. Using this slow method of communication, he reported the situation on the Ethiopian border and told about the three battles he had fought. It took a number of days to get a turn around on the message, but eventually he received a short message from the commander in Torit, encouraging Dick to continue putting pressure on the Italian forts. He was also overjoyed to receive a packet of letters from his beloved Nora. He climbed a rock above the pool at Loelli and spent hours reading through the letters. Some of the letters were weeks old. England seemed very far away and the daily life in England that Nora described seemed unreal. Dick and Nora had planned to marry after his two-year assignment with the Church Missionary Society. But now with the war looming, the marriage seemed far in the future. He wrote a response to Nora, but he could not tell her much of what he was doing since his assignment was classified. Instead he spent much of the letter describing the mountains, the animals and the local people he had met. As he closed the letter, he also spoke of his undying love and promised he would return as soon as the war was over. The next day he put the letter in a waterproof envelope and gave it to the messenger who would carry the letter back to Torit. When it would get to England was simply conjecture.

The Murle guides, Korok and Kireer, had stayed in the mountains, so Dick was without their valuable information. But the Didinga guide, Logoto, had come to Loelli with the soldiers. Dick spent some time with him trying to plan the next step. He needed to get his men back into action, but he knew the trail up the side of Moru Akippi would be watched by the Italian forces. Logoto told him about another approach from the south. It was seldom used by caravans because getting to the base of the mountains involved more time walking across harsh low country. Logoto said he had used this route once before with the English elephant hunter. The biggest problem would be carrying enough water. But Logoto went on to explain that at the base of the mountains there was a deep depression up in the rocks that contained permanent water. He referred to it in his language as *maam ci koli*, meaning "black water". From here they could ascend the gradual hills and end up on the banks of the Kibbish River.

Dick did not like the sound of a water hole containing black water. He imagined a dirty pond soiled with baboon droppings. But water was essential and there seemed to be no other options. Therefore plans were made to leave Loelli the following day and head for the Kibbish.

The remaining porters were ordered back to Kapoeta, along with several soldiers who were still suffering from their wounds. The active soldiers would now have to carry their own loads, food as well as ammunition. The newly commissioned soldiers carried exceptionally heavy loads. They were led by a sergeant named Tagoon. He was an Acholi soldier who had fought well and had shown leadership ability, so Dick gave him the position of sergeant to replace Loro.

They started off in the early dawn. Before leaving each man drank as much water as he could and carefully filled his two canteens. This water would have to last for several days. The men were ordered to drink no water until evening. This was a method used by the Sudan Defence Force in the northern deserts, so Dick decided to try it in the deserts around Loelli. They started walking southeast with Logoto leading them. There was no trail whatsoever. For the first few miles they worked their way carefully through large black rocks. Then they came to a plain covered with *sansaveria*, a type of wild sisal. These green succulents had a long, sharp thorn at the top of each blade. They were wicked plants and everyone had to slow down and step carefully to prevent themselves from getting stabbed in the legs by the vicious thorns. Dick had heard that elephants liked to chew *sansaveria* because they could get moisture from the juicy plants. It was obvious that elephants had been here because the area was covered with large balls of elephant dung. Since the strings of *sansaveria* were indigestible, they looked like balls of white twine. Eventually the caravan trekked out of the area of wild sisal and crossed a wide plain. This had once been covered with grass, but had recently been burnt by the local Nyangatom people. The result was black ash and sharp stubble. As the men marched, the ash rose up in a suffocating cloud, making it hard to breathe. It was also important that the men watch their steps because the burnt tussocks of grass were sharp and could pierce their ankles.

The men made periodic stops for rest, but did not drink. By evening they had covered over forty miles. Everyone was weary and grimy from the dirty ash. After resting each man drank a canteen of water. They drank slowly and enjoyed the feeling of the water re-hydrating their parched bodies.

That night they slept out in the open under the brilliant stars. The men slept on top of their ground sheets since there were no mosquitoes and there was no chance of rain. Dick was awakened once by a loud shout. A soldier had felt a movement against his leg and had leaped up from his primitive bed. Upon investigation he saw a large puff adder. Dick knew these loathsome snakes had long hypodermic fangs that could inject haemotoxic poison and easily kill a man. The adder was only looking for warmth, but the soldier dispatched it with a spear to its thick, triangular head.

The following day's trek brought them through a dry swamp. There was no standing water, just cracked earth. However, there was still a flush of green grass and the area was teeming with wildlife. Dick saw oryx, zebra, gazelle, warthog and giraffe. He broke away from the marching men and was able to shoot several zebras. Zebras are good keepers and these zebras were no exception, looking fat and healthy even though they were living in harsh country. Upon hearing the shots, Tagoon, with his newly trained soldiers, arrived quickly to cut up the zebras. That night the men ate well and each soldier drank another half canteen of water. They were now down to very little drinking water, but Logoto assured them they would reach the pool of black water the following evening.

The following day of walking was really difficult. The soldiers drank a little more of their water in the morning, leaving only a few swallows in their canteens. By afternoon the soldiers were all seriously dehydrated and weak. They had eaten nothing for breakfast since they knew food would suck water from their bodies into their stomachs to digest the food. Dick was following the basic rule for survival in the desert: if you have limited water, don't eat.

They were now trekking through a dense thicket of desiccated acacia bushes. Dick frequently saw dik dik skipping along ahead of him and then bolting into bushes to hide. He later learned these diminutive antelope lived in monogamous pairs and got enough moisture from the acacia leaves to survive without having to drink water. Dick also saw large flocks of helmeted guinea fowl running away with jerky strides. He was tempted to shoot some, but they were constantly on the move and hard to hit. It would be a waste of ammunition: a big bullet for very little meat.

By mid-afternoon Dick could see rocky hills on the horizon

and Logoto pointed out the hill and location of *maam ci koli*, the pool of black water. At that point Dick gave permission for the men to drink the remnants of the water in their canteens. With added energy they pushed on through the afternoon. At dusk they arrived at the base of the hill. Logoto led Dick up the rocks and showed him the pool. It was in a cleft between two gigantic boulders and water dripped down into the pool through a sheet of hanging green moss. The pool was very deep and contained clear, clean water. Dick was pleasantly surprised and learned that in the Didinga language "black water" meant clear water. "White water" was understood to be cloudy and therefore dirty. The men drank deeply at the pool and filled their containers. Dick was exhilarated by the presence of the water in the dry land. He climbed to a ledge thirty feet above the pool, posed for a minute and then executed a swan dive into the pool. His men thought he was a little crazy. This was not something they would do for fun. That night the men slept well with bellies full of zebra meat and sweet tea. Dick set sentries, but in this remote location he felt safe since they were bivouacked a long way from the Italian forts.

They were camped far to the south of the mountain named Moru Akippi and the following day the caravan trekked through broken country. There were many rocky hills to work through, but the men did not have to contend with climbing a steep escarpment. This was no-man's land referred to as the Ilemi Triangle. Technically the area belonged to the Sudan government, but it was so remote that the Sudan had no control over it. It bordered on northern Kenya. Since Kenya was also British-held territory, the Kenyan police occasionally visited it to put down any tribal disputes. But for the most part this remote corner of Africa was simply ignored. Only a few Nyangatom tribesmen lived in the area and they practiced a nomadic lifestyle, taking their herds of goats and cattle to and from the rare water sources.

The environment was arid, but not as harsh as the desert they had just covered. There were periodic waterholes and wells and Dick was able to slow down the daily marches. For the following days they marched through thickets of whistling thorns. These unique acacia bushes had two-inch long thorns and at the base of each pair of thorns was a large black gall. Pinching ants made their homes in these hollow galls. At the slightest movement of the branch, the ants would come pouring out of their homes and attack whatever had disturbed them. When the desert wind blew through these bushes it caught on the entrances to the galls and gave off a soft moaning sound. Each gall had a slightly different tone and altogether they made a strangely beautiful symphony in the harsh wilderness. The soldiers tried to avoid touching these acacia bushes as not to provoke the ants and get stung.

They eventually trekked into another stunted acacia forest and quickly discovered this area was infested with tsetse fly. These flies attacked the soldiers, making painful welts as they inserted their proboscises and mined for blood. The soldiers cut leafy branches and used them to swat away the persistent tsetse flies. Each soldier not only protected his own body, but also kept an eye on the back of the soldier in front of him, periodically beating his back to remove the biting flies. Dick understood why people avoided trekking through this area of Sudan. It was a relief to get out of the acacia scrub and back into open grass country. That afternoon they met some Nyangatom warriors who were taking their animals to water. They were all tall, lean men wearing only goatskins over their right shoulders. They had dressed their hair with mud so it was perfectly flat on top. Each warrior also had a hole in his lower lip and had inserted an ornament made out of elephant ivory. All of the warriors were well armed, carrying spears and well-used .303 rifles.

Logoto talked to the warriors and assured them that the caravan of soldiers was just passing through and intended no harm. That evening the soldiers camped by a well and Dick sat on a boulder and watched as different groups of Nyangatom warriors brought in their animals for water. The water was not easily accessible in a surface pool, but was only available at the bottom of a deep hand-dug well. Three warriors went down into the well where they balanced on narrow ledges cut into the walls of the well. The man at the bottom filled a skin bucket and handed it up to the man above him who handed it on to the man near the top. He in turn poured the water into a wooden trough. The thirsty animals patiently waited in line for their turn to drink from the trough. It was hot, sweaty work and the men sang an ancient song as they worked. As the orange sun set in the west Dick went back to camp for his evening meal. As he went to sleep he could hear the splashing of the water and the sound of the song as the pastoralists continued their work throughout the night.

The following day the soldiers continued marching eastward. Wildlife abounded in the area and Dick shot a number of antelope. Since the men were carrying a limited amount of sorghum flour, it was essential that Dick procure fresh meat on a daily basis. In the late afternoon Dick could see a dark line of trees in the distance and by sundown they arrived at the banks of the Kibbish River. This river marked the official border between Sudan and Ethiopia.

The Kibbish was a lazy, brown river flowing slowly from one pool to another. Dick saw large crocodiles slide ominously into the still water and he quickly warned the men to be careful and only to draw water from places where the water was shallow. Large *zyziphus* trees spread their glossy green leaves over the pools and as Dick sat on the bank he could hear the haunting call of an African fish eagle. He saw a pied kingfisher hovering over the water and watched it dive into the pool and emerge with a minnow in its beak. After all the days marching across the arid, hot plains, it was an idyllic spot. During the night Dick heard the honking of hippos in the distance. The next morning he was up early and taking Logoto he headed down river to the place he had heard the hippos. The hunters approached each pool quietly and upon approaching the fourth pool they saw a herd of hippos resting in the water close to the opposite bank. Only their nostrils, eyes and ears were showing above the surface of the muddy water. Dick aimed his rifle at the ear of the largest hippo and pulled the trigger. It was an easy shot from short range and the hippo sank silently under the surface of the pool.

Logoto stayed at the pool to watch for the dead hippo while Dick walked back to camp. He informed his sergeants about the successful hunt and they sent off a number of men to butcher the hippo and bring back the meat. By the time they got to the pool the current had pushed the dead hippo up to a bank and the men were able to roll it on to the shore. For the next few hours they butchered away happily and then carried the raw meat back to camp. That night the men reveled in the abundance of meat. They ate until their stomachs ached. The next day they cut the remaining meat into strips and smoked it into *biltong*. The three tons of good meat would feed the men for a long time and Dick was pleased.

The following day Dick sent Logoto north to try and make contact with Korok and Kireer, the two Murle scouts. He figured it would take Logoto a couple of days of hard walking to return to the area where they had had their earlier skirmishes. Meanwhile he kept hunting for meat. The soldiers took the opportunity to rest and build up their store of dried *biltong*. There was time for a little relaxation. Dick shot a few guinea fowl and Kuju cooked up the breasts by baking them in a hole in the ground. He served them with rice, a real treat offered up in the wilderness. Kuju also started serving Dick tea with milk. Milk was a rarity in the wilderness and Dick had resigned himself to drinking his tea black. Dick soon discovered there was a cow living in their camp. Kuju had traded some dried hippo meat to the Nyangatom warriors for a cow. Having fresh milk was a treat both to him and to the soldiers. Keeping a cow was not part of military protocol, but Dick informally inducted her into the militia.

Dick also had some time to build relationships with his men. His pidgin Arabic was improving and every evening he spent time sitting around a campfire and talking with his soldiers. Pidgin Arabic was a unique language. It was made up of a combination of languages, but it was fairly simple to learn and yet accurate in its capability to communicate. Dick used the language to ask questions and his men taught him about their traditional customs. Dick noticed that several of the older soldiers were smoking pipes. The aroma of the smoke smelled sweet and they explained they were smoking a leaf from an aromatic bush mixed with honey. Dick was intrigued and decided to try it himself. Tagoon cut him a branch and showed Dick how to carve it into a pipe bowl. Dick spent the next few days whittling away on his pipe and attaching a hollow stem. The men supplied him with the dried leaf and the honey. Dick enjoyed the flavor and each evening he smoked his pipe along with the men. He felt this created a positive bond with his soldiers. They were the teachers and he was the student. Yet when it came to military matters, Dick was obviously in control. He was always calm and never seemed hurried. As a result his men respected his leadership and willingly followed him into battle.

Nyangatom warriors visited the camp each day. There was limited conversation because of the language gap, but the two sides stood around and watched each other. The sharing of meat by the soldiers created reciprocal friendships. One day a tall warrior with a red goatee strode up to Dick and handed him a small brown puppy. It was a gift. Dick hesitated. What would he do with a puppy in a war zone? But he did not want to be offensive by refusing the gift. Grudgingly he took the puppy and gave the warrior a slab of dried hippo meat in return. That night as he lay under his ground sheet, the little pup snuggled up to his side for warmth. Dick liked the companionship. He named the pup Mary. Kuju took on the chore of feeding Mary every day. Mary grew quickly and tried to follow Dick wherever he went. Initially she was so small, she could not keep up. Kuju added the pup to his list of duties and frequently had to come to her rescue.

While he waited for the guides to appear, Dick spent the days sitting by the river. Each day he watched the pied kingfisher hovering and then diving into the brown water to seize small fish. It would land on a branch and bash the fish against the wood until it was dead. Then it would reposition the fish in its beak so it went down head first – thus avoiding the sharp spines. Again Dick thought of Nora and wished he could share the experience with her. He knew she would enjoy the tranquility and beauty of this place. He pulled out a scrap of paper and started to make a list of all the things he most loved about Nora:

Love for the Lord
Willingness for anything
A passion for souls
Missionary care and zeal
A soul winner
Makings of a prophetess
Sympathy
Personality
Humility
Looks
Strength and courage
Knowledge of how to dress well
Not minding roughing it
Love of poetry
An appreciation of the beautiful

It was a long list and he fully realized he was putting Nora on a pedestal. But for a lonely man in the wilderness it was a healthy exercise.

Five days later Logoto returned from his exploration trip to the north. He had Korok with him along with several other Murle men. Korok told Dick that the Italian forces were still moving around the valleys on Sudan territory. They had left Kireer in the area to keep abreast of their movements. Dick gave Logoto two days to rest and made plans for another attack.

9

Fighting in the Hills

They marched out two days later with Korok leading the way. It was a strange looking caravan heading off to war. Each soldier carried a rifle, a bandolier of ammunition over his shoulder and dried pieces of hippo meat balanced on top of his head. Kuju carried the pup Mary under his arm. The milk cow marched along with the soldiers bringing up the rear of the long procession. Dick had thought carefully about the battles ahead. He would not make the same mistake as the last time where he had set up a base camp and then returned to it – only to be ambushed by the waiting Italian forces. This time he planned to stay on the move, sleeping in a different place every night so the Italians would not be able to figure out where to find him.

Coming from the south there were no high escarpments to climb. Instead they marched through rough broken country. Periodically they walked through thick forests. Here they encountered ancient elephant trails. The footprints of some of the old bulls were enormous. They were the remnants of the great herds that once lived in the swamps of southern Sudan, but British ivory hunters and Ethiopian *shiftas* had over the years reduced these herds to a small number. The surviving bulls had moved into these forests where they could hide and live out their lives in peace. Dick gazed at the enormous footprints and was tempted to track down an old bull. But he had a bigger goal and the sound of shooting would alert the Italians to their presence in the area.

After three days of forced marching, they were back in the area where they had first encountered the Italians on Sudanese soil. Here Kireer, the Murle scout, met them. He sat down with Dick, Logoto and Korok and gave them an update on the movements of the Italian forces. They had strengthened their fortifications and small units were still making sorties into the Sudan. The various villagers in the area were quite aware of the locations of these units and had been passing on the information to Kireer. Dick realized information flowed both directions and he knew if he dallied, the Italians would soon hear he was back in the vicinity. He needed to attack quickly.

Kireer reported that one Italian unit was camped nearby and would be heading down a rocky valley the following day. Dick decided to set up an ambush. However, he was still concerned his men were few in number and he wanted to avoid a head-to-head battle. Therefore he opted to attack from the rear. That night he talked with his four sergeants and explained his plan.

Early the next morning while it was still dark they marched out, leaving only a handful of men behind to guard the food and supplies. The main body of soldiers proceeded to the rocky valley and took up positions behind the rocks. The men with rifles hid higher up so they could shoot down into the valley. Tagoon, with his newly trained soldiers, only had spears, so these men were positioned undercover in the valley itself. Everyone had strict orders to stay hidden until the Eritrean and Somali units had passed by. Then they were to attack from the rear.

The plan worked perfectly. From his vantage point high in the rocks Dick watched the approach of the Italian-led forces. They numbered over 200 men. In the vanguard were the heavily armed Eritreans, looking smart in their long, white tunics and red fezzes. They were followed by blue-coated Italian officers, riding on white mules. Lastly came the greater portion of the unit made up of Somali soldiers. Toward the end of the procession the Somalis were spread out and relaxed. Dick's soldiers kept perfectly still until most of the unit had marched past and turned a corner lower in the valley. At the sound of Dick's whistle, Tagoon and his men leaped out of the bushes and attacked with their spears. The Somalis were taken by surprise and a number of them were killed instantly in the first onslaught. But the Somalis had a reputation for being ferocious fighters and those not killed in the first wave of the attack quickly regrouped and fought back. Meanwhile Dick and the other soldiers fired rapidly into the other Italian forces. The Eritreans and Italian officers at the front of the column heard the sounds of battle and quickly returned to enter the fray. But they ran into their own Somali soldiers who were looking for cover, and for a few minutes they became a confused mass with the Italian officers shouting orders that nobody obeyed. From their high elevation Dick's men kept shooting bullets into the valley and men kept falling, fatally wounded. But within a few minutes the Italian officers got their men in order and started shooting back. They carried several machine guns that they set up and trained on the Sudanese troops. Dick quickly realized his soldiers were suffering serious casualties, so he blew the whistle for retreat.

Tagoon and his spearmen broke away from the battle and sprinted up the valley as Dick's men gave them covering fire. Then the Sudanese riflemen withdrew in an orderly fashion to the top of the ridges where they were safe from the Italian machine guns. Here they stood up and started running, all heading for the rendezvous where they had left their supplies. After a quick stop to pick up the food and to bind up the wounded they headed south at a fast march. They kept up this pace for the rest of the day, putting twenty miles behind them. That evening they camped by a small stream. Here they chewed on cold *biltong* because they dared not light any cooking fires.

Dick met with his sergeants and they reported on the condition of their platoons. Tagoon's men had done well in the hand-to-hand combat, but there had been casualties. Four men had been killed and twelve had been wounded. However, the wounds were not serious and they would heal. The men in Tagoon's platoon were proud of their accomplishment. They were now proven warriors.

Early the next morning Dick had his men up and moving. The wounded were stiff and sore, so they started out slowly. But as they warmed up they picked up the pace. Dick knew the

Italian-led forces would be infuriated and would be looking for them. Therefore he headed south away from the vicinity of the Italian forts.

Dick was near the front of the line when he heard a yell behind him. He looked back and saw the sergeant Bakir writhing on the ground, trying to rub his eyes. The men near him immediately grabbed him and held him down. Logoto was yelling, "*Kowat! Kowat!*" Dick realized a forest cobra had been frightened by the noise of the marching men. It had reared up, spread its hood, contracted its poison sacs and sprayed a vapor of poison into Bakir's eyes. The pain was terrible and Bakir naturally tried to rub his eyes to alleviate the pain. However, the other men knew if Bakir rubbed his eyes the poison would go into the blood vessels and could cause blindness or even death. The men had experience with cobras and they held Bakir firmly, so he could not rub his burning eyes. Dick immediately took his canteen and poured water into Bakir's eyes, trying to flush out the poison. Then he remembered the cow. He had heard that milk with its alkali base was a better treatment than water. He quickly gave an order and the cow was brought up from the rear of the caravan. A soldier milked out a cup of milk which they used to wash out Bakir's eyes. Within an hour the pain eased and Bakir was able to see vague shapes. The caravan proceeded onward to the next camping spot and by evening Bakir's eyes were able to focus again. The following day Bakir's eyes were sore and bloodshot, but he received no long-term damage to his sight. The cow had proved to be a valuable asset, providing milk for more than just their tea.

The men kept up the forced march, first heading west and

then north back toward the fighting zone. They were making their way up a gradual slope when suddenly they came under attack. Well-aimed bullets flew into the caravan and several men dropped to the ground. The others dived behind rocks and started shooting back. Dick and his men were in a bad situation, out in the open with limited places to hide. But his men were well trained and disciplined. They gathered in small groups and gave each other cover as they slipped from rock to rock. An extraordinary number of bullets were shot at Dick himself. It was quickly obvious that his white skin made him the primary target. He dodged from rock to rock and suddenly felt a tug at his left leg. He went down hard, thinking, "Why am I falling? I have to keep moving." Then the searing pain hit him. His leg was on fire and his first fear was that he could not move. He crawled behind a large rock and some of his men gathered around him and gave return fire. Dick looked down at his leg and saw blood dripping down from his thigh. Sergeant Musa ripped off a piece of cloth from his own shorts and quickly tied it around Dick's thigh to stem the bleeding. Then two men hoisted Dick up and put their arms around him. They supported and carried him down into a valley while the other soldiers provided cover by letting loose with a great barrage of bullets. Once into the edge of a thicket the sergeants organized their men into a line and continued to fire at the Italian forces. At this point the Italian forces were in the open and they were forced to withdraw. The battle was over for now with Dick's men having taken many casualties.

Dick looked closely at his thigh. Fortunately the bullet had not hit the bone and he was able to gingerly put his weight on the leg. But the incoming bullet had opened a long gaping wound,

Jon Arensen

starting above the knee and extending to the upper thigh. It definitely needed to be stitched. The medical kit was extremely basic. For antiseptic they carried only a bottle of iodine. Dick instructed the orderly to pour iodine into the wound. He knew it would burn, but it was essential to stop an infection. He lay down on his back and gritted his teeth. The iodine burned like fire and Dick groaned in pain. Within seconds the burning was over. However, the wound still needed to be stitched. Since they had no numbing medicine Dick decided he would rather sew it up himself than have somebody else do it. The orderly threaded a sewing needle with white thread and gave it to Dick. Kuju insisted on helping. As cook and valet, he felt that he was also responsible for Dick's health and wellbeing. So Kuju held the edges of the wound together while Dick pushed the needle in one side of the cut and out the other. It hurt badly, but not as much as he expected. He then pulled the thread through the wound and tied it off. Altogether he made sixteen separate stitches and sewed the gaping wound tightly together. A large bandage was then tied around Dick's thigh for support. Meanwhile, Tagoon cut him a strong walking stick to help support him as he walked.

Other men had been wounded as well and they were also stitched up and prepared to walk. They could not stay where they were. The Italian forces were in the field and would return. Dick gave the order for them to start moving. They were a small fighting force and could not just sit and wait for the Italian forces to track them down. The slow moving column was a sorry sight. The healthy soldiers spread out at the front of the line, making sure they did not walk into another ambush. At the rear of the line walked another well-armed contingent. They frequently checked the path to their rear to make sure the Eritreans and Somalis were not catching up to them. In the middle of the column limped the wounded. At least twenty men had serious wounds, but they had no option but to keep on walking. Dick's thigh hurt badly, but the stitches were holding and the supporting bandage made it possible to walk with the help of the walking stick. As he continued walking, the leg loosened up and gradually he was able to lengthen his stride. The caravan walked south all afternoon, trying to distance itself from the Italian forces. That night they slept in a dense thicket, making no fires and little noise. The next morning they awoke to find that one of the wounded men had died in the night. He had a bullet hole through his lung and the orderly had no training in how to handle such a traumatic case. They dug a shallow grave and wrapped the dead soldier in his ground sheet and interred him in the hole. As the men stood to attention Dick gave a prayer. Each man stepped forward with a stone and laid it on the grave. Then they were off again, limping their way south. They met no opposition over the next several days and eventually arrived back at the Kibbish River. Here they built a base camp in the shade of the *zyziphus* trees. Dick assigned a number of men to serve as sentries. Some were stationed several miles away to ensure the Italian soldiers could not sneak up on them unaware.

Dick's wound was a serious one, but it did not get infected. However, it limited his ability to walk long distances. He had to content himself to staying in camp while he sent out Musa to shoot meat for the camp. The pool near the camp was an idyllic spot during the day and Dick spent many hours a day watching the profuse bird life. He also spent many hours with the men, increasing his proficiency in speaking pidgin Arabic. Dick had made it a practice to read his New Testament every day, usually in the early morning while he was having his cup of tea. This routine was noticed by the men and they asked him questions about the teachings in the little book. He answered their questions, but did not push his Christian beliefs on to his men. However, a number of them expressed an interest in learning more. So several times a week Dick read them a passage of Scripture and translated it orally into pidgin Arabic. His orderly Kuju had been partly educated at the mission in Yambio. He had a strong belief in Christ and he took the simple Bible studies seriously. Sergeant Musa had also been exposed to Christianity in the Nuba Hills and his high moral values were a positive example to the other men.

The camp near the pool may have been idyllic during the day, but it was miserable at night. Everyone was plagued by the profusion of mosquitoes. One morning Dick woke up with a severe headache. By noon he had a high fever and was sweating profusely. He had caught a serious case of the dreaded malaria. He alternated between shivering with cold and burning up with fever. The soldiers were quite concerned. They knew well the dangers of malaria and there was a real possibility Dick could die in the night. Musa and Kuju came to talk to Dick. He was lying in a pool of sweat in a fever-induced stupor. Kuju shook him by the shoulder and finally got his attention by shouting, "You are very sick! We want to pray for you so God will make you well!"

Dick just groaned, but Kuju persevered. "The Bible tells us what to do when a person is sick. The Christians should gather together, anoint the sick person with oil and pray for him." Both

Kuju and Musa continued to insist that they needed to pray for Dick so he would get well. Dick groaned again, but he could see Kuju and Musa were serious. He nodded and told them to go ahead.

Kuju ran off to his kitchen supplies and returned with two containers. "I only have two kinds of oil: kerosene and hippo fat. Which one should I use?"

If Dick had been well enough he would have laughed. He lifted his head and pointed at the small piece of hippo fat. Kuju solemnly picked up the solidified hippo fat and made the shape of the cross on Dick's forehead and again on his chest. He prayed that God in his power would show mercy to Dick and make him well. Then Musa prayed as well. A number of the soldiers stood around to offer their support.

That night Dick's fever broke and by morning he was feeling well again. This was the only time Dick got ill in the entire campaign. Kuju and Musa were nonchalant about Dick's healing. They had prayed to God and of course God had answered. Dick was impressed by their faith.

After several weeks of rest Dick and his soldiers were fit again. Dick had spent some of this time training his dog Mary. She had grown quickly and had the long, lean look typical of Sudanese village dogs. Mary had a springy gait and could run for hours. It was no longer necessary for Kuju to carry her on the long marches. Mary was a one-person dog and always stayed close to Dick. He taught her some basic commands: Sit! Come! Be quiet! This final command was the most important since it was essential that Mary be quiet when the soldiers were hiding in ambush. Mary was also proving to be valuable as a guard dog.

Her senses were sharp and she growled softly if an intruder came into the area.

The sergeants and guides asked to meet with Dick and Musa led the delegation. "*Bimbashi*, we have been talking among ourselves. We insist that you darken your face when we go into battle."

Dick resisted their suggestion. He wanted to demonstrate that he was the leader and did not show fear. But it was obvious in the last battle that most of the enemy rifles were aimed at Dick. His white face made him the primary target. Finally Dick agreed. He experimented with mixing mud and hippo fat to make up a dark grease paint. He used this to rub on his face, neck and arms. Wearing his slouch felt to cover his blond shock of hair, he could hardly be distinguished from his men.

Together with his sergeants Dick came up with a new strategy. Having occasional battles with the mobile Italian forces in the valleys was not really accomplishing anything. The Italians were still entrenched in their forts and still held the high ground. Dick decided to attack these forts at night. More audaciously, he decided to attack two forts on the same night. He wanted to give the impression that the British had two large military units in the region. A combination of attacking and withdrawing would avoid casualties. If they were careful it would also extend their limited amount of ammunition. Mobility and endurance would be essential to their success. The sergeants assured Dick their men were fit and up to the task.

Dick calculated the night when there would be a full moon so his men could see and be able to move quickly. Based on the phase of the moon, he planned the first foray. The sergeants understood the new plans and passed the details on to their men. Several days before the actual attack they started moving north. Mary trotted happily along beside Dick. She was now strong and fit and could easily keep up with the men. But Dick decided the cow was not able to go on this trip. The men wanted to kill and eat her, but Dick thought otherwise. The cow had been a loyal member of the company, so Dick decided to retire her with honor. She was given to a passing Nyangatom herder.

The first march took place in the daytime because they were still a long way from the Italian forts and could not be observed. But after that they moved only at night, using the light of the half moon to brighten their path. During the days they laid up and hid in the dark thickets. Each night Korok and Kireer guided them carefully through the area. When they reached the escarpment where the Italian forts were located, they climbed quietly to the top and then hid all day in the hills above their chosen target.

That night after the sun had set in the west, Dick and his soldiers moved silently through the dark until they could look down on the fort. Dick had split his men into four platoons. Each approached the fort from a different angle. Dick could easily see the Italian officers sitting at a table, eating their meal by the light of a kerosene lamp. Sentries stood at the western walls of the fort, but they were relaxed and most of them had their rifles lying casually beside them. There was a big gun mounted on a wall and pointing west, down the escarpment. Dick quickly realized the big gun was really of no danger to him and his men since they were behind it and it would take a lot of effort and time to turn the big gun so it could shoot to the east. Most of the soldiers sat around two roaring fires, one for the Eritreans and one for the Somalis. The men talked and told stories. The last thing they expected was an attack during the night.

It was still very dark since the moon had not yet risen. Dick had briefed one of his best spear throwers to be ready with his grenade. While the four platoons lay in waiting, this soldier snaked down the hill on his belly until he was within thirty paces of the fort. When he was in place he stood quickly and lobbed the grenade into the middle of the fort. It landed near a fire and went off with a great explosion, sending hot shrapnel into the group of soldiers. Men fell to the ground screaming. This was the signal for the rest of Dick's men to open fire. Immediately all the Sudanese soldiers started shooting, pouring a withering wall of bullets into the fortifications below them. Dick fired his rifle at one of the Italian officers and he slumped over and fell to the ground. For several minutes there was pandemonium. Some of Dick's men had worked themselves quite close to the walls under cover of darkness and the sentries were taken out in the first volley. They then fired at the unarmed soldiers who had been sitting around the fires. A large number of the Eritreans and Somalis fell while the others scrambled for cover, ducking down behind the stone walls and running for the stone barracks. Within minutes they had found their weapons and were returning fire, shooting bullets into the darkness. The Italian officers were shouting orders, but without firm targets it was difficult to mount a counter attack, especially since Dick's men held the high ground and were shooting from four different positions. An Eritrean soldier doused the campfires and this reduced the obvious targets in the fort. But Tagoon had crept very near to the barracks. He lit a dry bundle of grass and lobbed it on to the grass roof of the barracks. Within minutes it was a flaring inferno. The Italian forces had to flee the burning barracks and the flames lit up the area making them once again exposed to the incoming bullets. Dick and his men kept shooting for a few more minutes. Suddenly the full moon popped up over the eastern horizon, shedding its pale, white light on the ground. This was the signal for retreat. Dick blew his whistle. A few of his men kept shooting while the rest crawled up to the higher ridges. They then supplied covering fire while the rest of the Sudanese soldiers withdrew. Within minutes they had all gotten out of harm's way. They regrouped on the back side of the hill and started running. After a couple of miles they slowed down to a lope, a pace that could cover five miles an hour and a speed they could keep up for hours. The full moon brightened the path so they could see where to put their feet. They were not trying to find a refuge where they could hide. They were heading for another Italian fort.

They arrived in the hills above the second fort at 4 am. Again Dick had the platoons approach the fort from four different directions, crawling quietly until they were in positions to look right down into the fort. Musa spotted a sentry whose job it was to guard the high ground. He was sleeping with his mouth open, periodically letting out a gentle snore. Musa sent one of his best Lotuxo hunters to deal with the sentry. Dick heard only a dull thud as the Lotuxo hunter smashed in the head of the guard with a stone. The Sudanese soldiers then lay in position for the next hour, getting some rest and storing up their endurance. At 5 am there was faint glimpse of gray on the eastern horizon. A red-chested cuckoo started heralding the dawn with its plaintive three-note song. The fort below them was perfectly silent. The fires were low and everyone was sleeping. Dick fired at a sleeping sentry. The bullet knocked him backward off the rampart where he had been sitting. Immediately Dick's men started shooting their .303 rifles, sending streams of bullets into the fort. There were few direct targets to aim at so the men shot at the tents and through the windows of the stone-walled barracks. Again there was pandemonium as the rudely awakened soldiers leaped up and scrambled to find their weapons. Soon the Italian forces organized themselves and started laying a hail of bullets at the hidden Sudanese soldiers. Dick could hear the dangerous rattle of a machine gun and the flying bullets knocked leaves off the trees above them. At once Dick signaled retreat and his men withdrew in an orderly fashion while it was still dark. Upon clearing the ridge they quickly reconvened and started running. This time they had to keep running. The coming dawn gave them good light so they could see their footing and they headed south at top speed. The long grass was heavy with drops of dew and within minutes all of the men were soaking wet. Korok led them through the back paths and the next two hours felt like a marathon. Dick's lungs burned and his legs ached, but he kept running. Mary bounded along beside him with her tail wagging, giving every indication this was a great outing. The Sudanese troops were extremely fit and they kept moving at a fast pace, but by mid-morning even they were feeling extremely tired. Korok led them up a rocky slope strewn with boulders. The troops followed, jumping from rock to rock so they would not leave tracks. At the top of the slope were some large boulders and here the soldiers stopped for a long rest, sucking long draughts from their canteens. Dick summoned Musa and told him, "Choose your best marksmen and have them set up an ambush. They can hide behind the rocks on the slope."

Then Dick laid down on a rock and scoped the valley below with his binoculars. About two hours later he saw a small group of Eritreans coming in their direction. They were being led by a local tribesman who was looking closely at the ground and following their footprints. When they got to the bottom of the slope below Musa, his marksmen let off an accurate volley of bullets. Several of the Eritreans fell to the ground and the rest bolted for cover. There was a short exchange of gunfire and then the Eritreans withdrew. They were a small force and their heart was not in it. They suspected they were up against a much larger Sudanese force that had the strength and numbers to attack their fort at night.

Dick called in Musa's men and they headed south again, moving out at a fast pace all day. That night they slept the sleep of the dead, but Dick had them up at dawn and again pushed them to move at a fast pace. By evening Dick felt they had outrun any pursuit. The men made small cooking fires and had a hot meal. The following day they arrived back at the Kibbish River. In the morning Dick hiked down to a large pool and shot another hippo for meat. For the following days the men ate, relaxed and regained their strength.

10

Domestic Interlude

Dick lay on his back under a *zyziphus* tree. He watched as a woodland kingfisher raised its red beak, beat its blue wings and let out its loud chattering call. He felt absolutely exhausted. His face was gaunt and his rib cage resembled an old-fashioned washboard. He looked over at the fire where his men sat. They too were gaunt and thin. And there were fewer of them now than there had been when they started the campaign against the Italian forts. For the past six months they had been making extensive forays into Italian territory. Dick had continued his method of attacking the forts at night, often attacking two forts on the same night. Sometimes he had divided his forces to make simultaneous attacks. But more often he made sequential attacks, shooting up one fort in the early evening and then running through the night to attack another fort in the early hours of the morning. The Italian forces fought back hard and during the many battles Dick had lost a number of his men. But the overall plan was working. The Italians had gotten the impression they were fighting several military battalions with a large number of soldiers. Dick wanted to know what the Italians forces were thinking. He offered his men a substantial reward for bringing in an enemy prisoner. He offered an even higher reward for bringing in an Italian officer. The reward was never collected. His men were fighters. When their blood was up they fought to kill. After six months of fighting his warriors had failed to bring in a single prisoner.

The Italians were no longer sending units into Sudan territory. They were now staying near their forts. They spent their time reinforcing their fortifications, so they could defend them better. Dick's overall plan was working. The Italian forces were still entrenched and in place within Ethiopian borders, but they were no longer threatening to come into Sudan and control transport down the Nile River.

Dick decided he needed a new strategy. His small group of remaining soldiers no longer had the strength to run up and down the border attacking the Italian forts.

First the men needed rest and good food. Some of them were showing signs of scurvy. Their skin color was an unhealthy-looking grey and many of them had open ulcers. Their gums were receding and their teeth were becoming loose. Dick himself had managed to avoid the problem. In his small store of kitchen supplies were several bottles of Rose's concentrated lime cordial.

He hoarded it carefully and dutifully took a spoonful a day at breakfast.

Dick sent for Logoto and asked about finding fresh vegetables. Logoto reported that the Dassanech people living near the Omo River had gardens. He knew the trail that led south to their villages. Dick called for volunteers. He chose a small group of the fittest men and told them to trek south to the Dassanech villages. It was the end of the rainy season and Logoto had assured Dick he would be able to trade bullets for fresh food. The trip was successful and after a few days the men returned carrying pumpkin leaves and green sorghum stalks. The leaves were cooked into a nutritious sauce and eaten with the *asiera*. The sorghum stalks were slightly sweet and the men chewed them like sugar cane. Within a few days the men started recovering and their skin returned to its natural dark color. But they also needed meat. Since it was rainy season the hippos had left the nearby pools and the game herds had moved away from the rivers and out onto the plains where they could benefit from the rich green grass. Dick decided to make a hunting trip to the pool of black water. He left Musa in charge of the base camp on the Kibbish River and he took Tagoon and his young warriors to help butcher and smoke the meat.

A fast day's walk brought them easily to the pool of black water. Due to the heavy rains it was full to overflowing and covered with a thick mat of lily pads with beautiful pink and yellow flowers. Blue dragonflies flitted from flower to flower, preying on the insects that came for the sweet nectar. The next morning Dick climbed the rocks behind the pool and scoped the surrounding area. He spotted oryx and then a large herd of buffalo. The buffalo would supply the most meat. Taking Tagoon with him, he crept up on the herd. The animals were unaware of his presence and he was able to get within fifty paces. Rising up from behind an anthill Dick took aim and shot into the neck of a large bull. His shot was accurate and it dropped immediately. As the herd took off running Dick sent a second bullet into a fleeing bull. It kept running and the entire herd disappeared into a thicket of acacia bushes. They needed the meat, but both Dick and Tagoon knew that a wounded buffalo was very dangerous. They tracked the wounded bull to the edge of the thickets and then stood and waited. Eventually they heard a mournful bellow. Both of them relaxed knowing they had heard the death call. They followed the blood spoor into the thicket and found the bull lying dead. The blood bubbling out of the small hole in the chest indicated Dick had hit the lungs. Dick's accurate shooting was proving invaluable in providing food in the wilderness. By noon Dick and Tagoon were back at the pool. Tagoon informed his men of the successful hunt and took them out to butcher the two buffalo.

Dick stayed in camp and walked to the pool to enjoy the tranquility of this oasis in the wilderness. As he crossed an area of wet sand he noticed two sets of human footprints. One set was made by a small adult, but the other set really got his attention. They were the small footprints of a child.

Dick had been at war for over eight months. During that time he had been living entirely with men, totally away from any contact with women and children. He had only received the rare letters that got through from Nora. Looking at the two sets of footprints Dick was strangely moved. He wanted to meet the pair that had made the tracks in this remote corner of Africa.

Dick started tracking, looking closely at the ground and following the faint footprints left by their passing. It was slow work because the ground was hard and stony, but Dick had been learning from Logoto and was able to make out the faintly marked trail. After several miles he lifted his head and on the horizon saw a stunted acacia tree. Under its sparse shade he saw a sitting human figure. As he drew closer he saw a second person – a small girl. The woman was young and had tightly braided hair. Around her neck was a profusion of red and blue beads. At her waist she wore a decorated goat skin. She regarded Dick solemnly and did not seem to be frightened. The little girl snuggled up to her mother and looked at Dick with big, dark eyes. Then Dick noticed that the woman had a small baby in her right arm. It was nursing from the mother's bare breast. The maternal scene was deeply moving to Dick. He edged slowly closer and the woman did not move. Dick greeted her in pidgin Arabic, but she made no response. She just kept looking calmly at Dick. She sensed Dick would do her no harm. Dick drew even closer and sat down. He was only ten feet away. He just sat and looked at the little family. It was somehow deeply satisfying for Dick to look at this woman and her children. In many ways it was a strange scene – a woman from a traditional culture with a different appearance, different language and different history. But in spite of the many differences Dick felt a close connection. He was seeing the universal human values of femininity, childhood, security and love.

Dick sat there in front of them for over an hour. Where had the woman come from? Where was she going? What confidence she had to traverse this hostile land with a young child and a baby! Over time the child relaxed and played with some sticks. The baby finished nursing, stared at Dick for a time and then went to sleep. After the hour was over Dick stood up, looked one last time at the little family and walked back to camp. That night he sat near the pool under the bright stars and thought about Nora. She was waiting for him back in cold dreary England. It was as if God had given him a little respite from the war and a small insight into his future when the war was finally over.

When the buffalo meat was dried properly, the hunting party returned to the base camp on the Kibbish River. Here Dick sat down with his sergeants and guides and laid out the next strategy. They reiterated the Italian forces were dug in at their forts and were no longer making forays into the Sudan. But Dick and his men were weary and could not keep up the pace of running up and down the border and periodically attacking the forts. So how could they keep the Italian forces where they were? Dick decided to build his own series of fortifications. These were not to be real forts, but were to give the impression the British forces were expanding and building up their numbers for a big attack. These forts needed to be built in the Sudan across the valleys from the Italian forts and placed strategically so they could be easily seen.

Plans were solidified and the camp on the Kibbish River was abandoned. The guides told Dick the Italians had hired their own scouts who were watching the trails heading north. If they used the usual routes, they might walk into an ambush. Therefore Dick decided that, instead of heading straight north into the hills, the whole company should trek west into the desert. They did so, eventually arriving at the pool of black water. From here they made their way north along the base of the mountains. It was rainy season, so it was very different from the usual dry season march. Water lay in puddles and low depressions and therefore finding drinking water was not an issue. But the black cotton soil had melted into a sticky goo that stuck to the sandals of the men. It built up so thickly they could hardly walk. The men quickly learned it was better to take off their sandals and walk barefoot. Wiggling one's toes helped get rid of the buildup of the heavy mud. The small *wadis* that were normally dry were now full of flowing water. The soldiers had to make human chains, holding arm to arm to get across the swirling currents. They were also plagued by irritating gnats that flew circles around the heads of the marching men, diving into their eyes, ears and nostrils. Progress was slow at best and at night sleep was hard to come by since everyone was lying in the wet mud.

On the third day they reached the base of the great cliffs of Moru Akippi and crossed over the trail they had originally used to climb the plateau. They did not take this path because they rightly assumed there would be enemy scouts in the mountains watching the trail, ready to report to the Italians. Instead Dick and his troops kept heading north around the base of the tall granite cliffs. They were heading north to the Kurun River. This river drained the area between Moru Akippi and the Boma plateau. As they passed the cliffs Dick could see the next set of towering cliffs to the north. That afternoon they reached the Kurun River where it flowed out of the divide between the two sets of cliffs. The Kurun was the major river in the southeastern Sudan, flowing west and then north, eventually becoming the mighty Pibor River.

They set up camp under some thick trees and Dick gave the men a two-day rest before ascending once more into the mountains. He and Logoto went out into the plains where they climbed a small rocky hill. Logoto had reported that the *kaja* were moving south. Dick had seen a few of the beautiful antelope further south, but as they climbed the small hill, he was awestruck by what lay in front of him. Thousands of white-eared kob were migrating south from their dry season location in the Jwom swamps. They walked in single file, each one following another with head held high. The males had lyre-shaped horns and shiny black coats with white patterns on their faces and bellies. The females were colored red. Stretching out in front of Dick to the far horizon were myriad trails filled with the migrating kob. Dick spent several hours sitting on the hill watching the great panorama unfolding in front of him: hundreds of thousands of antelope on the move. He and Logoto eventually hiked down the hill and crept quietly toward one of the trails. The kob were determined to keep trekking south and were not frightened with the approach of the two men. Dick approached within twenty paces. From this distance he was able to get a close look at the beautiful antelope. Dick did no shooting. He was content to simply stand there and enjoy the majestic scene in front of him.

The following day Dick and his troops started the ascent up to the plateau. There was no trail going up the gorge between Moru Akippi and the cliffs of Boma, but the roaring Kurun River had carved is way down the mountain in a series of falls and rapids. Along this steep gorge was a small gallery forest clinging precariously to the slippery rocks. The men slowly worked their way upward, jumping from rock to rock and holding on to vines and roots. Occasionally they ran into a sizable waterfall and had to work their way around the falls. Dick was entranced by the sheer beauty of this wild canyon. The men took their time. A slip into the rushing water could be fatal. As they ascended, the gorge got steeper, but at the same time the depth of the river lessened. By late afternoon Dick and Logoto climbed the last precipice and entered a beautiful valley. Here they lit a fire and boiled some water for tea while they waited for the rest of the men to arrive carrying the rifles, ammunition, food and camping gear. They all arrived safely and Dick hoped they had avoided detection by the scouts working for the Italians.

The following day they got on with their building projects. They first trekked in the direction of the Italian forts. There high on a ridge facing east they built the first make-believe fort. The men gathered stones and piled them up one upon another to form a curved wall about four feet high and forty feet long. They made no attempt to erect buildings – just basic walls with no mortar. That night they moved twenty miles north to another ridge and camped. The next day they built a similar wall. They continued this strenuous schedule for the next two weeks and altogether they built thirteen fortifications. Some were bigger than others, but all of them were placed in strategic locations where they were high in the hills and faced east. Each of them could potentially be manned by a few well-armed soldiers.

The last fortification was located at the top of a cliff. Behind the walls the men built some flimsy barracks and covered them with grass. From a distance it looked like a large fort that could hold many soldiers. Dick knew the Italians could see the newly erected fortifications. They knew he was in the area, but they had fought many battles and were weary, so they kept to their forts waiting for the British forces to take the next step.

With all the make-believe forts in place Dick set his plan into action. He broke his troops into thirteen units and each of them went to one of the primitive forts. Here they collected big piles of dry firewood and placed them behind the walls. They also mounted stones on the walls: two-foot stones topped by one-foot stones. From a far distance, backed by fire, these stones resembled human figures. On the designated night all thirteen fires were lit at the same time. Meanwhile Dick with Korok as his guide had hiked east and taken up a hiding place on a hill so he could look back at the false forts. The effect of the burning fires was impressive. Across the horizon the thirteen fires clearly revealed the stone fortifications. From a long distance using binoculars, the small stones placed on top of the walls looked very much like human figures manning the walls. Dick knew the Italians were also watching. He hoped they would get the impression that the British had brought many more troops into the area and were planning for a big invasion.

The Italians got the message. Two days later Dick heard the sound of an engine. It grew louder and from his hiding place he saw a fighter plane flying over the valley. Under each wing was a round white circle and on the tail was a white cross, indicating it was an Italian plane. Dick identified it as a Fiat CR-32. The pilot was heading for the largest fort where the barracks were made out of grass. The plane circled twice and on the second run it dropped a bomb on the make-believe fort. There was a great explosion and grass and rocks went flying everywhere. It was an accurate hit. The plane came back and made two more runs, strafing the ground with bullets. It then flew away to its base in Ethiopia thinking it had accomplished its mission. But nobody had been in the fort during the bombing, so no one was hurt. Later that morning Musa reported, "*Bimbashi*, I am sorry to inform you that the airplane caused the death of a goat and two chickens." The Sudanese soldiers had a good laugh and ate the goat and chickens for supper.

Dick planned no further attacks on the Italian forces. His men were exhausted and few in number. Instead they camped near the fake forts and periodically lit fires at night. In turn the Italians made no attacks on the Sudanese troops. It was a stalemate. This suited Dick. His assignment was not to defeat the Italians. He was vastly outnumbered. His assignment was to keep the Italians from entering the Sudan, which he was doing successfully. There was additional good news. His Murle scouts told him some of the Eritrean troops were unhappy being stuck in the Italian forts and playing a defensive game. Some of them were slipping away in small groups and heading south to Kenya, where they were turning themselves in to members of the Kenyan police.

Meanwhile the war in the outside world was progressing favorably for the British. They were now making serious plans to push the Italians out of Ethiopia. The big push was taking place 500 miles north of Dick's location. Here Colonel Boustead and his men of the Sudan Defence Force were marching east, taking one Italian fort after another. In January of 1941, a message reached Dick by runner from Kapoeta. The British were now preparing to invade Ethiopia from the south, starting with a major attack on the small Ethiopian town of Maji. From here they planned to march north to join the other Sudanese soldiers. The united forces would then take Addis Ababa from the Italians and put King Haile Selassie back on the throne. It was to be a major expedition called the East African Campaign. It was well planned and organized, but it did not work perfectly due to the vast spaces and hostile environment in southern Ethiopia.

Dick was informed that his small company was to be the hinge for a great pincer movement. A large British force was to come in from Sudan, entering Ethiopia at a location to the north of the Boma Plateau. Richard Whalley, the Frontier Agent living at Boma, had finally got the troops he had asked for two years earlier. He was chosen to guide the thousands of British-led troops into Ethiopia, cut the road to Jimma and march on Maji. Another force made up of troops from the King's African Rifles was to come in from the south, crossing the northern deserts of Kenya. A third group was to come from the southwest. It was made up of Ugandan troops with British officers and the Free Belgian Forces using Congolese troops led by Belgian officers.

However, the town of Maji was a difficult place to get to. It was located on a high plateau and protected by steep cliffs. The King's African Rifles coming from Kenya were attacked near the Omo River by Dassanech tribesmen and did not arrive on time. Meanwhile Whalley's group made gradual progress on the trek to Maji. They drove armored vehicles and carried heavy armaments. They were ready for serious battles, but these never materialized. As they progressed toward Maji, the Italian troops simply withdrew ahead of them. Nevertheless the allied troops had to be wary because they were periodically ambushed and there were land mines set into the roads. One British lieutenant tried to walk down the road using a minesweeper, but he was cut down by Italian snipers. After that event a heavily armored vehicle led the troops. This set off the mines without casualties to the troops following behind. However, in one instance an Eritrean unit set up an ambush and let the armored vehicle pass by. It then opened fire on the following infantry, killing every member of the platoon in the first volley. The land mines were hazardous to more than just the British troops. One day the scouts carried a dead lion into camp. It had stepped on a land mine while crossing the road during the night.

As for the Ugandan and Congolese troops, they were making slow progress on their trek toward Maji. They first had to cover miles of arid desert in southeastern Sudan. When they finally got into the rugged hills of Ethiopia, they discovered the footpaths leading to Maji had been heavily mined by the retreating Italian forces. This forced them to walk to the sides of the trails, clambering over obstacles such as rocks and trees, which seriously impeded their progress.

Meanwhile Dick made plans to start his march on Maji. He expected he would have to once more attack the Italian forts along the border with Sudan. He chose a date and once again had his soldiers light fires at all of his thirteen make-believe forts. Then he summoned all his men for one more big battle. But before Dick could initiate the attack, master sergeant Musa met with the Murle scouts and then reported to Dick. He saluted smartly and with a broad smile said, "*Bimbashi*, Sir! The Italians are pulling out of their forts. They are giving up and running away. They are retreating toward the town of Maji."

Dick canceled the planned attack. From a hilltop he focused

his binoculars on the distant forts. Musa was right. The Italian forces were dismantling the big guns, hooking them up to mules and dragging them away. So Dick had his men wait a few days until Korok and Kireer came in with reports that the Italian forts were now empty. Dick called his men together and praised them for the admirable job they had done. The following day they marched across the valley and entered the largest of the Italian forts. There was every indication of a quick retreat. They found torn tents, slashed cots, broken weapons, used clothing and piles of canned food. Dick's men promptly built fires and started cooking. That night they feasted on spaghetti and sardines, making up for the many weeks of limited food. Later in the evening one of the soldiers started beating a drum and the men danced far into the night, celebrating their victory over the Italian forces.

11

Scurvy and Bean Sprouts

The following days they marched east, following the trail of the retreating Italian troops. For the next sixty miles they moved slowly, allowing the Italians time to get away. When they got nearer to Maji Dick had his men avoid the roads and footpaths that had the potential of being mined. He eventually led his troops up to the top of a sharp ridge that ran all the way east to Maji. This ridge was the continental divide. All streams that flowed north went into rivers that eventually joined the Nile and flowed on to Egypt, ultimately reaching to the Mediterranean Sea. The water that flowed south of the ridge eventually ended up in Lake Turkana in Kenya.

Dick and his men were now at high altitude and they found

the air to be cool and crisp. The vegetation changed and they marched through fields of yellow flowers. They saw cattle feeding on the green pastures and the Nilotic soldiers were amazed at the size and fatness of the highland cows. As they got nearer to Maji, they found themselves walking in the shade of eucalyptus and cypress trees. They slowly worked their way along the ridge for several days and arrived in Maji district at the same time as Whalley's troops coming in from the north. They also met up with the Ugandan and Congolese units coming from the south. When the united troops finally got in sight of Maji town itself, there was no spirited defense by the Italian-led forces. Dick used his binoculars to look at the road leading northeast out of Maji. It was filled with vehicles and marching men heading toward Addis Ababa. The Italians were leaving without a fight, abandoning the empty town of Maji to the incoming British forces. Dick and his troops marched into the town with the other British forces. It was April 29, 1941. The campaign to take Maji had taken four months, but Dick and his men had been in the field for over a year. They were tired, hungry and footsore, but they marched proudly with heads held high. With thousands of soldiers arriving in Maji at the same time, the scene was chaotic. Initially nobody seemed to be in charge. Since Richard Whalley had been the British Consular Officer in Maji from 1930-1935, he was put in charge of administering the town. But the thousands of troops were under the authority of their separate commanders. They still had a job to do: to drive the Italians completely out of Ethiopia.

The soldiers from the various units needed a rest. Up to now the hardest part of the East African Campaign was not fighting battles against the Italian forces. It was moving the large numbers of soldiers through some of the most hostile environments in Africa. Even though they had fought no major battles, crossing the difficult terrain had taken time and had worn them out.

They set up tent cities in various parts of town. Maji had never been well built and there were few permanent structures. Most of the buildings were simple grass huts. As the leader of his small unit, Dick checked in with the temporary administration and was assigned a place to camp. In the high altitude it was very cold at night, but he solved the problem by obtaining a number of white canvas tents, essential for keeping out the rain and staying warm at night.

Dick found an open field edged with a few eucalyptus trees. These non-indigenous trees had tall white trunks with brown peeling bark. The trees would provide firewood and shade. Here he instructed his sergeants to set up the tents. Each sergeant instructed his men to put up their tents in a straight line. They wanted to look orderly like all the other troops in the area. Behind the tents each platoon even built its own latrine. This was a simple trench with a log suspended over it to use as a toilet seat. A grass wall was erected around each latrine for privacy.

Dick's primary concern was the health of his men. Over the past months they had trekked hundreds of miles on basic rations. Their legs and arms were thin and their faces were gaunt. Many had yellow-colored eyes and enlarged spleens due to frequent cases of malaria. But of greater concern to Dick were the obvious signs of scurvy. Most of the men had open ulcers and their skin was dull and rough. Their gums had receded and their teeth were loose. In some cases their teeth were actually falling out. Dick knew they needed a different diet with vitamins – and quickly.

Dick himself was craving vegetables. Every night he dreamed about red tomatoes, green lettuces and marvelous salads. Somehow his body knew what it needed. Unfortunately the food at Maji was limited to beans and what little they had carried with them. The military at Maji set up a two-way radio and Dick sent a message to his superiors at Kapoeta in Sudan. He reported his problem with scurvy due to the lack of vegetables and asked for help. He told them the only food available in Maji was black beans. These were nutritious, but were not helping cure the many serious cases of scurvy. He received a return message the next day. The doctor based in Kapoeta suggested an innovative cure. Dick should use the beans to make bean sprouts. Instructions were sent to soak the black beans in water overnight, then to lay them out on wet gunnysacks in a dark place and cover them with more wet gunnysacks. Within two days they would sprout and the men could eat the green tendrils. These were rich in vitamins and would cure the men of scurvy.

Dick promptly put the plan into action, laying out dozens of gunnysacks in a dark hut. The beans sprouted within two days and the long green tendrils tasted delicious. His men ate them with gusto, expecting an instant cure. Instead there was disaster. All of his men came down with violent attacks of diarrhea. Everyone rushed to the primitive latrines. Soon there was a long line of men in front of each latrine. As soon as a soldier completed his business in the latrine, he went to the back of the line and waited for another turn. This went on for hours. There was obviously something very wrong with the sprouts.

Dick radioed back to Kapoeta and explained what was happening. After a time the doctor got back to him. He was told it was not possible to eat sprouts made from black beans. The sprouts were poisonous. Dick was supposed to use mung beans. Since mung beans were not available at Maji, the idea of eating sprouts was not an option.

The following day Dick saw a lorry coming from the east. It was slowly making its way up the steep slope toward Maji town. Upon its arrival Dick discovered it was filled with fresh cabbages. Dick's soldiers were not traditionally lovers of vegetables. They normally preferred meat, milk and *asiera*. But at this point something in their bodies triggered a craving for fresh vegetables. They all grabbed as many cabbages as they could carry and took them back to their camp. Here they tore the cabbages apart with their hands and ate big chunks, chewing carefully with their sore, wiggly teeth. They continued to feast on cabbages for the next three days. Quickly the signs of scurvy disappeared. Their skin became smooth again and their gums firmed up.

At first Dick felt a little overwhelmed by all the activity at Maji. For the past months he had been living in the wilderness with only his own small contingent of soldiers. He had not spoken English for that entire period of time except for limited conversations with Musa and Kuju. Now suddenly there were dozens of different units bivouacked in the area and literally thousands of soldiers. Thankfully he quickly adjusted and enjoyed talking to some of the other officers. They were intrigued by the many tales Dick told them.

After a few days of rest at Maji, most of the allied troops headed northeast in pursuit of the Italian forces. Dick's unit was small. They had suffered serious casualties during their months in the field and were now down to less than sixty men. The primary role of the Sudan Defence Force was to guard the Sudan borders, not to invade another country. Dick and his men were ordered to stay at Maji for the time being until they received further instructions. Meanwhile, Richard Whalley, the British administrator in charge of Maji, followed the allied troops to Addis Ababa. Dick found himself temporarily in charge of administering the town of Maji.

The Italian headquarters in Maji were still largely in place. The Italian officers had left in a rush. Dick moved in and found himself sitting behind a wide mahogany desk, quite a change from sleeping on the ground with a hole for his hips. The radios and telegraph equipment had been destroyed, but there were still large maps on the walls and stacks of files and papers scattered around on the floor. As these were written in Italian, Dick could not read them, but he started organizing them by dates. An old Italian priest was still living in the Catholic compound in Maji. He had worked there a long time and had not been in favor of the fascist regime and how it treated the local people. When the Italians troops had fled Maji, he stayed behind to help his few parishioners. Dick befriended him and together they looked through some of the military dispatches. Dick was able to find files from the days when he was running up and down the border attacking two forts per night. The dispatches sent from the forts were enlightening. The Italian officers reported two British battalions in the area and said they were being attacked regularly by hundreds of British troops. In further dispatches they reported on the many new fortifications being built by the incoming British forces. Dick was both amused and gratified by the dispatches. His strategies had worked.

Within days Maji became quiet as most of the allied troops were now gone. One of the few units ordered to stay in Maji was a company made up of Congolese fighters from the Free Belgian Forces. Included in Dick's duties as administrator were supervision of the military Post Office and the stamping of outgoing mail. One day he was given a peculiar package from one of the Congolese soldiers who wanted it mailed to his father in Congo. Dick, deciding to investigate the contents, opened the package. It contained two dried hands covered in bark cloth and tied together with string. Dick checked the rulebook and found no rule barring the sending of human hands in the post. So he rewrapped the package, stamped it and sent it on its way.

Life at Maji was fairly dull after the many months spent trekking and fighting in the bush. Dick's Sudanese soldiers were all people of the hot savannahs and they did not like the cold and dampness of the Ethiopian highlands. But it was a good time for Dick and his men to rest up and get healthy again. The biggest bonus to Dick was a working mail system. He was now able to get mail regularly from England and the letters from Nora were something he looked forward to on a regular basis.

But it was not the responsibility of the Sudan Defence Force to administer parts of Ethiopia on a long term basis. Over the following weeks the British forces took Addis Ababa from the Italians and put Haile Selassie back on the throne. The Ethiopians were once more in charge of their own country. Dick's work at Maji was now done and he received a radio message from his superiors at Kapoeta ordering him and his men to return to Sudan, specifically to the Towath police post on the Boma Plateau.

Dick informed his soldiers. They were elated to be going back home. Two days later they marched out of Maji. The trek leading back to Boma was easy compared to the march going to Maji. This time his men were strong and well fed. They made the one hundred mile trek in easy stages following well-marked trails. They set up camps in the early afternoons and always bivouacked close to a source of good water. Near the Sudanese border they passed the now empty Italian forts and a day later they went past their simple make-believe fortifications. As they neared the east side of the Boma Plateau they passed a number of small villages built by the Kichepo people. With the help of Korok as translator, Dick stopped and talked to the headman of one of the larger villages. He was shy and hesitant at first, but Dick assured him the Italians were now gone. He also explained that British officers would now be in charge of the area and they would be fair and friendly. Upon climbing up the gradual slope on the east side of the Boma Plateau, Dick saw the landmark spire of ancient lava called Towoth. He knew he was back in Sudanese territory.

12

The Good Life on Boma

Dick and his troops arrived at the Boma fort in late afternoon. The fort was almost empty. Manning the fort was a single British officer named Cummings and ten local policemen. Cummings was pleased to see Dick and have some company, someone with whom he could speak English. Dick's soldiers bivouacked down for the night and the policemen found them some fresh food. Dick spent the evening with Cummings, sitting in a room with a real table and chairs and eating a good meal using silverware.

Cummings told Dick as much as he could about Boma and the people living in the area. However, he did not really know that much, having only been in the area for a few weeks. The following day Dick was shown around the fort. It was built in a marvelous location at the top of sheer cliffs where the rocks jutted out into space, forming two sides of a triangle. The main wall of the fort had been built across the third side of the triangle. Cummings, proud of the fort, stated, "Access to the fort can only be had from the fortified front wall and this makes it easy to defend. It is a no-back-door construction. Once soldiers are ensconced in the fort they have to fight to the death since there is no exit at the back of the fort."

Dick looked closely and saw that the cliffs at the back of the fort were solid granite and fell 250 feet straight down to the forest below. Inside the fort were more stone walls and two barracks used for sleeping. The Italians must have known that the fort was impregnable and therefore they had never made any attempt to take Boma.

The view from the back of the fort was spectacular, facing west with 270 degrees of unimpeded geography spread out below. Cummings told Dick, "The high cliffs come with a story. Former British officers used to urinate over the edge of the cliff, bragging they had the deepest latrine in the world. One day a visiting dignitary excused himself at supper and went out back to use the ledge. A minute later the officers at table heard a faint call, but ignored it. The call got louder and then became a desperate shout. They ran to the ledge and found their exalted guest hanging over the cliff, clutching a branch with one hand and his trousers with the other. They grabbed his arms and dragged him to safety." Both Dick and Cummings had a good laugh, but privately Dick resolved to avoid such an incident.

Dick was entranced by the beauty of Boma. It was located

at an elevation of 5,000 feet elevation, so the temperature was moderate. There was a grove of mango trees in the valley to the east of the fort and a clear spring of water bubbled out of the ground. In the morning Dick strolled around the area and greeted the Murle people in the surrounding villages. At midmorning Dick used the wireless radio to call his superiors at Kapoeta. He informed them of his arrival at Boma and said he was awaiting future orders. He received congratulations and was told to remain in Boma until they figured out what to do with him and his troops. For the next two days Dick relaxed. It was so good to be out of the war zone, not to be on the alert and watching over his shoulder all the time. He climbed to the top of several peaks, inspected some stone fortifications and walked in the cool forest. The hunter in him was excited when he spotted the deep footprints of a greater kudu, the tallest, most elegant antelope in Africa.

On the third day he got a return radio message from Kapoeta. His company of men fighting under the authority of the Sudan Defence Force was to be disbanded. With the Italians gone from the border area there was no longer a reason to have military troops patrolling the border. Moreover there was important administrative work to be done in the borderlands. The Sudan government had decided Dick should be withdrawn from the Sudan Defence Force and reassigned to the Sudan Political Service. His first posting was to be the Frontier Agent based at Boma. He was to start immediately.

Dick was elated. From the little he had seen of Boma it was a beautiful place to live and work. It was also located in one of the most remote corners of Africa and he would be relatively free to administer the area as he wished. His primary work would be relating to the local people and keeping the peace.

Before taking his new post Dick had to say goodbye to his troops. This was difficult after the many months they had spent together. He had bonded closely with his men. They were special people. Dick gathered his soldiers together and told them they were going home. They erupted in great shouts of joy. They had served long and hard as soldiers and they had shown their courage many times over. Now they could go home with honor, carrying their pay with them. In the future they could sit around their home fires at night, telling stories of battles they had fought and boasting of their prowess as warriors

The following day Dick and a group of his soldiers hiked down the escarpment to the plains below. In 1936 the Sudan Defence Force had built a fine road up the cliffs and Dick and his men used this road to walk down to the hot plains in an hour. Korok went with them as a guide and he led them to the clear stream the British officers had named Queen's Water. Here they rested while Korok went off scouting for game. He soon returned saying he had seen a herd of buffalo. Dick went with him and shot two young bulls. The men butchered them and carried the meat up the escarpment to the barracks. That night the soldiers held a great victory feast. They gorged on roasted buffalo meat and they danced long into the night. Dick danced with them, leaping up and down in time to the beating of the drums. But eventually he tired and went to bed. He drifted off with the sound of drums throbbing through the night.

The following morning the men were a bit bleary-eyed, but they hoisted their loads and rifles and headed down the escarpment, following the road to Mount Kathangor and on to Kapoeta. Cummings marched with them, going back to Kapoeta to take up a new assignment. The Didinga guide Logoto led them. He had proven to be an excellent scout and a good friend. Dick knew he would miss him. Even though he was an older man, he had kept the pace admirably. This would probably be his last great trek. All of the soldiers were to receive their pay in Kapoeta and from there they would disperse to their various villages. Dick had asked Logoto what he would do with his money. He said he would use his pay to buy cows from the Toposa living near Kapoeta. Then he would take these cattle up into the Didinga Hills where he would exchange the cattle for a second wife.

Kuju and Musa decided to stay at Boma with Dick. Kuju continued to work as Dick's cook and orderly. Musa had demonstrated definite leadership qualities and eventually could transfer into the local police force.

Dick felt sad as he saw his men trek down the hill and across the scorching plains. The place seemed empty without them, but he busied himself with talking to the local policemen and getting to know the Murle elders. A few days later a government messenger appeared at Boma. Since it was rainy season the road from Kapoeta to Boma was a sea of black, sticky mud – impossible for a vehicle to navigate. Therefore it was necessary to use messengers who walked the 125 miles through the mud. The messenger carried a small canvas bag. Dick opened it. It was from Geoffrey King, the District Commissioner in charge of Kapoeta. King was now Dick's direct superior. The box contained the pay for the ten policemen who were working at Boma. It also contained some coffee beans and two bars of chocolate. More importantly there was a manual, a book that set out the duties of a political officer in the Sudan. Dick was now the Frontier Agent for the Boma region, but had no training whatsoever as to his duties and responsibilities. Also in the box was a personal letter from the District Commissioner welcoming Dick into the Political Service. He wrote that Dick needed to make a mental change from being a military officer to being a political officer. As a soldier he had to make quick decisions and act on them right away. However, in the Political Service it was better to defer a decision until one was sure it was correct. He went on to write that many political crises worked themselves out over time with little interference. Dick appreciated this advice and proceeded with caution when he dealt with the tribal people in the area.

Over the next few days Dick read through the manual several times. Many of the instructions in the book did not apply to his situation. But he gleaned from it the most important aspects of his new job. Keeping the peace among the various ethnic groups would be the priority. Economically the people were fairly self-sufficient. In this remote corner of the Sudan there was little Dick could do in the way of improving health, schools and roads. But with the manual in hand, he was in charge.

Dick knew he might be in Boma for a long period of time, so he decided to settle in and make himself comfortable. He did not want to live in a room in the barracks. Instead he wanted his own space, a place to which he could retreat and be quiet. He decided to build himself a house. After walking around the area he chose a site one mile from the barracks. It was a sheltered nook located near the edge of a cliff, with a magnificent view to the west. At the rear of the site some large boulders and tall trees gave shelter from the wind.

Dick worked with the policemen to build the house. They cut straight poles in the forest and set them upright in the ground in the shape of a rectangle. On top of this frame they attached simple trusses. They used long grass to thatch the roof. Similar grass was tied to the walls, leaving a few gaps for windows. The floor was made of beaten earth. The evenings in Boma could be cool, so Dick wanted a fireplace with a chimney. He had the men collect small rocks. They made mortar out of mud that Dick puddled with his own bare feet. Dick had never made a chimney before, but his design worked well, drawing the smoke up the chimney. The finished result was a house with two rooms. The outer room was the sitting room with the fireplace at one end. The inner room was his bedroom. The toilet was an outhouse forty paces away. In addition Kuju built a grass hut nearby to be used as a kitchen, using three rocks to balance his precious pots over the wood fire. The entire construction was completed in a few days and Dick felt proud of his new house in the wilderness. It was such a pleasant change from all the primitive camping he had done over the previous months of war.

Next to his new house Dick planted a vegetable garden. Since he had no seeds he started out with local greens from the forest and some millet. Over time he got seeds sent in from Torit and grew carrots, tomatoes, eggplant, cabbages and okra. Around his house he planted flowers. The beds were soon bright with the colors of marigolds, zinnias, coreopsis and daisies. He built a trellis next to the door and this was eventually covered with light blue morning glories.

Near the cliff edge was a large smooth boulder. Dick designated this as his prayer rock. He retreated to this rock daily and in this marvelous setting he communed with his God. Upon returning from prayer he often made entries in his private diary. One morning he wrote, "I sought the Lord's face sitting out on my prayer rock. I sought Him and found Him and hid Him in the deep quiet places of my soul." On another date he made a further entry: "I am His, absolutely and forever. His to use or not to use . . . I will laugh with Him and I will weep with Him. Above all and in all and through all I will delight to do His will forever and ever."

The people living on top of the Boma Plateau were the highland Murle. Dick had already gotten to know Korok and Kireer who had worked with him as scouts during the months of fighting against the Italians. They had taught him a few words of the Murle language. But now surrounded by Murle villages he was committed to learning Murle. He wanted to be able to communicate face to face with his neighbors. There was an additional motive. His pay would go up if he could pass a language test proving he had learned a local language. With the house completed Dick focused on language study. He started learning from Korok. Dick pointed at various objects and Korok would say something. Dick listened carefully and wrote it down. But Dick was never sure if he was getting the right word. If he pointed at a tree, Korok might give him the generic word for tree. Or he might give him the name of that particular species of tree. Or he might be giving him the word for leaf. Or even the word for a bird perched in the tree. However, by trial and error Dick gradually built up a list of nouns in the Murle language. He had no training in linguistics, so he used the English alphabet. But because the Murle language had some unique vowel sounds he had to invent several alphabet symbols.

Korok was a family man with several wives and he had responsibilities other than teaching Murle to Dick. Korok suggested that Dick start taking language lessons from a young man named Lado. Lado had worked for several years as the official Murle translator to the officers of the Sudan Defence Force. Lado had a complicated history. He had been born on Boma, but as a boy he had been captured and taken into slavery by the Lotuxo people who lived near Torit. He was raised by the Lotuxo and learned their language and culture. When the British military entered the region he got a job as a gardener for the District Commissioner. In the process he learned pidgin Arabic from the local militia. When the Sudan Defence Force came and imposed British rule on Boma in 1936, they brought Lado with them to serve as guide and translator.

Lado had continued on as translator for the British officers working at Boma. Lado was a patient, gentle man and Dick liked him immediately. He hired him to be his Murle language teacher. Over the following months Dick made good progress with the Murle language and soon was walking around the Murle villages, conversing with the people in their own language. Over the following months he continued to expand his list of words, eventually making a comprehensive dictionary. He discovered the grammar of Murle was quite complicated, but gradually he unlocked the basic grammar rules.

Dick got to know Lado well and they struck up a close friendship. But at times Lado was withdrawn and sad. Dick finally discovered Lado's underlying issues. When Lado came back to Boma as the guide for the Sudan Defence Force, the local people initially saw him as a traitor, responsible for bringing in the conquering British troops. Even Lado's extended family rejected him. Moreover, Lado was trying to sort out why he had experienced so many troubles in his life. His father had been killed in battle. His mother had been captured and eventually died. He himself had been taken as a slave. Where was God in all of his suffering? Lado asked Dick many insightful questions and Dick realized Lado was seeking a deeper meaning in life.

Dick made it his practice to hold a regular small worship service in his grass house. Musa, Kuju and several of the local policemen attended. Dick invited Lado to join them. The next Sunday Lado came and sat on a stool in the corner of the room. He enjoyed the songs of worship and listened carefully as Dick gave a short talk about how a person could have a relationship with God through his son, Jesus Christ. After the little service everyone left, except Lado. He continued to sit on his stool with his head down. Dick just waited. Finally, Lado lifted his head and said, "I have finally found the truth." From that point onward Lado became a vibrant follower of Jesus Christ. He was full of questions and frequently came to Dick for answers.

During the following months, Dick spent much of his time out in the Murle villages. Because of the rough mountain terrain, land for cultivating was at a minimum. Therefore the villages were quite small, each one made up of only a few huts. These houses were built primarily by the women. They wove sticks together to form an inverted oval basket and thatched this framework with long grass. There were no walls needed since the grass roofs reached down to the ground. At the front door they built a small overhanging extension which they used as an entryway. In each village the houses were placed in a circle, facing inward toward a common courtyard with a fire pit. Encircling the pit was a rough circle of large stones used for sitting around the fire in the evening.

Dick was warmly welcomed at the Murle villages. The elders usually gave him a drink of mead, beer brewed from wild honey. At first the women and children were bashful, running and hiding in the houses when they saw Dick coming. But within minutes they surrounded Dick, asking him questions, touching his clothing and stroking his hair. The men were more dignified. No man was without his rifle: usually an old .303. Dick did not carry his rifle on these village walks. He wanted to establish that he came in peace and had no fear. In the early months Lado went with Dick on these walks to the Murle villages. Lado translated for Dick, listening to the Murle and translating it into pidgin Arabic. But Dick learned the Murle language quickly and soon his Murle was better than his pidgin Arabic. From this point onward Dick conversed directly with the Murle people.

Dick not only studied the Murle language, but he also studied the Murle culture. He asked them many questions about their history. He went into the fields with them and helped plant sorghum. He watched the women grind the grain using mortars and pestles. He learned how they made soft bark cloth for their clothing. Before many months had passed, Dick knew the location of every village and hamlet on the west side of the plateau.

For the next three years Dick was the only Englishman living at Boma. He did sometimes have radio contact with Geoffrey King, his supervisor based in Kapoeta. But this was sporadic since the radio often ran out of battery power. His lifeline was the road from Boma to Kapoeta that the Sudan Defence Force had built in 1936. Even during the dry season this was barely passable by vehicle, but this was the time of year Dick made a large annual order of supplies from Kapoeta. The order would be filled and loaded on to a grey Commer lorry. An old Arab soldier would then drive the lorry slowly to Boma. The lorry's arrival at the top of the escarpment was always greeted by hundreds of excited Murle, eager to look at the strange smelly vehicle and to see what it was carrying.

But for much of the year the road to Kapoeta was totally impassable. With the coming of the rains the black soil turned into sticky mud. To make it worse, the low-lying spots became vast shallow lakes. During these wet months the only way in and out of Boma was by foot, slogging through 125 miles of mud. Incoming supplies were non-existent. But periodically a messenger would walk in, carrying the official mail pouch containing pay and letters.

Dick looked forward to his letters from Nora. He sometimes had to wait several months between mail runs and then ten letters would come all at once in the mail pouch. Dick struggled with how to read the letters. Should he read them all at once? Or should he read them one letter a day, thus spreading out the joy? Dick tried to spread them out, but it usually did not work. He would organize the letters based on the dates they were written. Then he would read the first letter. Several hours later he could not resist, so he read the second one. By the end of two days he had them all read. Over the next few days he read them over and over until he had them virtually memorized.

Living on the Boma Plateau as the only Englishman was not lonely. Dick had much to do and he enjoyed being with the Murle people. Still, he did miss Nora. Every time he enjoyed a glorious sunset he wanted to show it to Nora. Every time he learned something interesting about the Murle culture, he wanted to explain it to Nora. Instead he wrote her letters – marvelous missives full of adventures and embedded with romantic statements of his undying love.

Dick had never walked the road from Boma to Kapoeta. The route passed through hot featureless country and during the dry season it lacked good water. Forty-five miles west of Boma the road went around the base of an ancient broken down volcano called Kathangor. It was here that the Sudan Defence Force had once built a heliograph station for sending signals to Boma. It was now abandoned, but Dick wanted to see what was left of the station, so he planned a trek to Kathangor with Musa and several of his policemen. Forty-five miles was possible in one day, so they started out early and after a fast march they arrived at the base of Kathangor by evening. Their camp was a rough one. The area around the base of Kathangor was nothing but gravel and they had to bed down on the hard stones. At night the wind blew hard, covering them with gritty grey dust. In the morning they found myriads of scorpions had taken up residence under their camping gear. They were fortunate not to get stung.

They spent the next several days climbing the mountain looking for water and caves. They quickly found the remnants of the heliograph station on a ridge facing east toward Boma.

It had held a large moveable mirror set up in such a way that it caught the rays of the sun and beamed them toward the Towath police post forty-five miles away. To send messages, a board had been used to break the sun's rays. This had to be inserted and removed rapidly to give short and long intervals of light creating Morse code. Short messages could be sent quite efficiently. It had been used to tell soldiers at Boma that vehicles were coming or that vehicles were stuck in the mud and needed help. However, stationing soldiers at Kathangor long term had not been feasible and the heliograph station had long been abandoned.

One of the Murle policemen said he knew the location of a pool with good water. He led them almost to the top of the mountain where he entered a deep ravine. At the upper end was a dark cave. They entered the cave and a few feet into the darkness was a deep pool of clear water. The air was moist and cool, quite a contrast from the blast furnace winds at the base of the mountain. The guide assured Dick the water remained here even in the driest time of the year. On the way down from the mountain the guide took them to another large cave. This cave did not have any water, but it had large metal rings embedded in the walls with rusty links of chain attached. The guide explained that this cave was once used for holding slaves. In recent memory Arabs had come from the Nile River and captured people to be taken north and sold into slavery. After capture the slaves were held in this cave, chained to the walls until enough slaves had been captured to fill the caravan. Then they were yoked together and marched east to the Nile River and on to Khartoum. Dick found the cave a depressing place, a place of suffering. He was happy to leave the cave and to go out into the brilliant sunshine.

On the way down through the sharp rocks they stumbled into a ravine and came upon yet another large cave. All around the entrance were piles of white feces. The guide told Dick this was the home cave for a large pack of spotted hyenas. The presence of these potentially dangerous predators made Kathangor feel even more ominous.

On the walk back to the camp Dick looked up and saw a pair of klipspringers looking down at them. He knew these unique little antelope lived only on the tops of rocky hills and had special soft hooves for getting around on the hard surface. As Dick and his men drew closer, the klipspringers bounded away, leaping from rock to rock until they were out of sight. Dick wondered how they had reached Kathangor in the first place. The rocky mountain was an ideal home for them, but it was an ecological island surrounded by hundreds of miles of hot lowland.

13

The Sacred Drums

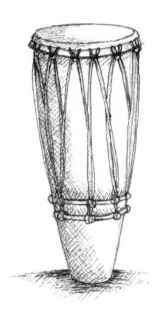

Upon returning to Boma, Dick continued roaming around the hills and visiting the Murle villages. He estimated there were about 3000 Murle inhabiting the area, making their living by growing crops. Whenever he entered a village, the men would ask him what *buul* he belonged to. Lado explained to him that a *buul* was an age-set. Dick began studying this part of the Murle culture and discovered every grown man belonged to an age-set. As teenagers they entered an age-set with other boys their own age and they stayed in this group for the rest of their lives. They took on the name of an animal, chose a color, scarred themselves with symbols, danced together and went to war as a fighting unit. Belonging to an age-set was the basic glue that held Murle society together. To be a man one had to identify with a specific age-set. When Dick was asked for his age-set, he had to admit he did not belong to one. He tried to explain this was not a custom practiced in England. When men found out Dick did not belong to any age-set, they invited Dick to join theirs. All the age-sets wanted him. It would be a real coup to have the white officer in their age-set. Dick had to make a choice and he chose to join the age-set called *Kelang* – the "Leopards". These were men in their early twenties who had not yet been married. They matched perfectly with Dick's station in life.

The Leopards were ecstatic. They planned a big dance. Word spread rapidly and Leopards came in from all the villages to the hard-baked dance floor. They spent the afternoon decorating themselves at a nearby spring. First they bathed and then they used white clay to draw white circles on their dark naked bodies. The circles represented the spots on leopards. Dick was taken to the spring and stripped down. The warriors carefully used the white clay to draw spots all over Dick's body. The white clay circles on his white skin were not especially dramatic, but it was obvious he was decorated like a *Kelang*. He was also given a headdress to wear, decorated with spotted guinea-fowl feathers. That night Dick danced with the warriors as a full member of the *Kelang* age-set. He stood in line with his Murle age-mates and jumped up and down in time to the rhythmic music. From that point onward when people asked Dick who he was, he replied that he was a *Kelang*. They would nod. He had a status in their society. He belonged.

Over the ensuing months Dick trekked to all the villages in the mountainous area. Most of these were within a day's walk. He could go and return the same day. The highland Murle people lived in the mountains and only went down to the hot plains when they wanted to hunt. Dick was told that most of the Murle actually lived in the hot floodplains where they practiced a migratory lifestyle looking for pasture and water for their cattle. These lowland Murle did not come within thirty miles of Boma. The area close to the hills contained tsetse flies and these were fatal to their beloved cattle.

Out in the plains were a series of granite kopjes called the Maruwa Hills. They were a holy site to the Murle and one of the red chiefs made his home in the area. Since the Maruwa Hills were under Dick's jurisdiction, he decided to pay the red chief a visit. He left Musa in charge of the Boma police post and took Lado and Korok with him. The difficult trek took two days. Once they left the deciduous forests at the base of the Boma plateau, they entered the floodplains. The grass had not yet been burned off and rose two feet above their heads. It was difficult to see more than one pace in front of their feet and they had to step carefully on the rough ground. The heat was intense and no wind moved in the tall grass. All of the men perspired heavily. Their bodies ran with sweat and the sharp grass seeds fell and stuck to their bodies.

By the afternoon of the second day they sighted the Maruwa hills. The land rose slightly in elevation and soon they walked on a well-trodden trail. Korok led them to a village at the base of the hills where Dick met the red chief named Keli. He was an old man with gray hair and he stood erect and tall, holding himself with great dignity. On his forehead he wore a cluster of bright red feathers collected from the breast of a black-headed gonolek. The red feathers were a symbol of his sacred office. Keli welcomed Dick and his men and showed them where they could set up camp. His wives brought pots of water so the men could drink and wash. A striped goat was killed in their honor and that evening they enjoyed the roasted meat. Dick was served the liver in a symbolic gesture of his authority. He sat and watched as the herd boys brought in hundreds of sleek cows and impounded them for the night in a well-built *zariba*. Keli reported they were having troubles with a couple of lions that were attacking the herd. He asked if Dick could shoot the lions with his rifle.

Dick agreed. During the night he heard shattering roars as the lions paced around the neighboring thickets. The next morning the warriors went out and found the lions' footprints. Dick loaded up his rifle and followed them. The tracks led to a dense acacia thicket. The warriors threw mud clods into the thicket and immediately two lions came bolting out, fleeing from the Murle spearmen. Dick took quick aim at the large male and hit it in the back. It went down in a heap. Dick swung his rifle back to the other lion and got off another shot. He saw the lion wince, but it kept running and disappeared into a patch of long grass. The warriors surrounded the grass and then waited, giving time for the lion to stiffen up from its wound. Then they threw clods of mud into the grass but got no response. The warriors carefully entered the long grass with spears at the ready. Dick went with them, rifle held tightly in his hands. But the lion was already dead. One of the warriors spotted the body. Its eyes were glazed over and flies were already buzzing about its head. Dick's bullet had entered the lion far back in the belly and then raked forward into the lungs. The Murle warriors were ecstatic. Their enemies were dead and their cattle would now be safe from the marauders. They skinned the mane off the big male lion and cut it into strips. These would be used to make new headdresses they could use at the next age-set dance.

Keli, the red chief, was also pleased. As a gift he gave Dick a large white ox with long curved horns and a red patch on its right flank. Keli explained that this was to be Dick's name-ox. That evening there was a short ceremony after which Dick took a spear and thrust it into the heart of the white ox. The ox bellowed and fell to the ground, dying fortuitously on its right side. Dick was then formally given a Murle name based on the color pattern of the ox. *Mer* was the word for red and *bong* was the word for a white pelican. The words were put together to form *Kemerbong*. From that day onward Dick was known by the Murle as Kemerbong, the Red Pelican.

Dick discovered Keli was not a chief in the political sense. He was believed to have direct contact with God and was considered to be a priest and a prophet. He prayed for rain, blessed people and asked God for help in raids. His position was inherited, passed on from father to son. Dick learned there were four chiefly families among the Murle. One lived at Boma and the other three lived in the lowlands.

Dick also learned that the Maruwa Hills had a large cave and this was a sacred place for all the red chiefs. Each of the four chiefly families was connected to a particular clan and every Murle person also belonged to one of these clans. The word for clan in Murle was *kidong*. This meant drum but could also be translated as drumship. Each of these clans had a sacred drum. These drums were used rarely and then only to announce war.

They were very old and Keli told Dick that these four drums were kept in the sacred cave in the hills above them. One reason Keli lived near the Maruwa Hills was to protect the site of the sacred drums.

Dick asked if he could see the drums. He did not use his authority as a British officer to force the issue, but he was curious. Keli hesitated at first. However, Dick was now one of them. He had a Murle name - *Kemerbong*. He was also a member of a Murle age-set – *Kelang*. Keli acquiesced, but told Dick that he must be respectful and he was not to touch anything in the cave.

Dick agreed and the next morning Keli led him up a rocky valley. They turned a corner in the rocks and climbed a narrow defile only three feet wide. At the top they squeezed through a narrow gap and stood on a flat ledge overlooking the landscape below. Behind the ledge was the entrance to a large cave. Keli told Dick to take off his shoes and again reiterated he was not to touch anything inside the cave. Dick complied, bending down to slip off his shoes. He then walked into the dark cave. His eyes slowly adjusted to the gloom. The cave was totally dry and gave off a faint musty smell. On a flat rock Dick saw the four sacred drums, covered with gray dust. They were small, only measuring two feet long. Dick looked closely at the largest of the drums and could see it was carved out of a single piece of wood. It was hollow and had a piece of skin stretched over both ends. The skin was old and torn. The drum had obviously been lying there for a very long time.

Dick also saw a number of clay pots lined up along the back wall of the cave. Looking closely he saw that each pot contained bones, the longest ones sticking out the top of the pots. Keli explained that the pots contained the bones of former red chiefs. Some of the pots had cracked with old age and the bones were disintegrating into dust. Dick understood he was looking at ancient relics from the past and he realized why this cave was so sacred to the Murle people.

Dick and Keli retreated to the entrance to the cave. Here they sat on a flat rock overlooking the plains below and Keli explained how the pots of bones got there. Whenever a red chief died, the whole clan went into mourning. A natural disaster was expected to mark the chief's passing into the next world. It could be lightning killing a person, the river going dry or the cattle getting sick. Social life came to a complete stop. The body of the red chief was dangerous because it contained a powerful spirit. After a week of mourning rituals, the body was put into a hut. The oldest son of the red chief was put in the hut with the body of his father. The hut was then sealed shut from the outside. The son stayed in the hut and over the coming weeks he cared for the body of his father as it rotted, brushing away the maggots. He did not leave the hut during this entire time. Food and water were passed in to him, but with the putrid conditions in the house, he ate very little. When the corpse was reduced to nothing but clean bones, the son called out and the door to the hut was opened. The son then came out bearing the clean bones of his father.

At this point there was a procession to the sacred cave in the Maruwa Hills. A large number of relatives joined this procession. Several black bulls were taken as well. The clean bones of the red chief were put in a clay pot and carried on the head of his first wife. Depending on where the red chief had died, the procession to the sacred cave could take several days. Each night the people stopped and made camp. One of the black bulls was sacrificed and eaten. When the extended family finally arrived at the base of the Maruwa hills, they set up a camp one last time. A final ceremony was held and the last of the black bulls was sacrificed and eaten. Then the son of the wife carrying the bones climbed up to the cave and placed the pot of bones with the other pots of those who had gone before. After this ceremonial trek health and happiness returned to the Murle drumship. Their red chief had gone to be with his ancestors. The son who had stayed in the hut and cleaned his father's bones inherited the religious power of his father and was installed as the next red chief.

Dick thanked Keli for showing him the cave and explaining its place in Murle belief and society. They made their way carefully down through the rocks. That night they feasted on the remains of Dick's name ox. In the morning they started on the long trek back to the coolness of Boma. Keli gave them several goats as gifts, something to eat on the long walk home.

14

The Peacemaker

Dick spent his first year at Boma focusing on the highland Murle people. They were the people who lived on top of the Boma Plateau and were closest to the fort and therefore he spent much of his time learning their language and culture. But there were two other ethnic groups that also fell under his jurisdiction – the Kichepo and the Anuak.

The Kichepo were also mountain people and lived to the east of Boma on the backside of the plateau. Dick made several treks back in the hills to visit their small villages. The Kichepo women practiced a highly unusual custom. Each lady wore a large labial plug in the lower lip. When a girl reached the age of twelve, an incision was made under her lower lip, reaching from one side to the other. The lip was then stretched and a small disk inserted. Over time larger and larger disks were inserted until the lower lip could encircle a disk as much as six inches in diameter. The bottom front teeth were also removed so part of the disk could rest on the lower gum. It seemed to be a bizarre and cruel custom and Dick asked the people why they did it. They insisted it was done for beauty. The girls with the largest lip plugs were considered to be the most beautiful.

The Kichepo warriors periodically held stick fights to try and win the hands of these duck-lipped beauties. Dick heard the news that a stick fight was being organized so on the given day he went to watch. At the fighting arena he found dozens of young men and hundreds of interested spectators. The fights were well organized with scheduled duels and referees. Each warrior carried a fighting stick, a strong smooth rod about six feet long. Before a duel a young man would wrap his arms and hands with thick rolls of cloth for protection. Further pieces of cloth were wrapped around his shins and head. To commence a duel the referee stood between the two warriors and indicated when it was time to start fighting. Each warrior held the end of his stick with both hands and swung it as hard as he could at his opponent, trying to hit him with a crippling blow. In turn the opponent would parry the incoming blow and then swing his own stick. These fighters were well trained and each had a variety of different moves. Whenever they got into close proximity or into a clinch, the referee intervened and pulled them apart. Blows were given and received. Limbs were broken and heads split open. Blood flowed. When it became obvious one fighter was getting the worst end of the duel, the referee stepped in and declared a winner. The winning warriors continued dueling with other winners until at the end of the day one fighter was declared the overall champion. Dick watched as the winning warrior was picked up and paraded around by his supporters. The young unmarried girls sidled up and gave him a small gift of beads: a token of their interest.

The Murle and the Kichepo were close neighbors and usually lived in an uneasy peace with each other. They spoke similar languages and practiced similar economies. Occasionally a Murle man would marry a Kichepo girl and vice versa. But historically there was enmity. For centuries the Ethiopians had taken slaves out of this region. During this time they had hired Kichepo warriors to capture people as slaves. Periodically Murle people disappeared, having been captured and sold into slavery by the Kichepo. In Dick's time slavery in Ethiopia was banned, but the people had long memories. Occasionally fighting would break out between the Kichepo and Murle. The Kichepo country was rocky and they needed better land for farming. So over time they were gradually moving west up the backside of the Boma Plateau, slowly encroaching on Murle land.

During Dick's second year at Boma the sporadic fighting between the Kichepo and the Murle increased until it became an outright war. Murle warriors came to Dick with spear wounds and bullet holes, asking for medicine. Men from both ethnic groups walked around in groups so they would not be ambushed. Women and children went into hiding. Dick realized he must do something. One of his primary responsibilities as Frontier Agent was to keep the peace.

Dick convened the older Murle men and they agreed things

had gotten out of hand. There needed to be a peace ceremony. The elders talked to the Murle warriors, telling them to back off and stop being so aggressive.

Then Dick and Musa made a trek out to the Kichepo villages. As they walked through the area Dick could see the devastation caused by the fighting: burnt houses and overgrown fields. He met with various Kichepo elders and they too agreed the fighting had gotten out of control. But they did not trust the Murle. If the Kichepo warriors laid down their weapons, they might be attacked.

Dick offered himself as the peacemaker. The elders on both sides considered this carefully and then agreed. On the chosen day they all met at a large granite boulder on the main path that led between the two tribes. Here a white goat was sacrificed. Its blood was poured on the rock. Then the stomach was opened and the chyme (green undigested grass) taken out. Some of this was thrown on the boulder. Each elder took a small bit of the chyme and rubbed it on his forehead. Dick stripped off his shirt and the green ooze was smeared all over his chest and face. This indicated that Kemerbong was the peacemaker. The boulder was now the official border between the Murle and the Kichepo. A Murle warrior going into Kichepo territory had to lay down his weapons at the rock and enter Kichepo territory unarmed. It was the same for Kichepo warriors going into Murle territory. Both sides vowed to keep the agreement. As long as Kemerbong was in the region they promised they would keep the peace.

The warriors on both sides were informed of the peace agreement and abruptly all fighting stopped. People on both sides rebuilt their houses and got back to tilling their fields. Dick was pleased with the result of the ceremony. He had made peace using the traditional process, not using the force of the Sudanese police.

Life at Boma never fell into a routine. There was always something interesting happening. Dick still had his dog Mary with him as his constant companion. She went with him on all his treks and at Boma she slept on a rug by the side of his bed. Mary had a litter of five pups and Dick opted to keep two of them. He named one Bite and the other Koli – the Murle word for black.

Leopards lived in the hills and occasionally Dick heard one walking around his house at night, making its unique call that sounded like a saw cutting through wood. The leopard became increasingly bold and started breaking into Dick's hen house and taking the chickens. The Murle pointed out that the leopards in the hills had a reputation for eating dogs so Dick was concerned for the safety of his pets. With the help of Musa he built a trap. They made a dead fall using a large tree trunk. It was lifted up on one end and they set an elaborate trigger in place. They tied a live chicken to this trigger as bait. That night the leopard grabbed the chicken and the log came down, pinning the leopard to the ground. Dick heard the angry snarling of the wounded leopard and ran out with his revolver, shooting the leopard in the head from close range. Now he could sleep at night knowing his dogs were safe.

Lions tended to stay in the lowlands away from the Murle villages. But one morning Dick got up and saw large pugmarks in the flowerbeds. Some of these footprints led right to the open window of Dicks' bedroom and Dick realized the lion had stood within two feet of where he was sleeping. Even the watchdog Mary had not been aware of its silent visit.

During the war years Dick had not been allowed to keep a journal. It was prohibited by the British government for fear that secret information might fall into enemy hands. But during his assignment to Boma, Dick began keeping a journal again. In his writing he indicated he thoroughly enjoyed his life at Boma. The only thing he regretted was not having Nora with him. He knew Nora would enjoy life at Boma as much as he did. She had taken training as a nurse in England and was committed to returning and working in Africa. Dick and Nora planned to get married as soon as the war was over and Dick could return to Britain. Meanwhile all he could do was write letters, so write letters he did. Eventually there was a fairly well organized system of mail coming in and out from Kapoeta and Dick appreciated Nora's regular missives.

But it was still hard to be so far away from Nora. For a period of nine months Dick was totally isolated from the outside world, with no chance to speak to somebody from his own culture. Then a government doctor visited Boma: somebody who spoke Dick's mother tongue. The doctor was a patient, understanding man and Dick talked to him hour after hour, unleashing a torrent of rapid English. He talked about his life at Boma and about the Murle culture. He described his administrative work and the long treks he had made. But mostly he talked about Nora. He told the doctor about Nora's background. Her grandfather was Stanley Smith and he had been one of the famous Cambridge Seven who had gone to China to work as missionaries with Hudson Taylor. Her grandfather had learned the Chinese language, donned Chinese clothing and wore his hair in a long pigtail. Nora's father Algy had been born in China and as an adult he had worked as a missionary in Uganda and Rwanda. Dick emphatically stated, "Nora was born to live and work overseas. It's in her blood."

After the government doctor left, Dick wrote in his diary, "We talked about love and the future, about Nora and married life. I am too much of a coward to think about such things. The only way I keep happy is by working hard and concentrating on the present. The pull of home is very hard when I allow myself to think about it. That is why I seldom do so."

Dick also continued to find solace at his prayer rock. This beautiful spot overlooking the vast plains below was a perfect place to connect with God.

In his role as Frontier Agent, Dick was well received by his Murle neighbors. They saw him as a fair and just man. He was also seen as a spiritual man with a connection to God. People wanted to be his friend. One of the Murle elders named Kamalong came to Dick and told him his wife had just given birth to a baby boy. Dick paid a visit to the newborn baby and the baby was promptly christened Kemerbong in honor of Dick. Dick was now his godfather – whether he liked the child or not. Dick gave the baby a string of beads, but in his diary he referred to him as a "revolting little creature." However, as the baby grew Dick became fond of him and called him a "sturdy little chap." Dick visited his godson periodically, spitting on his tummy and tickling him in the orthodox Murle manner.

The region around Boma had never been properly surveyed, so one of Dick's assignments was to trek through the entire region and make cursory maps. Dick loved this part of his job.

He would plan a trip and organize a caravan of police and porters. Kuju always came along, bringing his pots and pans. The porters carried the camping gear so they could be comfortable after a long day of hiking. Dick said it best in his journals: "What a joy it is to experience once again the rich thrills of the march, the sights and sounds which never lose their power to fascinate. The long black and khaki line winding away and away, up over the crest of the hill, over the world's rim, to disappear in the very heart of the furnace of the sunset. And always the creak, creak, creak of accouterments, the soft click, click, click of equipment as metal kisses metal at every stride. The heavy breathing, the crunch of many footsteps and the slap, slap, slap of polished black bayonet scabbards against polished black thighs."

There were no roads in the region except for the track to Kapoeta. But people used faintly marked footpaths and these gave Dick a sense of comfort, knowing someone had previously passed that way. He noted this in his journal, writing, "There is something remarkably comforting about marching along a path after a number of days of making one's own way . . . I suppose it is the sudden assurance that one is not alone in the world after all; that there are other human beings in villages not so far away."

To make maps Dick would camp at the base of a hill. He then climbed to the crest and took a compass bearing on another hill, carefully recording the direction indicated by the compass. Afterwards he hiked to the second hill, estimating the mileage between the two locations. He then climbed the second hill and took another compass reading on a third hill. Then he would hike to the third hill to continue the process, making a rough map by triangulation. It was slow, painstaking work. Over a number of months he walked hundreds of miles and climbed all the hills in the region and drew them into a master map. This map was eventually turned over to the survey department in Khartoum and it became the officially accepted map for the region.

The Anuak people lived north of the Boma Plateau along the Akobo River. Since these people were also under Dick's jurisdiction, he organized a large caravan to go and visit their paramount chief who was named Ogada. The caravan marched north through rough country and the first night they camped on the Raprap River. It was a small, rocky stream where many animals came to drink so it was necessary to set a guard to protect the sleeping men. Dick took the first watch and entered the experience in his journal the following morning: "I took the first two-hour watch and sat cross-legged with my back against a tree and with my rifle across my knees to enjoy the solemn majesty of the night. Now and again I got up to throw a log on the fire. A shower of Lilliputian meteors flashed their bright courses through the night. The red glow and the dancing reflections of the fire gave to the surrounding objects an appearance at once constant and inconstant, certain and yet uncertain. A breath of air set the trees and grasses whispering to each other and spread a plume of sweet wood smoke across the stars. The glow of my pipe vied with the redness and the steadiness of Mars. Strips of meat lay drying on a barbecue over the fire. The great and the lesser beasts of the bush trod softly around their waterhole and stampeded thunderously as they caught the scent of man. Hyenas laughed as they found food and howled as they failed. Cicadas chirped and screeched endlessly. Somewhere up in the hills a lion grunted as he drove game to his waiting mate. And so

I sat on through the early night until a double span of the finger and the thumb against the moon's silver track told me that my two hours had passed away."

Four days of trekking brought them to chief Ogada's village. The Anuak were a Nilotic people who had a highly organized political system. Ogada was the paramount chief over all the Anuak people. He lived in a large grass house surrounded by hundreds of other grass houses. In the center of the village was an enormous palace made of grass. The caravan set up camp just outside the village and Dick was invited to meet the chief the following morning. He was ushered to the palace and bent low to go through the small door. When his eyes adjusted to the gloom he saw a slight elderly man sitting on a large chair. Dick walked up to him and shook his hand and they exchanged a few words of greeting in pidgin Arabic. Dick was then given his own chair. He liked chief Ogada immediately. He held himself with dignity, but there was a twinkle in his eye. Through a translator Dick asked the chief many questions and was impressed with his answers. The Anuak people had a well-structured society and the chief was truly in control. They lived primarily off their well-tilled fields, but they also kept some cattle. When the kob migration came through their area they hunted the antelope for meat. In addition, the rivers were full of fish.

After talking for a period of time, chief Ogada called for his elders. Within minutes old men started entering the cavernous palace. Each man had to stoop to enter the low door. Then they immediately sat on the ground facing away from the chief and began crawling backwards across the dirt floor. Only when they got close to the chief did they swivel around and face Ogada.

Dick was amazed by the respect they showed toward their chief. Nobody was allowed to stand in his presence. Dick counted a total of 72 elders. When they were all gathered, Ogada spoke quietly to them. Every time the chief stopped speaking, the elders politely clapped several times to acknowledge they heard what he was saying. Dick and his caravan camped out for three days next to the Anuak village. He met with chief Ogada several times and explained the role of the British government. He discovered working through chief Ogada was much easier than working through the Murle chiefs, who did not have much control over their constituencies.

On the way back to Boma, Dick took another route south following the Akobo River. Dick stopped and visited each Anuak village along the river. Showing the British flag while on patrol was one of his jobs. The daily treks were short and Dick thoroughly enjoyed getting to know the area. There was plenty of game around and Dick kept his police and porters happy with plenty of fresh meat. He shot several Roan antelope, large ungulates he had never seen before.

Every evening Dick swam in the Akobo River, keeping a sharp eye out for crocodiles. Often the local village boys joined Dick in the water. Dick dove underwater and grabbed the boys' legs, pretending to be a crocodile. The game was made even more exciting because of the real crocodiles in the river. The boys screamed and shouted when Dick grabbed their legs, hoping it was just the strange white man and not something much more dangerous. In the lowlands the temperatures were hot and the grass was long, but Dick flourished. At the end of the 150-mile trek he wrote in his journal that he had thoroughly enjoyed "fishing, bathing, shooting, basking in the sun and generally lotus-eating."

Dick spent a total of three years based on the Boma Plateau, only rarely seeing a fellow Englishman. Only twice during this time did he get away and have a short vacation. Over time he became fluent in the Murle language and made many close Murle friends. He felt so at home he thought he could live there forever except that he missed Nora. If only Nora had been with him, life would have been perfect.

However, Dick was in limbo with the British government that ruled the southern Sudan. He had left the military position of *Bimbashi* with the Sudan Defence Force and was now acting as Frontier Agent with the Sudan Political Service. However, he had never been vetted or trained for the job. He received a salary, but was regarded as a temporary. He sent numerous letters to Sir Douglas Newbold in Khartoum asking for a clear answer on his status. He wrote, "Either accept me as a full working officer or reject me so I can move on to other things."

But he received no answer. The officers in Khartoum seemed to have more important things to do than sort out the status of a minor local officer in the farthest corner of Sudan.

In 1944 the war in Europe was finally coming to a close and Dick eagerly monitored the progress on his wireless radio. He knew when the war was over he could go back to England and marry Nora. On October 21 he finally received a message from Khartoum stating, "You are ordered to leave your post at Boma and report to Khartoum by October 30th."

15

Job Interview

Dick's orders to report to Khartoum in eight days did not give him much time. He spent a busy day putting his affairs in order and he turned over the responsibilities on Boma to his sergeant, Musa. The following day he took Kuju and several policemen and marched to Kathangor where they spent the night. It was a delightful day. They passed through herds of migrating kob and the large numbers of beautiful antelope never ceased to thrill Dick. In spite of the sticky mud, Dick's feet felt light and he was full of energy. He was finally going to see Nora! It had been six long years since they had been together. They had both been loyal to each other over the many years. The time for marriage was finally here.

The following day they trekked onward to Kapoeta. It was a very long day. That night Dick met with his superior Geoffrey King, the District Commissioner for the area. King had been impressed with Dick's work at Boma and said he would write him a recommendation to become a full member of the Sudan Political Service. He also offered Dick a ride to Torit the next day – on a lorry. Dick's legs could finally have a rest.

Riding in the cab the next morning was like flying. An Arab sergeant did the driving and Dick relaxed and enjoyed the scenery, thinking forward to the days ahead. Kuju rode in the back of the truck. He was going back to his family in Zandeland. He had a pocket full of pay and a head full of exciting stories. He knew he was going to be a popular man.

The ride to Torit took only three hours. In the afternoon Dick met with the commander of the Sudan Defence Force and gave him an oral report. After a scintillating conversation, the officer offered to give Dick letters of recommendation to be presented to officials in Khartoum. In the evening Dick was invited to have dinner with the officers. Dick felt underdressed at this formal dinner. His khaki uniform was frayed along the edges and his boots were falling apart. But his commander assured him, "I understand the circumstances. You can get new uniforms made when you arrive in Khartoum." This put Dick at ease and he spent the evening regaling the officers with stories of life on the Boma Plateau.

The next day the military lorry proceeded onward toward Juba, the capital of the southern Sudan. The red laterite road was corrugated and the truck shuddered along, making Dick's teeth rattle. They eventually came to the mighty Nile River and crossed it on a rickety metal bridge. The town of Juba lay on the west bank. The truck driver dropped off Dick and Kuju at the government offices and they were given places to stay for the night. The next morning Dick said good-bye to Kuju and helped him find a ride westward to his home in Zandeland. Kuju had been a loyal companion and friend for many years and Dick knew he would miss him. But it was time for Kuju to get on with his life back in his homeland.

At 2 pm Dick boarded an old Hudson airplane to take him north. Dick did not trust airplanes. The sky was full of dark clouds and the plane had to maneuver through them, twisting first one direction and then the other. Dick felt sick and his hands clenched the armrests. He prayed fervently he would make it safely. Two hours later the plane landed with a bump on the muddy airstrip at the little town of Malakal, located near the junction of the Sobat and the Nile rivers. Dick was relieved to be back on the ground. The area was perfectly flat and in the evening Dick walked along the riverbank and watched the flocks of white cattle egrets flying in to roost for the night.

The following day he boarded the Hudson again. This time the skies were clear and the plane headed north towards Khartoum. Heat rising off the desert made for a bumpy flight, but Dick was happy not to be swerving around big clouds. As they approached the airfield in Khartoum, Dick looked down on the expansive city that held millions of people. It was actually three cities in one, located at the junction of the White Nile and the Blue Nile. South of the confluence was Khartoum proper with its high buildings and government offices. To the west of the Nile was the sprawling city of Omdurman where most of the

Arabs had their traditional mud-walled houses. North Khartoum was on the east bank and was essentially an industrial city with factories dominating the scene. The plane landed safely and Dick was driven to his quarters.

After settling in, Dick walked around the bustling city. The shops were full of food. He saw pyramids of dried dates, lentils, string cheese and apricot leather. Dick stopped at a street café and bought some barbecued chicken. He ate his chicken on a bench overlooking the confluence of the two mighty rivers and tried to take it all in. It was so different from his isolated home on the Boma Plateau.

Dick had arrived in Khartoum in time to keep his appointment. He reported to government headquarters the following morning where he met with three senior officers. They held a sheaf of documents and recommendations. The meeting was cordial. After an hour of questions the senior officer concluded, "You have done an exemplary work holding back the Italian forces along the Sudan/Ethiopian border. We are also pleased with your work as Frontier Agent at Boma. Therefore we are offering you a long-term position as a District Commissioner in the southern Sudan."

He went on to point out these positions were only given to people who had proved to be of good character and had demonstrated leadership ability. Dick had proved himself both on the battlefield and as an administrator at Boma. But the officer had one stipulation: "We are short handed and need you to start work soon. We can give you only two months of leave and then you are to report back here to Khartoum."

Dick gratefully accepted the position. A position as District

Commissioner in southern Sudan was considered to be one of the best assignments anywhere in the British Empire. The men who were awarded these positions were well educated, usually at Oxford or Cambridge University. It was often said that southern Sudan was a nation of "blacks ruled by blues." A blue was a sports award given at Oxford or Cambridge for athletic prowess. Dick fit the criteria. He had earned his degree at Oxford and he had earned his blue in squash.

District Commissioners in southern Sudan represented all that was best in the British Empire and were selected carefully. The selection committee looked for men of strong moral character. As a District Commissioner, Dick would be given heavy responsibility over a vast amount of territory. He would also be given the authority and freedom to do the work with a minimum of interference from headquarters. In joking terms these District Commissioners were often referred to as Bog Barons – powerful men ruling over the people of the floodplains.

16

Married at Last

Dick spent the next seven days in Khartoum. He went to an Indian tailor and was measured up for a new uniform. He had lost a lot of weight over the many years of trekking. He looked thin, but he was actually in superb condition. He wanted to get married in the khaki uniform of the Sudan Defence Force. The Indian tailor assured him the uniform would meet the standard, right down to the slouch hat.

A week later with the new uniform in his suitcase, Dick caught the train heading north. He sat by the window and looked out over the Sahara desert, mile after mile of gravel and sand. At Wadi Haifa he disembarked from the train and boarded a steamer that took him north down the Nile River to Egypt. Here he took the virtually obligatory camel ride to see the pyramids and then proceeded to Port Said where he boarded a ship named the *Dunolthan Castle* heading for England.

Dick found life on board the ship boring. He was eager to get to England and see Nora. But there was still danger from German U-boats so the *Dunolthan Castle* was part of a convoy with military ships shepherding the passenger ships. Since all of the ships had to stay together they could only proceed at the pace of the slowest ship. This was much too slow for Dick. He spent his 28th birthday in the Bay of Biscay, standing at the railing as the ship plodded along. Then he came down with a fever for several days. Malaria had finally caught up with him. However, he was well enough to get up and see the great rock of Gibraltar as they sailed out of the Mediterranean.

In the early morning of December 5th the ship pulled into port in the city of Glasgow. Dick stood at the rail in the drizzling rain and looked at the drab, gray lines of warehouses and factories. The heavy smoke in the air limited his vision. It was nothing like the long vistas from his prayer rock on top of Boma. As soon as the gangplank was connected to the ship, Dick hurried off the boat. Clearing customs took only a minute. All he owned were a few worn pieces of clothing and his new uniform. He caught the 9 am train to York where he was reunited with his mother and father. They were a little older and grayer than when he had left them six years before, but otherwise much the same. His mother cooked him some beans on toast and it almost felt like he had never been away.

Dick pulled away from the conversation with his parents and rang up Nora on the telephone. They talked and talked and talked. Four days later Dick went to see Nora. It was a joyful reunion. Dick wrote in his diary, "Nora was just as I remembered her." As they talked face to face, the intervening years slipped away "like snowflakes in sunshine." Their exchange of letters over the years had kept them loving and connected. The only sad event that took place at this time was the death of Dick's granny. She had willed herself to stay alive so she could see Dick again. She recognized Dick and died soon thereafter.

Dick and Nora were married on December 15, exactly ten days after he returned to England. They were not going to spend any more time apart. Nora was stately and beautiful in her long, white gown and Dick proudly wore his new khaki uniform with the slouch hat of the Sudan Defence Force. They went on a short honeymoon and returned to Dick's home to spend Christmas. The house was full of family and friends and Dick told them intriguing stories of his years in the Sudan.

Dick was going back to Sudan as a District Commissioner and the colonial government needed him immediately. Nora had applied and been accepted as a nurse with the Sudan Medical Corp. Travel to Sudan was still dangerous and highly restricted and Dick and Nora were given separate orders. Dick was told to report to London where he was attached to the transit camp at the Great Central Hotel in Paddington. Every day he had to report in, waiting word on when he was to sail. Meanwhile Nora was ordered to report to Newport and there she was put on a ship heading for Egypt. Dick and Nora were apart once again, but fully expecting to be reunited in Egypt.

While waiting for his ship in London, Dick met regularly with Dr. Archie Tucker: the famous linguist who knew more about Sudanese languages than any man alive. One of the few languages that Tucker had not studied was Murle and therefore Tucker had many questions. Dick enjoyed passing on his knowledge of the Murle language to the great linguist.

Dick also had the opportunity to visit with B.A. Lewis. He was a former District Commissioner who had spent time at Pibor Post with the lowland Murle. He had just written his Master's thesis at Oxford University on Murle culture and the two men had an enjoyable time comparing the customs of the lowland Murle of the plains and the highland Murle of the Boma Plateau.

Dick's ship finally sailed. In the Atlantic it joined a large convoy. Nora's ship was supposed to be part of the same convoy and Dick expected they would arrive in Egypt together. It was a weary trip for Dick. The ship was severely overcrowded. There was little space to move about and 24 people shared Dick's cabin. The seas were choppy and many of Dick's fellow travelers were seasick, making the conditions even more appalling. Dick did not enjoy being away from his new bride and wrote in his diary, "I miss my wife desperately." He was used to being alone at Boma, but found it lonely on the crowded ship.

Then he discovered Nora's ship was not in the convoy. Nobody seemed to know where it was. He eventually found out it had never joined the convoy. But the officers assured him there were no reports of an attack on any ship in the region. They told Dick that Nora's ship would arrive at a later date. The entire situation had Dick very worried. What would happen when he arrived in Alexandria? How would they connect? Could he stay in Alexandria and wait for Nora? Or would he be shipped south, leaving Nora to find her own way?

Dick's ship arrived in Egypt on March 4 and he was put up in the Royal Oak Hotel. He promptly went to the Cook travel company that kept a list of all ships and their schedules. They were sympathetic and assured Dick that Nora's ship was expected in three days. Dick got permission to wait for Nora, but after three days the ship had still not arrived. Dick checked again and was now told Nora's ship would not arrive until March 18. Dick was not allowed to wait that long and he was ordered to proceed south to Khartoum. Nora would have to follow on her own.

Dick left Cairo on a steamer named *The Britain*. It was an old boat that chugged and panted its way up the broad brown waterway of the Nile River. It would have been romantic if Nora had been with him. Dick decided to share the experience by writing the following poem:

The Lotus Eater

I sail the ageless Nile,
And float past palm-girt strand
And boundless wastes where smile
Infinities of sand.
I feel the sweet sun's kiss
On limbs, on mouth, on eyes
And know a lizard's bliss
In lizard's paradise.

On March 17 Dick arrived back in Khartoum. He was given a day to rest and spent the time visiting the site of the famous Battle of Omdurman. It was on this open plain that 80,000 dervishes armed with swords ran on to the British machine guns.

It had been a massacre, the last great battle between a medieval army and soldiers using modern weaponry.

The following day Dick kept his appointment at the war office since he was still technically a military officer in the Sudan Defence Force. Here he was released from the military so he could be transferred to the Sudan Political Service. The Civil Secretary, Sir Douglas Newbold, summoned Dick to his office. A contract was drawn up on the spot for Dick to be appointed a District Commissioner. It was made out for a ten-year commitment and Dick was asked to sign it. Dick hesitated and then politely refused. He had originally come to Sudan as a missionary and he still felt that was his ultimate calling. The Civil Secretary was taken aback at Dick's refusal. Dick explained, "I am ready and eager to take the position of District Commissioner. I am simply refusing the stated time commitment." He left the office without a signed contract. He felt strongly, however, that he had done the right thing. That night he wrote in his diary, "I was led by the Lord not to commit myself for so long. They adjourned to consider the matter and I will go back tomorrow to hear what they have to say. I have joy and peace."

The Civil Secretary never got back to Dick about signing the ten-year contract. So Dick prepared to head south and begin work without a signed contract. He checked in with the Sudan Medical Corps and they talked about assigning Nora to work in Khartoum for a period of time. This did not please Dick at all. He was beginning to wonder if he was not going to see his beloved wife for a long time.

On March 21 Dick received a wire from Nora, who had

finally arrived in Egypt. She said she was flying to Khartoum and would be there in three days. Dick was ecstatic. To celebrate he rented a small boat and went sailing on the Nile River. He wrote in his diary, "It was ecstasy to feel the tug of the sheet and the tiller once again . . . and to hear the water chuckling under the bow."

Nora flew in right on schedule and it was like a second honeymoon. Dick wrote, "How well she looks and how brown and bonnie . . . How happy we are . . . It is as though she had come gliding down the rainbow into my arms."

Nora explained why her ship was so late. While her ship was loitering in the Atlantic waiting for the convoy to form up, they had been suddenly attacked by a German U-boat. The ship had fled into the open ocean and made its way down to the Azores. There the ship spent a number of days hiding in the harbor until the danger from the U-boat had passed. They then had to wait for a second convoy before they could proceed to Egypt.

To celebrate their reunion Dick took Nora sailing on the Nile. It was a wondrous day and that night Dick wrote, "The water matched my Nora's eyes and the sunlight her hair. We stripped naked and loved and laughed and jibbed and all but sank."

Four days later they were invited to the palace as guests at a banquet held by His Excellency, The Governor of Sudan. For the rest of her life Nora remembered the grand occasion when she walked down the white marble staircase, arm in arm with her handsome husband. Afterwards came the good news. Nora was to be assigned to Juba, the capital of the southern Sudan. Dick got permission for himself and Nora to travel together to

Juba, riding on the same steamer that had taken Dick south six years earlier.

17

Apprenticing as District Commissioner

Nora and Dick traveled to Kosti by train and boarded the paddle wheel steamer named the *Rejaf*. They had a nice cabin in first class and day after day they sat on the wooden deck in canvas chairs and watched the scenery go by. Nora reveled in the bird life and Dick enjoyed teaching her the names of the many water birds along the banks of the Nile. Nora found the intense heat trying, but fortunately the nights were cooler and there was a breeze in their cabin.

The *Rejaf* stopped in Malakal for a day and Dick and Nora went ashore to stretch their legs. Dick met several policemen: men who had once fought with him in the battles with the Italians. They were all delighted to see each other and to reminisce about life in the good old days. Leaving Malakal, the *Rejaf* continued to chug up the Nile. The river was at its lowest in recorded history and the steamer constantly got stuck on mud bars. Great green crocodiles were a common sight, sunning themselves on the banks and rushing into the water as the steamer went by. Dick thrilled at the sight of all the wildlife and entered his observations in his journal: "At every deep spot hippos came surging to the surface, snorting the water in rainbow showers from their nostrils, twiddling their little ears and honking at us with eyes full of wisdom and wonder."

The *Rejaf* arrived in Juba on April 8 and the next evening Dick and Nora were invited to have dinner with Governor Marwood, who held the highest office in the province of Equatoria. He was a cordial host and he gave Dick many insights into administration in the southern Sudan. Dick learned his specific assignment was still to be decided. The paperwork moving him from the Sudan Defence Force to the Sudan Political Service was still slowly working its way through the halls of bureaucracy. Meanwhile the governor assigned Dick to the town of Yei in the southwest. Here he would be the Acting District Commissioner for a few months to fill in for Cullen who was going on leave. In the process he would learn about the responsibilities and duties of being a District Commissioner.

Nora was assigned to work at the hospital in Juba. It meant separation again, but both Dick and Nora prayed the separation would only be temporary. Dick drove Nora around the little town of Juba. Nora was fairly impressed. There were enough Greek and Arab shops to provide basic food and supplies. She would be able to stay at the sisters' mess where she would have a room and companionship. The only thing that troubled her was the constant heat. On Sunday they went to the Anglican Church where Dick met several of his former soldiers. They had a joyful reunion and Dick was pleased to see they were progressing well in their Christian faith.

Dick had left most of his personal gear in Boma so he needed to return there to collect it. Leaving Nora to settle in at Juba, he retraced his steps to Kapoeta by lorry and hiked the final 125 miles into Boma. He enjoyed marching across the floodplains again and soon he could see the high cliffs of Boma rising up on the horizon. He arrived at the top of the escarpment with mixed emotions. It felt good to be back on the plateau and to see his many friends. Musa and Lado and Kireer were there to welcome him back. But he discovered his dog Mary had died in his absence. She had missed Dick and simply stopped eating. This news caused Dick great grief. Koli had also died, leaving only Bite alive. Dick decided to take Bite with him when he returned to Juba.

Dick spent many hours talking with Lado. He was still committed to his new faith in God. Dick recognized his potential but knew he needed further education. They discussed the options and Lado eventually agreed to go with Dick to Juba and Dick promised to get him into a training program.

The return trek out of Boma was a difficult one. It had rained hard in the lowlands and Dick and his porters had to spend three days camping at Kathangor Mountain until the mud dried enough that they could continue walking to Kapoeta.

Upon arriving back in Juba, Dick learned that World War II was officially over. It was a time of rejoicing and Dick felt he had played a small but meaningful part in winning the war. Nora had settled into her work at the Juba hospital. Dick spent only a couple of days with her and then headed off to Yei to take over from Cullen. The District Commissioner was tired and eager to get away. Therefore he arranged a hasty hand-over of responsibilities. Dick had to learn a multitude of responsibilities and he dug in with enthusiasm. The more he learned now the better, since he would soon have his own district to administrate.

Several weeks later Nora caught a ride to Yei to visit Dick. She had special news. She was pregnant. Both Dick and Nora were excited, but several days later Nora came down with a serious case of the measles. She was in bed for several days with cramps and there was concern she might miscarry. Many prayers were made on her behalf. Nora gradually got better and returned to Juba to resume her nursing duties.

Meanwhile Dick learned what it was like to be a District Commissioner. He took a trip to Maridi, a town with a large cathedral and hundreds of mango trees. Here he met with the local chiefs, inspected the roads, collected sorghum grain as a form of taxation and exhorted people to grow more food. Overall he found life to be too tame. He wrote in his diary, "I am glad I am to be here only five months. It is a desperately soft and civilized district. If I stayed, I would become soft and civilized myself."

But life was not all soft. Dick made a long foot safari to Kajo Keji on the banks of the Nile River. Here he fished and caught large Nile perch and also shot two elephant that were destroying peoples' gardens. Later Governor Marwood visited Yei on his annual tour and was pleased with Dick's work. However, during his visit Dick started feeling nauseous and woke up one morning with yellow eyes. He had contracted a bad case of jaundice. The governor took Dick back to Juba in his car where he was put in the hospital. There Dick had the most caring nurse possible – his wife, Nora.

He gradually got well and was told to take an extensive rest. Nora was released from her work for a few days to make sure he rested. The two of them caught a ride southeast into the Immatong Mountains. These heavily wooded slopes made up the tallest mountains in all of Sudan. The government agricultural department had planted extensive stands of Mexican pine near the tops of the mountains and had also built a lovely stone guesthouse called Colobus Cottage. It was named after the beautiful black and white monkeys that inhabited the area. The cottage was located at 7,000 foot altitude so the climate was cool, an ideal place for Dick to recover his health. He and Nora spent hours walking slowly through the pine forests. Dick always carried his bird book – *Robert's Birds of South Africa*. Even the dullest walk became exciting when they were spotting new species of birds. In the evenings they luxuriated in a deep tub of hot water before sitting in front of a roaring fire. But they could not stay in paradise forever and after two weeks they returned to the heat of Juba.

Here Governor Marwood summoned Dick and informed him his orders had come through. "You are being assigned to Upper Nile Province with headquarters in Malakal. Your eventual posting will be the little town of Akobo on the Ethiopian border." Dick was very pleased. He couldn't have asked for a better assignment. His district would encompass people from the Anuak, Murle and Kichepo tribes. It was guaranteed not to be dull. He was to be in charge of the wildest district in all of Sudan. To Dick, the appointment could not have been more ideal. It was just what he wanted.

It was nearing time for Nora to give birth. Juba did not have good birthing facilities at the hospital. Therefore Nora was ordered to go to Kampala in Uganda to have her baby. Dick borrowed a government car and drove Nora south into northern Uganda. He drove slowly, not wanting the rough corrugated road to bring on the birth prematurely. After passing the rapids on the Nile River, he put Nora on a steamer and she proceeded on to Kampala on her own. She made the trip without incident and sent a wire back to Dick in Juba stating that she had arrived and was comfortable. She stayed with some C.M.S. missionaries until the baby came.

Meanwhile Dick received a letter of welcome from Governor Kingdon, the governor of Upper Nile Province. He described the district Dick would administrate, an area of over 50,000 square miles and containing three different ethnic groups. Dick wrote in his diary, "How perfect that sounds."

Dick took a quick trip back to Yei where he was happy to turn the administration back over to Cullen who had returned from his leave. Dick packed up his gear and returned to Juba where he caught the first steamer heading north to Malakal. He had Lado with him and his dog Bite. While on the steamer he received a wire from Nora: "Michael born October 1. Baby and mother doing fine." Dick was extremely pleased that it was a boy. It just seemed so right. He worked out the date of birth and realized Michael was born exactly nine months after he and Nora had wed.

Upon arriving in Malakal, Dick was met at the pier by Governor Kingdon. The governor was gracious and hospitable and Dick knew immediately he would be happy working under his administration. Dick's one big concern was Nora and Michael. Most District Commissioners were either single or had wives who lived in central towns. But neither Dick nor Nora liked this arrangement. They wanted to be together, living full time in the place of Dick's assignment. Dick brought up the issue with Governor Kingdon and Doctor Bloss, who oversaw the medical work of Upper Nile. They were both reasonable men and did not have any objections to Nora and the baby joining Dick at Akobo. However, the governor did point out that official permission would have to be granted from higher authorities based in Khartoum, commenting, "What you are asking for is highly irregular."

The more Dick got to know the officials in Malakal, the happier he was. There was a loose camaraderie among them and they did not stand on protocol. Dick wrote in his diary: "There was a most agreeable atmosphere after the organized formality of Equatoria." In one conversation with Kingdon, the governor pointed out he was committed to assisting missionaries in the region. With a twinkle in his eye he said to Dick, "I assume this will not be distasteful to you."

The more Dick heard about Akobo the happier he became. He ignored a written message from a former District Commissioner saying Akobo was by far the worst posting in the entire Sudan: nothing but boredom, heat, mud, mosquitoes and wild tribesmen. The eight days Dick spent in Malakal were delightful. He took long walks out to the groves of majestic doleib palms and watched the falcons making their nests high in the fronds. Dick got to know his superiors and played some exciting games of squash, the game that had earned him a blue at Oxford University. He also learned that Akobo was unique in having a small unit of mounted police. He would have his own horse and in the evenings he could also teach Nora to ride.

He boarded the gunboat that would take him up the Sobat River to Akobo. The river ran through flat floodplains without a hint of a hill. Other than the water birds and crocodiles, there was not much to look at. Dick spent his time on board playing chess with Captain Romilly, who was the District Commissioner for the Nuer region. Occasionally they steamed past a Nuer village with its thatched huts. The tall, naked tribesmen occasionally raised their hands in greeting, but for the most part they stayed aloof, ignoring the noisy chugging gunboat.

On October 17 the steamer pulled into the dirt landing at Akobo. Dick had arrived. This was to be his home for the years to come. He was pleased with what he saw. The house was located a little way out of town and faced the Pibor River. It was a large house built on brick stilts so it would not be inundated by the periodic floodwaters. He was met by the local missionary, Don McClure, who took Dick to the nearby Presbyterian mission station to meet his family and have a hearty meal. Don was an old African hand with vast experience and Dick liked him immediately. Don informed him about the growth of Christianity among the Anuak. There was a small school in Akobo for training Christian leaders and Dick asked if Lado could join the school. Don readily agreed and Lado enrolled for two years of Bible study.

Dick moved into his house. It contained only some basic

furniture and was quite austere. Up until now it had only been occupied by bachelors. Dust and cobwebs covered everything. Dick promptly hired servants and put them to work cleaning and scrubbing. Dick wanted it perfect, ready for Nora and the new baby, Michael. Then he went to his office in the government compound and met the clerks, police and other staff. He gathered them together and gave an opening speech in pidgin Arabic, assuring them he needed their expertise and help over the coming years. Where to start? One of the clerks informed him the local Anuak chiefs had been collecting taxes in the form of cattle and the government herd now numbered 235. It was becoming too big a job to take care of that many cattle. Dick immediately decided his first point of business was to sell off most of the herd at auction. He sold over 200 cows to Arab traders and they were trucked off to the abattoir in Malakal. Dick had the benefit of starting his job as District Commissioner with plenty of money in the office safe.

After ten days of office work and meeting various Anuak chiefs, Dick decided to trek south to Pibor Post. This small village was the administrative center for the lowland Murle. The Anuak situation was under control, but the lowland Murle were still making raids on their Dinka neighbors to the west. Dick decided he needed to make his presence felt early in his administration and stop the raiding. He took several policemen and porters and hiked south along the Pibor River. There was no road, so they simply followed the footpath along the riverbank. At night they camped by the river and were inundated by the voracious mosquitoes. Unable to sleep Dick got up, sat in the smoke of the campfire and wrote a poem.

The Night Raider
It roves the allied countries through
And raids the guardian empire too,
Of Benito.

Attacking all that comes its way
Both white man, black man and they say
The negrito.
It wanders at its own sweet will,
Traversing forest, vale and hill
Without veto.

And slips through every known defence
With little short of impudence.
Incognito.

It flies with drone, or hum or buzz
Or some say whirr, but fly it does.
THE MOSQUITO

It took five days to walk the 85 miles to Pibor Post. Much of this trek was spent pushing through long grass and skirting flooded depressions. It became obvious to Dick that one of his first jobs was to build a proper road from Akobo to Pibor Post. Dick's arrival at Pibor Post was received with great joy by the Murle people. That night they held a dance in his honor and sang a special praise song in which Dick was featured as the hero. Some of the Murle had formerly met Dick when he was living at Boma and all of the Murle had heard of the exploits of the man they called Kemerbong – The Red Pelican.

Dick was pleased to be back in Murle country. He spoke their language and understood their culture. He convened the Murle chiefs and talked to them about administration and taxation. He also sat as judge in some criminal cases. The lowland Murle still lived very traditional lives, more so than anywhere else in Sudan. They had been the last people in southern Sudan to be pacified by the British. In the dry season of 1912 the incoming British government had sent three separate forces simultaneously to conquer the Murle. Getting there proved to be a serious problem since their area was remote and protected by the all-encompassing swamps. One of the military units tried to enter Murle land from the south. But they ran out of drinking water before they got there and had to retreat. The units marching in from the north and the west did manage to reach the Pibor River, but they encountered only empty villages. The Murle warriors kept pulling back into the tall grass, only occasionally throwing a spear at the incoming British troops. Eventually the British did find large herds of Murle cattle and confiscated them. They sent out word that the Murle could have their cattle back only if they agreed to be under the authority of the British government. The Murle loved their cattle so they agreed. Peace was established and the British troops built a small base of mud and grass at the confluence of the Pibor and Lotilla Rivers. They named it Fort Bruce. Here they left two British officers with a handful of local militia to keep the peace. However, when the rains came, Fort Bruce went underwater. The soldiers had to move two miles north to a small rise and there they established Pibor Post.

This was the location Dick now visited. Administration over the lowland Murle had always been cursory. After talking to some of the Murle chiefs, Dick realized there was plenty of work ahead. He was delighted with Pibor itself and knew Nora would like it too. He spent an enjoyable week camping by the Pibor River under the shade of the jorghan trees and spent some of his time shooting, fishing and canoeing. The kob migration was beginning its annual trek north and the Murle hunters were bringing in plenty of fresh meat. Former administrators had seen Pibor district as a flat, ugly, inhospitable land. But Dick fell in love with it immediately. In his diary he described the abundant bird life: "In come vee after vee of ducks and geese and egrets, leaving their roosts inland for their early morning feeding grounds. Pelicans come slanting down out of the sunrise, their great wings outstretched and with feet and legs thrust forward as they glide down to the water with all the grace of a flying boat. Solitary herons are to be seen and crowned cranes and storks, driving their strong way through the cool upper air."

During his stay in Pibor Post, Dick wrote the following poem for his beloved wife:

If you were here, my darling
These stars would stay to see you
For fear that they would miss you.
If you were here.

The sky would buy new dresses
And put them on to please you.
The breeze would search for beauty

And find it in your hair.
If you were here.

The river thinks of something
That it could do for your sake
If you were here.

And I should take and kiss you
And tell them you were mine dear
And shout and tell the morning
That you were mine forever.
If you were here.
If you were here.

Dick returned to Akobo by canoe, floating north on the slow current of the Pibor River. He found the five-day trip to be boring: nothing but grass as far as he could see. Upon finally arriving back in Akobo, he got involved in the daily work of a District Commissioner. There was no end of possible activities and he was young and energetic. However, he quickly realized if he tried to do everything he would work himself to a shadow. There was a danger he could spread himself so thin he would accomplish nothing of significance. He had to decide which parts of his job description were the most important and which jobs to leave undone.

Every Monday morning Dick put on his uniform, mounted his horse and did an official inspection of Akobo town. He first inspected the police. All ten of them lined up and presented arms. Then he rode around the town visiting the merchant shops, the clinic, the school, the prison, the gardens, the cattle herd, the milking house, the abattoir, the garbage heap and finally the latrines. The rest of the week was engaged primarily in office work with many side jobs such as brick-making, breaking in bullocks, letter-writing, riding, reading, fishing, fixing the house, carpentry, tax collecting, poisoning hyenas, counting ammunition, paying salaries, killing locusts, planting mango trees, sharpening his saw and oiling his tools. The list went on and on. For most people living in such a place would be the ultimate in boredom, but for Dick it was an exciting life with a great deal of variety. There was always something new to see and do.

After a month of living by himself, Dick received a message brought by the incoming steamer. Approval for Nora to live in Akobo had been sent from Khartoum. They could truly live together at last! Dick caught the return run of the steamer back to Malakal. Nora and baby Michael were supposed to fly into Malakal on BOAC on December 25th. Their arrival would be the greatest Christmas present in the world.

The plane came right on schedule. Dick waited with anticipation as passengers climbed down the ladder. The last passengers disembarked, but Nora was not among them. BOAC had overbooked and Nora and Michael had been bumped. Dick was not happy. He spent the next days living with the governor and taking out his frustration on the squash court. Nobody could beat him. Then he decided to do something useful – to take his language exam in the Murle language. He would get an increase in pay of 50 pounds a month if he passed the language test. There was a problem, however. There was no other government officer in all of Sudan who knew the Murle language, so there was nobody to make up and grade the exam. Dick went to the Malakal jail and found a Murle man who was incarcerated for murder. He got the man out of jail and brought him to the governor. As the governor listened, Dick and the Murle prisoner had an animated discussion on how to collect honey from wild bees. The governor did not understand a word of what they were saying, but it was obvious Dick knew the Murle language well. After the Murle conversation had taken place the governor smiled and said, "I assume you knew what you were talking about. I will give you a passing grade and you will get your pay raise." Meanwhile the Murle prisoner went back to jail to serve his time.

The next BOAC plane was scheduled for December 27 and Dick went to meet the plane – hoping. His hope was rewarded. Nora with baby Michael in her arms descended from the plane and Dick made the acquaintance of his son for the first time. He was not overly impressed. That night Dick wrote in his diary, "Michael looks surprisingly like any other baby."

18

Flying the Flag

Dick and Nora settled into their house at Akobo. Having a baby in the house added a new dimension to family dynamics. Meanwhile Dick continued making the acquaintances of various Anuak chiefs and figuring out his responsibilities as District Commissioner. Dick's assignment was to administer an area covering 50,000 square miles. This region was located in one of the most remote corners of the Sudan, butting up against the western border of Ethiopia. Virtually the entire area was composed of flat floodplains covered with long grass. The only exception was the Boma Plateau in the far southeastern corner. During the rainy season the rivers burst their banks and the entire area became a bottomless bog. In contrast, during the dry season the rivers receded and often went totally dry, leaving only isolated water holes for wildlife, cattle and people. When Dick took over the area the only access to and from the region was via the paddle wheel gunboats that made their slow way from Malakal to Akobo on the Sobat River. When the river was running deep, a small medical steamer, named the *Lady Baker*, could proceed south as far as Pibor Post. There were no roads within the region so initially Dick had to move around the area on foot or by horseback.

The three ethnic groups living in the region still practiced their traditional cultures in much the same way they had for centuries. During his stint at Boma as Frontier Agent, Dick had already learned something about all three groups. The Anuak lived along the rivers that bordered Ethiopia, some of them living in Ethiopia and others in Sudan. The lowland Murle lived on the vast flood plains with Pibor Post at the center. On the Boma Plateau lived the highland Murle and the Kichepo. To administrate this entire region there were only four police posts. The main post was located at Akobo at the northernmost point of the region. This was headquarters for the district so it not only had the most policemen, but it also had mounted police. Using horses was the only way to move quickly around the region, but they were only useful in the dry season. Pibor Post had ten policemen and Boma had nine. The fourth location was the post at Pochala. It was located on the border with Ethiopia and the ten policemen stationed there were in close contact with the southernmost Anuak people.

All counted Dick had less than fifty police to control 50,000 square miles. Dick often said he ruled largely by bluff. At any time the local people could have easily taken over any of the small police posts. But as long as Dick was fair and just, he was accepted as the authority in the region. His primary responsibility was trying to stop inter-tribal fighting and cattle raiding. The British government insisted this type of behavior was simply not acceptable and the penalties set by the government were severe.

However, there was no way one District Commissioner with his miniature police force could control the whole region. Therefore Dick ruled through local chiefs, allowing them to make most of the local decisions. This was termed Indirect Rule and was a policy the British used in many African countries. It worked well among the Anuaks. Dick had already met their traditional paramount chief named Ogada. Under Ogada were many sub-chiefs. The Anuak people were used to living under a hierarchy of leaders and tended to obey these leaders.

But Dick quickly discovered that working with the lowland Murle was a different proposition altogether. The Murle red chiefs were actually religious leaders and did not pay attention to political matters. The society was organized into families. The highest political position was the head of a family and each headman made decisions only for his own family.

Initially Dick found it difficult to identify chiefs who were willing to interface between the Murle people and the British-run government. Being a government chief was not a popular position since part of the work of a chief was to collect taxes and to assign work details. The naturally competent men refused the positions of chief. Instead they often put forward incompetent fools, just to make the government's job that much harder. The Murle people referred to these chiefs as "government dogs" and gave them no respect. However, over time Dick identified some older men who were respected and convinced them to serve as chiefs. These men swore loyalty to the government and each was given a green silk sash as a symbol of his authority. This was worn over the right shoulder and tied at the left waist. These chiefs were also given a monthly salary if they did their work in a timely manner.

The primary role of Dick and the chiefs was to keep the peace. This often meant resolving disputes. When people had disagreements they could take them to court. Here the disputes or accusations could be heard and justice served. A traditional court system already existed within Murle culture, but now these courts had official government backing. Most cases had to do with cattle, dishonor and adultery. The local chiefs were quite competent in adjudicating such cases.

As District Commissioner, Dick was at the top of the justice system. He studied Sudanese law as it pertained to the southern Sudan and then sat a law exam. He passed the exam and received the position of magistrate. This gave him the authority to act as judge in serious cases. Accusations of murder could not be handled at the traditional local court level and these cases were brought before Dick. In such cases Dick always had two assessors sit with him. These were Murle chiefs he trusted and they helped Dick make sure justice was served. Dick was in the awkward position of holding four roles at once. If the police brought an official accusation against a person for breaking a law, Dick was the prosecutor. He also acted as the defense, making sure the accused got to speak and explain his position. After hearing all the evidence he then acted as jury and made the decision as to whether a person was innocent or guilty. Then as the judge he set the penalty. As an outsider, Dick was independent from pressures within the Murle culture and was convinced he could be fair in his decisions. In western societies this mingling of judicial roles would not have been tolerated since separation of these roles was deemed essential for a person to have a fair trial. However, the system allowed Dick to listen to both the accusers and the defense in full context and make his decisions accordingly. But it also laid great pressure on Dick to be scrupulously neutral and fair.

Punishment varied with the crimes. Small crimes earned the guilty person a stint in the Pibor jail. This was actually considered a bit of a holiday to many prisoners. They got fed every day and had a place to sleep. Prison was sometimes referred to as King George's Hotel. On most days the prisoners were released from jail to go out and work on a government project, coming back at the end of the day to spend the night in jail. If a man was proven to be a murderer, Dick had the authority to condemn him to death by hanging. In order to be fair, such murderers were sent to Malakal where they were held in a maximum security prison. At this time they could appeal the penalty. The court papers were sent on to Khartoum for final clearance. If an appeal failed and it was deemed everything had been done properly and in an orderly manner, the murderer was hung in Malakal.

Since Akobo was the district headquarters Dick knew he needed to maintain this as his base of operations. However, he was entranced by Pibor Post. He also knew he needed to spend extensive time among the lowland Murle. It was essential to work closely with the Murle government chiefs. So his first project was to improve communications between Akobo and Pibor Post. Dick decided the first priority was building a road. Dick assigned workers at the Akobo end and they worked their way south toward Pibor Post, following the west bank of the Pibor River. Most of the area was open floodplains so clearing trees and grass took a minimum of time. But there were a number of small *wadis* and feeder streams that had to be crossed. This necessitated cutting trees, laying them down as a bed and then piling soil on top. The basic road was completed in a few weeks, but because all the soil in the area was black clay it was doubtful if the road could be used in the rainy season. However, as long as the road was dry, Dick could now get to Pibor Post using the government lorry.

With the road completed Dick organized an inaugural trip. The lorry was loaded with grain and other supplies for the police based at Pibor Post. On top sat nine policemen with their families. They were being transferred to police posts at Pibor Post and Boma. Ahmed was the official driver of the lorry and Dick sat in the cab wearing his official District Commissioner's uniform with pith helmet and white feather. The 85 miles to Pibor Post took only three hours on the newly made road. When the lorry pulled into Pibor Post it was greeted by cheering children. It was the first time they had seen such a big smelly monster. Dick made an official inspection of the ten policemen and checked their rifles and counted the ammunition. All was in order. He announced the various transfers and postings and some of the policemen based at Pibor Post began packing up to return to Akobo. Dick talked to the local sergeant in charge who complained about lack of buildings and other facilities. Dick took the complaint seriously and began making plans to upgrade the police post, including new offices, barracks and jail. He also made plans to build a central courthouse. He decided on a design that used no walls, but only simple pillars supporting a grass roof. This way the court would operate out in the open and not be seen as something done in secret. On the ride back to Akobo Dick kept thinking up designs for all the building projects that needed to be done.

Dick was happy to get back to Akobo and reunite with Nora and Michael. He told her about the trip to Pibor Post and promised she could go with him on the next trip. The following months were spent settling in at Akobo and making it home. Nora planted flowers around the house. Vegetables and fruit were hard to come by in the small market area so Dick made plans for a large garden. He designated a two-acre spot near the river and assigned workers to turn over the soil and to dig furrows. He also had manure brought in from the *zariba* where they kept the government cattle. Dick then set up a pump that sucked water out of the Pibor River and brought it to the top end of the garden. From this point the water flowed by gravity through the furrows to the lower parts of the garden. With permanent water the garden flourished. They soon had abundant vegetables such as okra, eggplant, carrots and cabbage. Dick also planted an orchard of orange, lemon, guava and papaya trees. These also flourished with the combination of water and heat.

The months passed and Michael began learning to walk. After watching his efforts Dick wrote in his diary, "Michael is now strutting about with great confidence. Too much so, because he tries to run and dance as well. There usually follows an increasing look of horror on his face, a final stagger, a despairing clutch at the air and then descent – sudden and devastating. However, he is a gutsy little chap and only dissolves into tears when his head comes in contact with the hard cement floor."

Dick gave Nora her own horse. He looked the herd over carefully and chose a brown mare with a gentle disposition and a smooth gait. Nora learned quickly and proved to be a good rider. Within days she was trotting and cantering in full control of her steed. In the cool of the evenings the syce brought the saddled horses to the front of the house. Dick and Nora would mount up and go for a ride along the river. In the dry season the edges of the river were firm and flat and it was possible to let the horses run. On the return trip they walked the horses, letting them cool down. Both Dick and Nora loved this time of evening as the sun set in a plethora of reds and golds and the long skeins of water birds covered the sky.

One of the first things Dick discovered at Akobo was a squash court. A former District Commissioner had built the court out of burnt brick and the inside floor and walls had been smoothly cemented. It had not been used for many years. There was dirt and sand on the floor and lizards lived in the cracks. The wooden door had disappeared. Dick ordered racquets and balls from Khartoum. Meanwhile he had the court thoroughly swept, painted lines on the floor and repaired the door. The court was ready for use by the time the racquets were delivered. Dick quickly discovered that playing in the court was extremely hot. There was no roof and the equatorial sun beat down all day, heating the walls and floors. By late afternoon they radiated heat. But the intense heat did make for a lively ball. Dick taught

Nora how to play and she was a natural, soon giving Dick good competition. After half an hour of chasing the ball around the hot court they were both covered in sweat. They continued this exercise for all the years they lived at Akobo. Even when Nora was pregnant they continued to play. Dick would spot her one point for each month she was pregnant. Dick also taught some of the local policemen to play squash and several of them became quite proficient.

At the end of the first year at Akobo Dick received a message from Governor Kingdon in Malakal. He and Nora were invited to Malakal for the Christmas holidays. The big event was the annual polo match. Dick was advised to bring his horse and be ready to play. Dick was delighted with the invitation. He went out to the horse kraal and inspected the horses, trying to select one that would be a good polo pony. He wanted a horse that was eager to run and could turn quickly. There were three horses that looked like they had potential. Dick tried all three, pushing them as hard as they could run and making them turn tight corners. In the end he chose a small gray mare. She was not the most beautiful of the three. She had a rough coat and a bullet shaped head. But she was eager and that was what Dick was looking for. Dick named her Zigir, which meant donkey in the Arabic language.

Dick made himself a polo mallet out of a tree branch and borrowed a rubber ball from baby Michael. Every afternoon he mounted his pony and practiced hitting the ball with his mallet and then charging after it. Zigir quickly got the idea and eagerly chased after the ball as fast as she could run. After several weeks of practice Dick decided they were ready for the big match. The monthly paddle wheel steamer arrived at Akobo and Dick and his little family booked rooms for the return run to Malakal. Zigir was put in a quickly erected stable on the attached barge, together with a herd of cattle being taken to the abattoir in Malakal.

Dick and Nora enjoyed the slow ride down the Sobat River to Malakal. There were always flocks of herons and storks standing on the banks of the river and Nora especially enjoyed the white pelicans swimming in a line. They worked together to force the fish into the shallows where they bobbed their heads underwater and caught the fish in their large pouches.

Upon arriving at Malakal, Governor Kingdon welcomed them and offered them a room in the governor's large house. The big polo match was scheduled to take place in two days. Dick took Zigir out for a run each day to stretch her legs after the long boat ride. Other officials were also arriving at Malakal for the grand polo match and all of them spent time getting their horses fit and in shape for the big game. The governor had ordered the prisoners from the local jail to clear a patch of land near the soccer field and goals were put in place. On the afternoon of the match crowds of Shilluk people gathered to watch the strange event in which white men galloped horses around the field and tried to hit a small white ball. Teams were drawn up. There were enough riders for two full teams. Dick had never played polo before, but he did have some idea of what he was to do. He even managed to score a goal, but in the end his team lost by one point. Zigir ran with great eagerness and Dick stated later she was one of the best polo ponies in the entire game. The day after the polo match the officials returned to their remote posts around the Upper

Nile region. Having taken part in a little English culture, they were now re-energized for another year of living and working in the bog.

19

Enraging the Governor

Back at Akobo, Nora kept asking to visit Pibor Post, so Dick finally arranged a trip. The rains were approaching, but the new road was still open. Dick planned to use the government lorry. However, it had broken down on a trip to Malakal and was awaiting an essential part. Consequently Dick arranged to ride with an Arab merchant who was driving to Pibor Post. His lorry was old and in very bad condition. Dick and Nora, holding baby Michael, sat in the cab with the driver. The back of the lorry was seriously overloaded with bags of grain and people perching on top. The battered vehicle had a top speed of only a few miles an hour. The springs were broken, so they felt every bump on the rough road. Before many miles were completed

Dick heard a hissing sound. Soon he saw steam spouting out of the radiator. The driver stopped the vehicle and poured in some water. Dick noticed there was no radiator cap and pointed this out to the driver. But the old Arab insisted if he put on a cap, the radiator would build pressure and blow up. As a result they continued their drive with steam shooting into the air. The lorry had no windscreen and hot drops of water came flying into the cab. Nora had to cover herself and baby Michael with a blanket to keep from getting scalded. The driver kept stopping to add water. Soon his jerry can was empty and he started using drinking water to put into the radiator. By late afternoon he had used all the drinking water in the lorry and Dick and Nora were getting very thirsty. The lorry stopped for a final time. With no water they could go no further. Dick sent off a party of police to search for water. They returned three hours later with containers of dirty river water. Dick boiled up some of the water and made hot tea. By now it was dark and Dick discovered the lorry had no working headlights. They all ended up sleeping in the cab for the night since the lorry could not proceed in the darkness. The sad vehicle limped into Pibor Post the next morning and Dick vowed never again to ride in a merchant's lorry.

Nora fell in love with Pibor Post at once. There was something enchanting about the extensive floodplains with the shallow rivers and the great flocks of birds. She also enjoyed the bold, inquisitive Murle people. It was a nice change from the more structured life in Akobo. Nora and her husband moved into a small thatched hut that served as the official guesthouse. It contained only two string beds and had no door. Nora hung a piece of cloth over the doorway to give them some privacy from peeping eyes. Meals were cooked outside and they ate at a table set up under a *neem* tree. The hut was located on a bank facing the Pibor River. Nora was happy just to sit in the shade and watch life on the river. She enjoyed the sight of the majestic fish eagles swooping down to seize fish in their yellow talons. Rafts of hyacinth plants floated by with their spires of pink and purple flowers, bringing a splash of color to the brown muddy water. In the evenings she went out riding with Dick. He taught her to use a shotgun and most nights they returned with several white-headed tree ducks for their supper.

Dick promptly got to work at Pibor Post. He held the first central court, including as many of the Murle chiefs as possible. He paid the clerks their salaries, auctioned off some of the government herd and met with the Arab merchants. On Sunday he held a small church service with some of the policemen who were Christian. Some curious Murle also came to the service, attracted by the singing. Dick gave a short talk in the Murle language, explaining the good news of the gospel.

Dick stationed several of the mounted police at Pibor Post. Periodically he took them out on a ride to assess their ability. They proved to be good riders. One morning he told them to bring spears and they rode out to the Kongkong River. Here they found herds of white-eared kob grazing in the short green grass. Dick and his men chased the antelope trying to spear them from horseback. They utterly failed. The kob fled into the tall grass and it was not possible to chase them in the grass without hurting the horses. On the return trip they encountered a warthog. Dick chased it until it tired. He then galloped abreast of the wild pig and bending low in the saddle he thrust his spear into its chest.

The policemen were Moslem so they would not touch such an unclean animal. Dick butchered the hog himself and for the next two days he and Nora feasted on the tasty white meat.

Several weeks later Dick got word of a fight between the Murle and the Jiye on the Kengen River. Leaving Nora at Pibor Post, he quickly organized the mounted police and galloped south. It took two days of hard riding to get to the location of the fight. By the time they got there the fighting was already over and the Jiye had withdrawn. Dick spent some time bandaging up some 40 Murle warriors who had been wounded in the fracas. The Murle had successfully protected their grazing territory, but Dick realized the skirmishing was an ongoing problem he would eventually have to solve.

Meanwhile Nora and baby Michael had stayed in Pibor Post waiting for Dick's return. One morning she heard a loud, piercing whistle and saw a commotion as Murle people ran down to the docking area. Nora walked to the riverbank and observed a paddle wheel steamer pulling in to the landing. From a distance she saw the tall, erect figure of Governor Kingdon standing in the prow of the boat. He was wearing his white dress uniform with the white feather in his helmet. He had initially sailed from Malakal to Akobo to make a spot inspection. Upon arriving at Akobo he discovered Dick and Nora were at Pibor Post. Since the Pibor River was flowing deep he had decided to proceed to Pibor Post and pay a surprise visit. It would be his first visit to Pibor Post and he planned to confer with Dick and make an official inspection of the police post.

The local sergeant met him at the landing and informed him Dick was out with the mounted police trying to stop a fight.

The police quickly lined up and presented arms. The inspection did not take long since there were only eight at the post and there was only one police building. The sergeant then escorted the governor to the guesthouse where Nora was staying. Nora came out of her hut carrying baby Michael. She curtsied to the governor. Governor Kingdon was appalled. He became angry and berated her, "What are you doing living in this filthy hut with no door? You are the wife of a British officer! What kind of image does this project to the local people? What is Dick thinking? How dare he leave you in such abject surroundings? You are not safe living on your own – especially with a small baby!"

Nora answered politely but firmly, "Dick has not abandoned me! I am safe and happy. The local Murle people are taking good care of me. I have plenty to eat and people come to visit every day to check on my welfare."

But the governor would have none of it. "I am ordering you to pack up your things within the hour. I am returning to Akobo on the steamer and you are going with me." Nora had no choice. Hurriedly she put some clothing in a bag and carrying Michael in her arms she boarded the steamer. Meanwhile the governor wrote a harsh letter to Dick, admonishing him, "I am greatly displeased that you have left your wife and child alone. As per this letter I am informing you that I am taking Nora back to Akobo. You have let down the standards of British officialdom. Nora is forbidden to return to Pibor Post until you have built a proper guesthouse where she could live as a proper white lady: the wife of a District Commissioner."

When Dick returned to Pibor Post the following day, he found Nora and Michael were gone. He read the letter the governor had left for him. He accepted the fact he needed to build a proper guesthouse. He assigned some Murle prisoners the job of making burnt bricks out of the black clay. He worked with them for several days, actually puddling the mud with his own bare feet and showing them how to mold the bricks and stack them for eventual firing. Leaving the crew hard at work, he returned to Akobo by horseback.

Dick worked out a special method for riding long distances. In the intense heat he knew he could not push a horse too hard. He would mount his horse and have it walk for five minutes. Then he would have the horse canter for five minutes. Finally he would dismount and walk – leading the horse for the next five minutes. Then he would remount and start the whole cycle again. Using this method he could travel all day. He traveled the distance of 85 miles from Pibor Post to Akobo in twelve hours. There he was happy to be reunited with Nora. That night he wrote in his diary, "Separations if they aren't too long and frequent are good for us. They make us appreciate each other so much more."

A month later Dick returned to Pibor Post. He took the government lorry with a load of cement and a trained mason, hoping to make progress on building the guesthouse. However, when he arrived in Pibor Post he was disappointed by the work of the prisoners. The bricks they had made were soft and crumbly. But he admitted it wasn't their fault. The black soil was simply not good material for making burnt bricks.

Dick went ahead and laid out the plans for the guesthouse and assigned the mason the job of laying the cement foundations. He drove the lorry ten miles to a small granite hill called Lothir.

Here he had the workers break up boulders and load the pieces into the back of the lorry. Lothir was the only source of rock closer than Boma and those hills were located 90 miles away. Leaving the mason with cement and stones, Dick proceeded by lorry to the Boma Plateau to make an official inspection of the police post. The road from Pibor to Boma had not yet been built so they drove slowly, making their own rough road as they went. Upon arriving at the base of Boma they discovered the old road up the escarpment had received no maintenance since the beginning of the war and was badly eroded. So they parked the lorry at the base of the cliffs and walked up the steep slope. It was the first time Dick had visited Boma since he had become the District Commissioner. By the time Dick reached the edge of the plateau Sergeant Musa and his nine policemen were ready for his inspection. They were all lined up in immaculate uniforms with their puttees wound firmly around their legs. Dick greeted his many friends and moved back into his old house. There were still some blossoms brightening up the flowerbeds. This place held such a firm place in his heart. He really wanted to share it with Nora. He vowed that on the next trip to Boma he would bring her with him.

Dick spent the next few days hearing major cases in the local court. Musa was doing a good job keeping the peace in Boma. Dick also talked to the Kichepo to the east of Boma. It seemed the peace was still holding between the Murle and the Kichepo. In the evening Musa came for a talk. They reminisced about the experiences they had shared in the war. Then Musa brought up a new topic. "I am tired of police work and I am also afraid of being transferred to another location. I like living here at Boma and want to make it my home. I've found a young Murle girl whom I like and I want to marry her. I want to leave the police force and become a coffee merchant. I have discovered many of the Murle and Kichepo drink coffee. They pick the leaves from wild coffee trees that grow in the valleys and boil up the leaves to make a strong drink. But they throw away the coffee beans."

Dick knew coffee had originated in Ethiopia and got its name from the Gaffa province located just across the border from Boma. Musa took Dick on a walk and showed him the wild bushes, laden with red coffee beans simply falling unused to the ground. Musa had devised a scheme for collecting the coffee beans, drying them and selling them to merchants in the northern Sudan. Dick thought it was an excellent idea. Part of his work as District Commissioner was to promote economic advancement in the region. He suggested, "Perhaps the local people could be taught to plant coffee trees in their gardens. In the long run it would be easier than collecting coffee beans in the forest." Musa had already collected and dried a gunnysack of coffee beans and Dick agreed to take them to Pibor Post and sell them to the Arab merchants.

The trip out of Boma was a rough one. It had rained hard and the sticky mud built up on the tires of the lorry until it wedged against the fenders, bringing the lorry to an abrupt halt. Everyone had to pile out and use their machetes and bayonets to scrape the mud off the tires. With the tires free of the clinging mud they started off a second time. But within minutes the lorry jerked to a stop and the men went through the whole process again – and again – and again. Eventually the lorry broke through the soft surface. All four wheels sank into the oozing mud and the

lorry ended up resting on its chassis. Dick realized the only way
to get back to Pibor Post was to walk. He started off with two
policemen, carrying his rifle for protection. There was no food
available so he did not take a porter. He figured he was still 80
miles away from Pibor Post. Walking in the sticky mud meant
taking short strides with frequent stops to scrape the mud off
the bottom of his boots. It took Dick five days of walking to
get back to Pibor Post and he arrived very hungry. After resting
for several days to regain his strength, he rode a horse back to
Akobo. Using his ride/canter/walk system, he made it home in
one long day.

The rains were heavy that year and the rivers broke their
banks and inundated the entire region. Even Dick's garden at
Akobo went underwater, killing most of his precious fruit trees.
There was little Dick could do about building the guesthouse
at Pibor Post. But Dick planned ahead and ordered a load of
burnt bricks from Nasir, a little town located on the Sobat River
halfway to Malakal. These were made and eventually loaded on
the paddle wheel steamer and brought to Akobo. Here they sat
waiting for transport. As soon as the waters receded and the
road to Pibor Post was passable Dick had the bricks loaded on
the government lorry. The trip to Pibor Post took several days.
The floods had done serious damage to the road and the lorry
had some major problems crossing the washed-out *wadis*. But
it eventually arrived. The cement foundations of the guesthouse
were completed, but Dick discovered the floodwaters had risen
three feet above the new foundations. That meant every time
there was a major flood the guesthouse would be inundated with
water. But there was no higher ground in the area so Dick went

ahead with his building project. The local workers unloaded the bricks and the mason started laying rows of bricks around the edge of the cement foundations.

The guesthouse was to be 40 feet long and 20 feet wide with curved ends. It was to have a total of three large rooms. The central room was designated to be the living/sitting room and there were two bedrooms: one on each end. Dick gave the mason instructions to build the walls up to a height of six feet, leaving gaps for the doors and windows. Then he returned to Akobo and informed Nora about the progress of the guesthouse. The building now needed a thatch roof. Finding long grass and workers to do the thatching was not an issue. But Dick knew a grass roof of this size would be very heavy. The house needed strong trusses to hold up the roof. However, building strong trusses was a major problem. There were no cut boards in all of the Upper Nile. The few local trees were bent and gnarled and totally unsuitable for such a project. He was stuck on how to proceed and shared the problem with Nora. She continued to think about the need for strong trusses and then remembered seeing a pile of metal water pipes lying in the grass near the mechanics' workshop. She went to the workshop with a tape measure where she counted the pipes and measured their lengths. Asking around she discovered they were left over from a government well-building project. Using his authority as District Commissioner, Dick gave her permission to use them for the guesthouse. Nora spent the next few days measuring and fitting the pipes together. There were male and female sockets available. Nora cut the pipes when needed and screwed the pipes into place, eventually coming up with a framework of interlocking pipes. Dick looked it over and agreed

Nora's efforts were successful. She had built a framework strong enough to hold a heavy thatch roof. Nora drew up a blueprint of the framework and coded all the joints with numbers. Then she took it all apart and laid it out on the ground. It was ready for transport to Pibor Post.

The pipes were long and heavy so Dick decided to send them to Pibor Post on the *Lady Baker* the next time she came to Akobo. The old paddle wheeler arrived the following month and Dick made his request to the Arab captain. He agreed and the pipes were loaded on to the deck of the boat and strapped down. The Pibor River was receding, but the captain thought there was enough water to float his boat. The trip south went slowly with the steamer hitting various mud banks. As they proceeded south the river became more and more shallow. The old boat got within fifteen miles of Pibor Post and was grounded one last time. The captain announced it was impossible to go any further. Everything was off-loaded on to the riverbank. The loss of weight helped the steamer to float once again and the captain turned it around, heading back to Akobo. Dick gave orders for his policemen to find local canoes and transport most of the gear south to Pibor Post. But the pipes were too heavy and awkward to transport by canoe so they were put in a pile and abandoned. Dick picked up his rifle and walked the fifteen miles into Pibor Post.

The pipes sat rusting in the long grass for the next few months. No further progress was made on the guesthouse. The following rainy season, as soon as the Pibor River flooded again, Dick once again requested the *Lady Baker* for a trip to Pibor. This time he took Nora and Michael with him and the trip took only a few hours. They found the metal pipes lying in the long grass right where they had left them. They were loaded on to the deck and taken on to Pibor Post. Here Nora went to work. She laid out the pipes according to their code marks and screwed them together like a little boy putting together an erector set. Everything fit together perfectly. But since the framework was made out of metal pipes it was quite heavy. Dick ordered a number of prisoners to be released from the jail and working together they lifted the metal framework so that it rested on top of the brick walls. Workers then went and cut sheaves of long grass and began the tedious job of thatching the house.

With the guesthouse nearing completion there was only one more major project. The toilet. A normal outhouse placed over a hole in the ground did not work at Pibor Post. The earth was black clay and the fluctuation between dry season and wet season was extreme. During the wet season the entire area flooded and the water table rose to the point that whatever was in the toilet pit floated out the door. To counter this problem Nora reverted to a technique that was once used in India. The honey-bucket system. A small room was built at the back of the guesthouse. Here the mason constructed a series of five steps rising to an elevated toilet seat. Under the toilet seat was placed a large zinc-coated bucket. Behind the bucket was a metal trap door opening to the outside. Once a day the honey-dew man would open the trap door and take out the full bucket, emptying the stinking contents into his own container. The now empty bucket was replaced under the toilet seat. The honey-dew man then lifted his container onto his head and went and dumped the contents somewhere out in the bush, as far from town as possible.

With the roof thatched and the toilet complete the Lyth family moved into the finished guesthouse. It was a great improvement over their little mud hut. Now they could entertain guests in Pibor Post to the level that the governor demanded of them. The honey-bucket system proved to be quite efficient, but Nora did complain that it was somewhat odiferous. It did have another down side. On one occasion a female guest was sitting on the throne when she suddenly felt a cool breeze on her nether end. She was horrified to hear a rattle as the honey-dew man opened the trap door and withdrew the honey-bucket out from under her. She simply froze in place, hoping the man would not notice. In turn the honey-dew man proceeded with his work, pretending nothing was amiss. The bucket was duly replaced under her and both proceeded with their business.

The guesthouse at Pibor Post became a retreat for Dick and Nora. The guesthouse had a long open veranda that faced a deep pool in the Pibor River. In the evenings they sat in their canvas safari chairs and enjoyed the tranquility of the river and the myriads of water birds. When their children got older they often fished from the bank, catching catfish and occasionally Nile perch. They also swam in the soft brown water. When the water was low they made slides on the steep mud banks. Together with their Murle friends they poured water on the black clay until it was slippery and then slid at high speed down the bank and into the water. When Dick and Nora were living at Pibor Post they felt like they were living at the end of the world. But in front of the guesthouse was a reminder that they were connected to the outside. Descending into the pool were three marble columns. Arabic numbers were etched deeply into the white marble.

These columns had been placed there by the Egyptian Irrigation Department. Periodically an Arab clerk would come and read the height of the Pibor River, using the numbers on the white marble columns. This was done on all the major tributaries leading into the Nile River. Using this information the Egyptians could predict how much water would arrive in Egypt several months later.

The natural beauty of the Pibor area appealed to both Dick and Nora. Dick kept several horses at Pibor Post. Initially they did not flourish in the intense heat and the coarse grass did not meet their nutritional needs. So Dick started buying sorghum grain from the Murle and added this to their diet. The grain gave them added energy. They were also rubbed down twice a day by the syce who also removed any ticks clinging to their rough hides. Periodically Dick and Nora took rides out along the rivers, always carrying their shotguns in leather scabbards. Nora had become a good marksman with her .410 shotgun and it became somewhat of a contest to see who could shoot the most ducks or guinea fowl.

Their favorite ride was along the course of the Kongkong River. As the water receded in the dry season it left open flats of short green grass alternating with shallow lakes. Animals and birds flocked to these green pastures and it was a good place to let the horses run.

On one ride Dick and Nora approached the river quietly, wanting to see the black crowned cranes that habitually roosted on the far bank. During the day this flock of beautiful cranes broke up into pairs and flew off to feed on grass seeds. But in the evening they all flew back to their usual roosting spot. As many as 5000 birds would congregate on the same bit of ground and here they spent the night together. Dick and Nora sat on their horses and watched the spectacular show as hundreds of incoming cranes covered the sky. The evening was filled with the sound of their mournful cries as they came flying in to roost.

After the cranes had landed, Nora challenged Dick to a race. Before he could reply she whipped up her horse and went galloping south across the flat plain. Her long blonde hair was loose and flowed behind her. She handled her horse well and it took Dick some serious riding before he finally caught up with her. They both had a good laugh and then walked the horses slowly to let them cool down. They approached an oxbow that was still holding water. It was covered with lily pads and the pink and purple flowers were starting to close. The honeybees were working hard trying to get as much nectar as possible before the coming night. Dick and Nora stopped and viewed the lovely sight.

Dick noticed some white-faced tree ducks landing at the end of the shallow lake. He dismounted and tied his horse to an acacia bush. Then taking his shotgun he began to stalk the swimming birds.

As he was creeping up to the ducks he suddenly heard the loud sound of a shotgun go off behind him. The ducks he was stalking flew up in front of him before he could get off a shot. He was not too pleased with the situation. He trudged back to the horses to protest, but Nora was not there. Then he heard a splashing sound and turning around he saw Nora wading toward him through the pink water lilies. She was completely naked. In one hand she carried her shotgun and in the other she carried two dead ducks. The sun was setting and the red color reflected off her statuesque body. On her face she had an impish smile of success. She knew she looked good. It was a memorable sight that Dick carried with him for the rest of his life.

20

Darkening the Sun

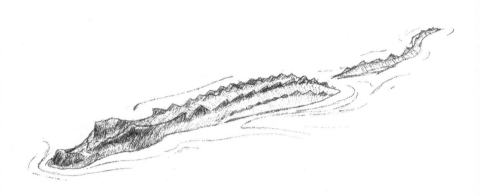

With Dick now spending more time at Pibor Post, he was able to work more closely with the Murle government chiefs and they began to take the court work more seriously. As they proved themselves capable Dick gave them increasing authority to adjudicate cases. The policy of Indirect Rule allowed the chiefs to settle most minor cases using their own traditional customs. This policy was well received by the Murle people and also allowed Dick to move on to other aspects of his work as District Commissioner. The chiefs appreciated their salaries and overall the system proved to be economical and efficient.

The one big issue was setting dates for the courts or other meetings. The Murle had no calendar. They simply moved with the natural rhythm of the seasons. One month a chief could be living on the Kengen River and the next month he could be out in the cattle camps. Getting a chief to come for a specific court case on a specific day was problematic. Dick finally worked out a solution. He would set a court for a certain date, perhaps ten days away. Then he took a short leather thong and tied ten knots into it. The thong was given to a messenger who hung it around his neck and headed out to find the chief. Each evening on the road he would untie one knot indicating the passage of one day. He would eventually find the chief and give him the knotted thong saying, *Aroong Kemerbong ineet* – "Kemerbong wants you." Each evening the chief would untie another knot. When the last knot was untied the chief was due at the court location to adjudicate a case. Dick reported the system worked perfectly with the chiefs showing up on time.

Court cases were always handled in the shade of a large tree. Certain trees in each area were identified as judgment trees. Holding court under these specific trees was not something started by Dick as the magistrate. The judgment trees were already in place in Murle culture and Dick merely continued their use in his administration. The chiefs were also allowed to adjudicate cases in the traditional manner. When one person brought an accusation against another, it was usually solved informally within the family structure. But more complicated cases were brought to the chiefs who served as judges.

A court case was a public affair and everybody was welcome to attend. The chief himself sat up against the trunk of the judgment tree. The accusers and defenders never spoke to him directly. Instead they spoke to a man called *bacoi*. This man had to be both wise and eloquent. The accusing party would sit in a group on one side of the court and make their case to the *bacoi*. He would listen carefully and then turn to the chief and summarize the argument. Anybody in the accusing party could speak and background information was welcomed so the case could be set in the proper context. There was sometimes a problem with people getting excited and speaking at the same time. There was real potential for chaos. Dick introduced a speaker's stick. The person holding the stick had the exclusive right to speak. He would hold the stick in his right hand and walk around swinging it for emphasis as he spoke. When he was done, the *bacoi* would turn to the judge and summarize the gist of his speech. Then another man would take the speaker's stick and give his view. Of course the judge could hear and understand every word of the accusers. But the rewording of the speeches gave him an opportunity to hear them again. More importantly it kept him at an objective distance and out of the verbal fray.

After the accusations were made, the accused party made its defense. Again anyone could speak and people made use of the speaker's stick. Their speeches were also summarized by the *bacoi* who passed them on to the judge. When both sides had presented all their evidence, the judge could then ask questions. The *bacoi* rephrased these questions for the listening audience. When the judge was content he had all the relevant information, he made his ruling. Again the *bacoi* was involved, rewording the words of the penalty and passing them on to the litigants.

In most cases the punishment was a payment of recompense: a fine of cattle or goats. In more serious cases such as murder, Dick himself took over as judge. His clerks set up a canvas chair and folding table under a judgment tree. Dick would be seated, taking care to wear his symbol of authority: the official District Commissioner's helmet with a brass badge and white feather. This became the official high court. Dick also used an eloquent *bacoi* who interpreted the evidence for Dick and helped him understand the case so he could make an accurate decision.

Some court cases were tough for Dick to handle. In one case a Dinka family came from Bor to bring an accusation. They said their young son had been stolen by the Murle many years before. They had finally located him and wanted him back. The boy was now a teenager and had bonded to his Murle family. The boy did not want to return to his Dinka parents. He now spoke Murle and had Murle friends. But Dick felt he had to uphold the law and he ordered the boy to be given back to his original Dinka parents. His decision caused great consternation and sorrow. Over time Dick dealt with many such cases. If a Dinka child was fathered by a close relative, the baby was considered a child born of incest. These children were often sold to the Murle in exchange for cattle. They were adopted and considered to be full members of the Murle tribe. But often a Dinka relative would come find the child when he was in his teens and demand his return. The Murle adoptive parents would refuse to give him back, having paid for him and invested care and expenses in the raising of the boy. In these cases the boys considered themselves to be Murle and did not want to return to Dinka culture. Dick weighed these cases carefully, trying to do what was best for the welfare of each boy.

Another case involved two women who were co-wives. One of the women gave birth to a child. She had a nasty disposition and was always gloating and disparaging to the other wife who was barren. Finally the barren woman had enough. She killed the child, cut up the body and served it for supper. The mother ate it unknowingly and then the barren woman smiled and said, "Did you enjoy your supper? You just ate your son." The murderer was brought to trial and openly confessed what she had done. Dick had to condemn her and gave her the penalty of death. She was taken to Malakal, but her execution was never carried out. The British administration had a policy of never hanging women, so her sentence was commuted to life imprisonment.

In yet another case a Murle elder was accused of murder. He admitted the crime, but claimed it was in self-defense. He was an old man with a good reputation in the Murle community. Dick hesitated to send him to Malakal to be executed. Instead Dick gave him a unique punishment – to pull a punkah. A punkah was a type of fan used in India. It was a large piece of cloth mounted on the ceiling of a room and attached to a rope and pulley. The operator stood outside the room and pulled the rope up and down, causing the cloth inside to rise and fall. This moved the air and cooled the room. Dick set up a punkah in his office. Every day the old prisoner was released from the local jail and pulled the rope up and down during the hot hours of the day. Dick also built a punkah in the bedroom of his house. Nora was bothered by the heat, especially when she was pregnant. The old prisoner would sit outside the bedroom and pull the punkah to keep Nora comfortable. Normally a pukah puller would pull the rope with his arms, but one day Dick returned home to find the old prisoner lying on his back sound asleep. He had tied the rope to his foot and was using his leg to pull the punkah up and down, all the while having a good nap.

Some cases erred on the side of being humorous. Hassan was the man who had the horrible job of emptying the honey-buckets at Pibor Post. Daily he would go from latrine to latrine where he opened the trap doors and dumped the stinking contents into a large metal container. This he would carry on his head as he went from location to location. When it was full he would go dump the contents out in the bush. It was a filthy job and people could smell Hassan coming from over one hundred paces. Everyone stayed clear of poor Hassan. If a person even hinted at laughter, he might find a pile of human dung dumped in front of his door. One day Hassan was brought to Dick's office and various charges were brought against him. But Hassan was prepared to defend himself. He set a letter in front of Dick, a letter he had dictated to a local scribe with limited English.

"Dear Sir, I quoted my words in this list because I am poor in talking. This case was held by sergeant Samson, but unfortunately he could not hear my expression. This incident was in this wise. The Public Health says that nobody doing the work I am doing can pour the human dung into the 1) river 2) gardens 3) courtyards. I know these rules before I come to work in Pibor. Ali excused me to the sergeant saying I did such a thing but I could not admit it. Ali relieved himself from excreta in the river and was caught and reported. Nothing was done about it and no cutting of his salary as has been done to me. I shall probably be transferred to Malakal because of Ali."

Dick handled the case personally. He was sympathetic toward Hassan and cleared him of all charges. Good honey-bucket men were difficult to find.

District Commissioners in southern Sudan had many

responsibilities and were overworked. So each officer had to prioritize. Dick was totally absorbed in getting to know the chiefs and the people under his authority. He firmly believed that earning the trust of the people was the underlying basis for all of his work. This involved much travel from place to place. Dick's happiest days were spent out on trek, flying the flag and showing his presence. In the early days this was done mostly by foot. Dick thoroughly enjoyed these treks. He usually traveled with a small contingent of police, porters and a cook. In the morning he would set a destination and the porters would take off carrying the gear. Dick was then free to visit villages, explore or go hunting – whatever pleased his fancy. At the end of the day he would rendezvous with his men. He would find his tent set up, a chair beside a crackling fire and a hot meal ready to eat.

In the dry season Dick rode his horse to the farther locations. But it soon became obvious to Dick there needed to be roads connecting the various police posts. Therefore building roads became an important part of Dick's work. He eventually created a network of roads connecting all four police posts. To build the roads the various chiefs had to conscript young men to do the physical work. In open country the work went quickly. It simply involved setting a direction and then digging out the tussocks of grass so a vehicle could drive relatively smoothly. However, building roads in the gallery forests along the rivers took much more work. The footpaths made by the Murle bypassed any obstacle so the paths were anything but straight. Dick would have a member of the crew walk down a path for about a mile. Then he would fire off a rifle. Dick took a compass reading toward the sound of the rifle shot. Using the compass bearing the men would walk in a straight line, blazing the trees as they walked. Using this blaze line they would then cut down trees and dig out the stumps. The result was a relatively straight road through the forest.

These roads did not stay open from year to year without maintenance. Branches quickly grew across the roads and these had to be cut back at the beginning of each dry season. Each chief was responsible for clearing a certain number of miles of road. On one hunting trip Dick noticed the road from Pibor Post to Kongkong had gotten overgrown. Chief Yankor was in charge of that section of road. Dick called him to headquarters and told him to clear the road. But Yankor insisted the road had already been cleared and it was in fine condition. Dick had Yankor and some of his elders climb into the back of an open lorry. Then Dick drove down the overgrown road, driving as fast as he could. The overhanging branches contained hooked thorns and the naked passengers in the back of the lorry started howling for him to stop. Dick finally brought the lorry to a halt and asked Yankor what he thought of the road. Yankor thought it could use some more clearing and promised to do it right away.

Another time Dick was riding his horse from Akobo to Pibor and found the road so overgrown that even the horse could hardly find a way through. Dick rode to the chief's house where he reprimanded the chief and fined him two cows. Earlier in the week Dick had looked at his calendar and noticed there was going to be an eclipse of the sun. The timing was perfect. As Dick mounted his horse to leave the village, he said to the chief that the entire world had never seen a road as bad as this one. The whole of heaven was probably gazing down and looking at this appalling road. Dick went on to say he would not be surprised if the heavens showed their anger.

As Dick rode away the shadow of the moon started covering the sun and the day began to turn dark. From behind him Dick heard an appalling wail and people started beating on cans and drums. The next time Dick rode through that way, the road was cleared and open. It remained smooth and open year after year. Dick's devious plot had worked. But he felt a little badly that he had deceived the chief.

Over time Dick had earned a bit of a reputation. At Pibor Post he started to build a cement retaining wall in front of the police station. The purpose of the wall was to prevent water from going into the building if the river flooded too high in the rainy season. The chiefs sent a delegation to Dick and asked him what he was building. Dick explained the wall and its purpose. The chiefs became very upset. They presumed Dick was actually going to cause a large flood. They begged him not to bring the high waters and inundate the area. Dick had a hard time explaining he did not have this kind of power and the wall was purely precautionary.

Wherever Dick went on his treks as the District Commissioner, he held regular worship services. His commitment to God was very real and personal and he was eager to pass his faith to others. Usually these services were small and impromptu. Dick would sing a couple of songs and give a short message. He would tell a parable from the Bible and apply it to the local culture. He never pushed people to attend these services: the propagation of his Christian faith was a natural thing. In Pibor Post several of his policemen and clerks were Christians so Dick met with them each Sunday morning. Some Murle men were attracted to these meetings and over time some of them became Christians. Dick was not a missionary trying to set up a church of a particular denomination. But as the number of people coming to the worship services began to grow he thought they needed some sort of organization. So he called together a few of the long-term Christians and they elected themselves as leaders.

Dick's friend Lado sometimes served as the preacher in the newly founded church at Pibor Post. But Lado was only one man and he was often away working on the Boma Plateau. So Dick met with the missionaries based at Akobo and invited them to start a work among the Murle. After negotiations with the governor in Malakal, the missionaries were given permission to start a new mission station at Pibor Post. Dick gave the missionaries a tract of land one mile east of the police post. It was on the curve of the Kengen River and had a beautiful gallery forest of tamarind and jorghan trees. Several American missionary families moved from Akobo to Pibor Post and built homes overlooking the river. They also built a clinic and established a medical work with the Murle people. Whenever Dick and Nora came to Pibor Post, they would meet socially with the missionaries and the children would get together to play. Both sides benefited from the mutual friendships and they became a tightly knit community.

The missionaries were well received because of all the help they offered the local Murle people. They learned the Murle language and even began a translation of the Bible. Gradually over time a number of Murle people became Christians and their new beliefs began to have an impact on their lives.

Dick got up early one morning for the ride from Pibor Post

to Akobo. He had informed the syce the day before and his horse was saddled and ready to run. Dick chose to travel alone and figured he could make the whole trip in about eight hours. He put his foot into the stirrup and swung himself up into the saddle. Waving goodbye to his servants he clucked to the horse and rode away at a canter. About one mile out of Pibor Post he suddenly felt an intense pain on the inside of his thigh. He pulled the horse to a stop and dismounted. The pain quickly got worse, radiating up into his groin. Dick untied the girth and took the saddle off the horse. There between the saddle and the blanket he found an angry, bruised scorpion. Now he knew why he was hurting. He had been badly stung by the yellow arachnid.

Thus began one of the longest days of Dick's life. After dispatching the scorpion he put the saddle back on the horse and cinched it tight. He remounted but his thigh rubbed directly on the saddle and every movement of the horse accentuated the pain. After a few miles of agony he got off and tried to walk. But walking was not much better since his khaki shorts rubbed against his aching thigh. So it was back on the horse. Periodically he would have the horse increase its pace from a walk to a canter. The pain was much more intense, but Dick gritted his teeth and bore the pain with the knowledge he was covering ground more quickly. Eventually he would have to stop the horse, dismount and just stand in one place until the pain lessened. Then he would remount and canter again. In late evening he finally arrived at his house in Akobo, absolutely knackered. Nora treated the sting with ice and aspirin and Dick went to bed where he slept the sleep of the dead. He had never liked scorpions, but from this point onward he had an even stronger dislike for the beasts.

One of Dick's primary assignments as District Commissioner was trying to keep the peace in the region. One of the primary trouble areas was the buffer zone between the Murle and the Jiye. The Jiye were an offshoot of the Toposa people. They were aggressive pastoralists and were constantly pushing north into pastures the Murle considered to be theirs. While on a trip south of Pibor Post, Dick heard a rumor that a major fight was brewing. The Murle warriors were planning a major attack on the Jiye. Dick called together the Murle chiefs who were in charge of the southern region. He fined them 200 cows for allowing the fight to take place. Then he mounted his horse and galloped south. By riding hard he managed to get to the location before the fighting started. He found a large cohort of Murle warriors lined up and ready to fight. Coming toward them was a line of fully armed Jiye warriors. Dick dismounted and taking his flywhisk, the local symbol of authority, he stood between the two lines of advancing warriors. He waved his flywhisk and ordered everyone to go home. The advancing lines slowed, hesitated, stopped and then withdrew. The fight was averted - for now. The incident also proved Dick was in control of the region, relying largely on the force of his character and personality. In talking again with the Murle chiefs Dick was able to reassess the situation. They confirmed the Jiye had provoked the situation by entering Murle territory and stealing some cattle. The Murle warriors were only trying to protect their land from the invaders. After listening Dick agreed with them and returned the 200 cattle. The chiefs were pleased with Dick's decision and his reputation as a capable District Commissioner was elevated to an even higher level.

The ride back to Pibor Post was long and hot. Dick kept going, alternating walking and riding, looking forward to reuniting with his family. He finally arrived back at the guesthouse, dirty and exhausted. After greeting Nora he took a quick swim in the Pibor River to wash away the grime of travel. Then he enjoyed a wholesome meal of roast duck prepared by Nora. Lastly he did one of his favorite activities. He took out his precious old gramophone, inserted a new needle and put on a favorite record of Bach's sonatas. He lay back in his chair and let the magnificent music sweep over him as Nora rubbed his aching shoulders. Home again. There was no better way to relax after a tough safari.

However, the problems with the Jiye continued. They kept pushing north into Murle territory. Finally Dick arranged a meeting with Geoffrey King, the District Commissioner of the Kapoeta area. Since the Jiye were operating in the border region between Kapoeta District and Pibor District, they were somewhat in no-man's land. The meeting was set to take place during the dry season on the vague border between the two districts. Dick took a government vehicle and drove slowly south along the Kengen River, clearing a track as he went. The trip took five days. He met up with King on the appointed day and they spent three days setting a firm border and establishing grazing territories. Both Murle and Jiye chiefs were present at the meeting and ultimately they all agreed to the newly established boundaries. The Jiye were to stay south of the boundary at all times and they were to be under the administration of the District Commissioner based at Kapoeta. The Murle were to stay north of the border and they were under the control of the District Commissioner at Pibor Post. It was a good clear agreement and one that solved the fighting in the region for many years to come.

On the drive home there was a light rain and the track became tacky. Dick saw a large thunderstorm heading their way. The black clouds boiled thousands of feet into the sky. He knew if the storm hit them with full force the sticky clay would turn into liquid mud and they would be stranded for weeks. There seemed to be no way to avoid the oncoming storm. He wanted to pray with his men and ask God to stop the oncoming storm. But he hesitated. If he prayed publicly and the storm still hit them, he would look like a fool. He mentioned his hesitation to Paulo, one of his sergeants who was a member of the church in Akobo.

Paulo had no hesitation. "Let us pray!" he exclaimed.

So Dick held a prayer meeting with his men and asked God to stop the rain. Almost immediately the wind shifted and the great thunderheads blew east, leaving the track in front of them fairly dry. The Christian men in Dick's party were convinced their prayers had been heard and God had responded in their favor.

Even so the long trip back to Pibor Post was a tough one. Two of the tires sprung serious leaks and would no longer hold air. Dick opened up the tires and stuffed old gunnysacks into them. This made for a rough ride, but the lorry was able to keep going. They had to cross some soft *wadis* where the lorry bogged down. The men lay coconut matting in front of the vehicle to keep it from sinking. The driver carefully drove the lorry on to the matting and proceeded to the front edge. Here he stopped and waited while the men moved the used matting from the rear of the lorry and placed it at the front so it could move forward a few more paces. This leap-frogging system finally got them to drier ground and eventually they limped back into Pibor Post. Dick was pleased to stretch out in his canvas chair, hold Michael in his lap and listen once again to the pleasant tones of Bach playing in the wilderness.

Nora did not know how to drive. She pointed out to Dick this was something she needed to learn. There might well be a situation where Dick was absent and she would need to drive a vehicle. Dick agreed, so he commandeered one of the old Commer trucks and gave Nora driving lessons. The lorry had no power steering and it took considerable strength to keep the vehicle heading in the right direction. The Commer was also stick shift, so there was also heavy work involved in compressing the clutch and shifting gears. But Nora was strong and capable and soon mastered the skill of driving. As the magistrate of the region, Dick gave her a driving test. He had her drive the truck out to the granite hill named Lothir and bring back a load of rocks. She returned successfully with the lorry full of granite stones. She passed the test. In his role as District Commissioner Dick issued her with an official Sudanese driver's license. She kept this license. Years later when she returned to England she presented her Sudanese license to the local authorities and was automatically given an up-graded English driver's license. There were definitely some benefits to having a husband who was an all-powerful government officer.

Pibor Post became the favorite place for the Lyths to live and they went there several times a year. On one of the earlier trips Nora began feeling ill. She could not decide if she had a stomach disorder or if she was pregnant. This went on for several months until she finally decided she really was pregnant. However, because of the initial confusion she did not know when the baby was due. She had to make a general calculation. When the time came, the Lyths made a family trip and went on vacation to Uganda where they visited a numbers of friends. Then Dick returned to his post in Akobo, leaving Nora and Michael in Uganda. In due time she gave birth to another son. He was named David. Dick received the news by wire and several weeks later he took the paddle wheeler down the Sobat River to Malakal. Here he stayed at the governor's house and waited until Nora and the babies arrived on the plane from Uganda. Nora was tired, but happy to be back with her husband. They returned to Akobo by boat and then proceeded on to Pibor Post.

At certain times of the year the region around Pibor Post was full of wildlife. These animals, birds and fish provided Dick and his family with all the meat they could eat. Dick had been a crack shot in Oxford University and this skill served him well when he went hunting for the pot. On a survey trip beyond the Kongkong River he spotted a herd of zebra. These were fairly rare in the area, so he took a shot. The bullet passed through the neck of the closest zebra and hit a second zebra in the chest. They both went down. As the mounted police were butchering the animals a young Murle warrior ran up to Dick. After he got his breath he reported he had found Dick's little book. Dick reached into his shirt pocket and realized his daily diary was missing. He had not even been aware he had lost it. He was greatly relieved and asked the warrior for the diary. The warrior said he did not have it. It was back in the village Dick had visited the day before. After butchering the zebras Dick and his men retraced their steps to the village. Here he found an old man squatting in the cattle kraal. The diary was lying in the mud and the old man was carefully guarding it so the cows could not step on it.

Later in the month Dick was sitting on the front porch of the Pibor Post guesthouse when a messenger ran up to him. He reported that the crocodile hunters had come. Dick was bewildered by the message, but he followed the messenger down to the government office. Here he found a dilapidated lorry with a number of passengers sitting on the ground. They were a tough-looking lot with dirty robes, soiled turbans and bandoliers of bullets over their shoulders. In talking with them Dick soon learned they were a specialized clan of hunters who focused on killing crocodiles for their skins. They hailed from Nigeria, a country well over 2000 miles away. Dick was intrigued and discovered this clan of specialized hunters traveled all over central Africa looking for crocodiles. They had been doing this for generations, initially using donkeys and camels to carry the loads of dried crocodile skins. Now that the world was getting more modern, they were doing the trips with an old lorry. They were not licensed to kill crocodiles in Sudan, but they had been doing it for decades, so traditional law was on their side.

Dick gave them permission to hunt crocodiles in the Pibor region, but only if he went with them. The Nigerians readily agreed and said they would be ready to leave the following morning. Dick knew there were very few crocodiles in the Pibor River, so he wondered where these Nigerian hunters would find enough of the reptiles to make their trip viable. The next morning Dick got in the front of the cab and the hunters climbed up on top of the lorry. They were a motley-looking crew. Some of the hunters had deep scars on their arms and several had only one eye. They held their old rifles at the ready. Dick wondered what he was getting into. But the Nigerians were very cordial and eager to show Dick their hunting technique. They drove east across the plains and eventually stopped near the Raprap River. At this time of the year the river was not flowing and had receded into long shallow pools. The Nigerians made camp on the banks of the river. They took large boards off the top of the lorry, placed them side by side and started sewing them together. Dick was amazed to see these were quickly made into two serviceable canoes. That evening they pushed the canoes out into the shallow pools. Dick got into one of the canoes and the man in the rear started rowing quietly along the banks. One hunter pulled out a large torch and shone it ahead of them. The rays reflected back in the form of red lights – the eyes of dozens of crocodiles. The oarsman edged the canoe up close to a pair of eyes and the hunter in front of the canoe threw a harpoon into the back of the waiting crocodile. With a great splash of its muscular tail, the crocodile dove to the bottom of the pool and the attached rope ran out the front of the canoe. For a short period the wounded crocodile pulled the canoe around the pool, but it quickly tired. The harpooner then pulled on the rope and drew the wounded crocodile close to the boat, dispatching it with an axe to the back of the skull. It was then lifted into the boat. Dick noticed the other canoe was having similar success on the other side of the pool.

After several kills the red eyes disappeared. The remaining crocodiles were now cautious and keeping out of sight. One of the Nigerians started making a low humming sound. This in some way attracted the crocodiles and almost immediately the red eyes reappeared. The Nigerians proceeded with the hunt. Within two hours both canoes were full of dead crocodiles and the canoes returned to the base camp.

The next morning the crocodiles were carefully skinned. Only the stomach skin was valuable so cuts were made on the side of each crocodile and the stomach skin removed as a single piece. The skins were then pegged out on the ground and covered with a liberal sprinkling of salt to keep them from rotting.

Night after night the Nigerians went out and came back with more crocodiles. Dick was amazed by the large numbers of crocodiles in the area. He knew the Raprap River stopped flowing every year. He also knew the pools eventually dried up into stagnant puddles of mud. How did so many crocodiles survive in such a hostile environment? He later learned crocodiles had the ability to estivate. When the pools dried they simply dug down into the mud and went into a long sleep. Their metabolism slowed down and they lived off their reserves of fat. A crocodile had the ability to sleep for many months until the rains came back and filled up the pools.

After a few days of hunting the Nigerians had collected hundreds of skins, all they could carry in the lorry. They dismantled their wooden canoes, loaded up the skins and headed back to Pibor Post. The next day Dick said goodbye to his new-found friends and they headed west, starting their long trip back to their families in Nigeria.

21

A Price on His Head

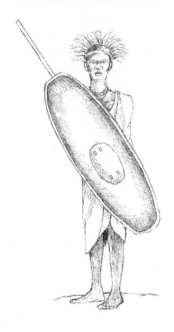

The Boma Plateau had a special place in Dick's heart. Having spent several years in the beautiful highlands, it held many good memories. Each dry season he made the long trek out to the area to inspect the police manning the post. It was always a relief to be back in the cool hills. After one arduous walk from Pibor to Boma, he wrote the following statement in his diary: "It is such a joy to me to lift my eyes up unto the purple hills, each one known and loved so well. And then to climb up into them and receive the welcome that was waiting for me from all my old friends. Then to walk through the villages, recognizing every tree and stone. And then to go sit out on the old rock looking out over the great panorama below and lift up my heart in praise prayer for it all."

His grass-roofed house was still there but a little run down from lack of use. Sitting in front of the crackling fire at night gave him the sense of coming home after being away for a long time. But as always he wanted to share it all with his beloved Nora.

A year later the opportunity finally came. With the road to Boma completed, it was now possible to drive the government lorry from Pibor Post to Boma. A meeting of government officials was set up to firmly establish the status of Boma. For many years the Towath police post on the Boma Plateau was in an administrative conundrum. The stone fort was located right on the line between Kapoeta District and Pibor District. In the early years it was administered from Kapoeta since the only route to Boma was the faint track from Kapoeta. When Dick was the Frontier Agent at Boma during the war, he had reported to Geoffrey King, the District Commissioner for the Kapoeta region. However, the Murle people living at Boma were affiliated with the lowland Murle in the Pibor District. They shared a common culture and language and regarded themselves to be one people. Therefore a decision needed to be made. There was a date set for the discussion. Dick and Nora came to Boma from the north, driving the old Commer lorry along the new track. It was dry season so the road was dry. But it was so hot Dick removed the front window and the doors from the lorry so they could get maximum airflow. After placing Nora and the babies in the front seat, he tied a rope across the space so they did not fall out.

The other officials drove up from the south. They included Marwood, the Governor of Equatoria, King, the District

Commissioner of Kapoeta District and a number of other officials – both police and military. Dick had never seen so many white people at Boma at the same time. He compared the gathering with a vacation in Blackpool, England. The meetings were cordial and after long discussions it was decided the military out of Kapoeta would withdraw and have no more jurisdiction on the Boma Plateau. Boma would be occupied only by the police and these police would be under the authority of Dick Lyth as the District Commissioner of Pibor.

With the decision made the officials left. Dick stayed on with Nora for a few days. For the first time he could show Nora where he had lived for the years during the war. Hand in hand they walked the mountain paths, enjoying the fresh air and the spectacular views. Dick wrote in his diary, "I have dreamed so often of being here together." They also walked out to the villages where Dick introduced his wife to his many Murle friends.

Lado, the evangelist, had come out to Boma by foot a few months earlier. As was his practice he was going from village to village telling people about God. On Sunday Lado organized a church service. Over 100 people attended and Dick spoke to the congregation, using as his text the parable of the prodigal son. In talking to Lado Dick learned he had recently taken a trip down to Kapoeta. From there he had gone back to the Lotuxo village where he had once lived as a slave. Here he contacted the family that had adopted him and shared with them the news of Jesus Christ.

Dick held court at Boma using his authority as the chief magistrate. The local chiefs presented several complicated cases and Dick listened carefully before making his decisions. Dick and Nora also walked out to see some Kichepo villages. Nora was amazed at the size of the lip plugs worn by the young women. Dick was pleased to see the peace agreement between the Murle and Kichepo was still holding. Before leaving Boma he met with the police and set out their new responsibilities. Musa the sergeant again asked if he could be released from the police force. Dick assented and chose another Nuba man to serve as sergeant. Musa was now free to pursue his new vocation – trading in coffee.

The return trip to Pibor Post went well. Nora enjoyed watching the many herds of animals. She especially liked the graceful giraffes that ran away from the vehicle with their tails curled up over their rumps. Upon arriving back at Pibor Post Dick wrote in his diary that all was well "except for a couple of murders."

Having abundant wildlife in the area was not always enjoyable. Upon settling back into Pibor Post, Nora noticed the area was inundated with mice. Over the following weeks they rapidly increased in numbers until they literally carpeted the ground. Walking down a path Nora could see hundreds of them scurrying out of her way. These thousands of mice were voraciously hungry. They climbed the sorghum stalks in the fields and ate the grain before the Murle could harvest it. Then the mice moved into Pibor Post looking for scraps and refuse to eat. They entered houses and soon Nora's home was invaded by mice. She did her best to keep them out, putting stockings filled with sand across the bottoms of the doors. She also kept the doors and windows closed, but each time a door was opened a few mice would scoot into the house. Nora had to keep her food in sealed containers, but it was disconcerting to have droves of mice streaking around the floor. One night she accidentally left out a bucket half full of water. In the morning she found 30 mice had fallen into the bucket and drowned.

Since Nora was a trained nurse, the Murle women often brought their children to her for medicine. During the mice plague many mothers carried in their children with sore feet. While the children were asleep the mice had eaten the calluses off their feet. Their calluses were so tough the children did not feel the mice chewing away until they bit into raw flesh. These bites got easily infected and Nora was kept busy putting mercurochrome on the children's wounds.

After a few days of fighting the mice, Dick and Nora returned to headquarters at Akobo. The Akobo River marked the border between Sudan and Ethiopia. It ran from the police post at Akobo southeast to the base of the Boma Plateau. The Anuak people lived on both sides of this river and this brought many headaches to Dick. If an Anuak man committed a crime in Sudan, he simply crossed the river in a canoe and was out of reach of the authorities. Pochala was an Anuak village on the bank of the Akobo River that had a police post. The eight policemen who worked there tried to monitor who crossed in and out Ethiopia.

One of the Anuak policemen based at Pochala proved to be a thief. His name was Abuja and Dick caught him stealing guns and ammunition from the police armory. He was dismissed from his job and promptly crossed the river into Ethiopia. He swore vengeance against Dick and over the following months raised a fighting force of 150 men. They based themselves in Ethiopia and made raids into Sudan to attack villages and steal cattle. Abuja put a price on Dick's head, offering 50 Sudanese pounds to anyone who killed Dick and produced his body. Dick was actually quite offended he was only worth 50 pounds. In turn he put out the offer of 100 Sudanese pounds for anyone who brought in Abuja.

The raids increased and Dick brought in his small force of mounted police. Dick rode with the men and he spent many weeks patrolling the Sudan/Ethiopian border, hoping to catch Abuja and his men on the Sudan side of the river. But Abuja proved to be an able guerilla leader and he continued to attack and withdraw. Only once did the mounted police catch up to the raiders. They shot three of them, but Abuja managed to escape into the long grass.

These weeks on patrol were difficult for Dick. As the only white man in the region he knew he was an obvious target. But he was the District Commissioner so he did not want to show fear. Evenings were especially difficult. Dick would sit at his camp table and write by the light of a kerosene lantern. Here he was silhouetted by the glow of the wick and he felt a constant itch between his shoulder blades - just waiting to feel a bullet tear into him. It never happened. His men saw him as a fearless leader who worked diligently to try and catch the rebel.

When Dick returned home to Akobo after these extensive patrols, he was totally exhausted. Nora plied him with love and healthy food and he spent hours listening to his beloved classical music on the gramophone. Over time Abuja got bolder and while Dick was in Akobo he made an open attack on the police post at Pochala. The police were caught unprepared, but they handled the situation well. Instead of running to the forest to hide, they dashed to the guardhouse with bullets kicking up dust around their feet. Once in the guardhouse they grabbed their rifles and started shooting. A fierce firefight took place and several of Abuja's men were killed before they withdrew across the river. The sergeant had a bullet through his thigh, but he recovered. Dick later awarded him a medal for his bravery.

At this point Dick requested the help of the Sudan Defence Force. A contingent of soldiers arrived from Malakal on the paddle wheel steamer. They were made up of hardened Sudanese troops led by a British officer. Dick gave them guides and they marched off through the long grass. It was a long march through swamp and mud, but after several days of trekking they eventually arrived at Pochala and set up camp. Abuja and his men were aware of the troops and stayed in hiding in Ethiopia. The Sudan Defence Force did not have permission to enter Ethiopia so they simply sat and waited. Over the ensuing weeks they became increasingly frustrated by the lack of action. They did make contact with all the Anuak villages and warned them there would be dire consequences if they assisted Abuja and his men. The troops eventually broke camp and marched back to Akobo, having never met the enemy.

Although the rebels never engaged in battle with the Sudan Defence Force, their presence did make the Anuak aware of the strength of the British government. Nobody gave any food or aid to Abuja and his men and it was increasingly difficult for them to live off the land. Things became quiet and in Dick's reports he stated Abuja had "gone to earth" – using the fox and hound terminology for losing the fox.

Several months later Dick received a message from Pochala that Abuja had turned himself in. He was hungry and ill. He stated he was tired of living in the mud and being eaten by hordes of mosquitoes. The police put him in chains and walked him to Akobo where he was jailed.

Over the next months Dick traveled around Anuak country on his horse and interviewed various people who had personal knowledge of Abuja and his atrocities. He carefully rounded up witnesses who could testify at the trial of Abuja. Because of the open enmity between Dick and Abuja, Dick did not want to sit as judge on the case. He invited a superior judge, Billy Mesowall, to come from Malakal to Akobo and serve as magistrate judging the case. The court case was a big production. Many people came to listen and it took a full two days. Witnesses were called forward and they testified to the crimes Abuja had committed. The magistrate listened carefully to the evidence and made his judgment. Abuja was guilty on all counts and condemned to death.

Abuja was taken to Malakal on the steamer. Here he had the opportunity to appeal his case, but the guilty verdict was upheld and he was eventually hanged. Dick was just happy to have it all behind him. Never again during his time in Sudan did he have another case like Abuja. With the trial over Dick took his family and went to their favorite place for a vacation – Pibor Post.

22

Donkeys Hate Ducks

While they were staying at Pibor Post, Dick heard that a financial accountant was coming to inspect the books. Over the next few days Dick spent a substantial amount of time getting the financial reports ready and doing inventory on all the supplies in the storerooms. It was a tedious process and one Dick did not enjoy. The accountant arrived on the government lorry – with his wife. They were both enthusiastic travelers and enjoyed riding around the area on horseback and seeing the wildlife. The accountant was not really interested in the bookkeeping and took only a cursory look at the financial records. Dick was a bit disgusted since he had put in so much preparation time. The couple had heard about the beauty of the Boma Plateau and were eager to see it for themselves. So Dick arranged for an inspection trip, taking two lorries and including Nora on the trip.

On the track to Boma they stopped to make camp and the accountant had the opportunity to shoot a buffalo. The following day he woke up with a bad case of food poisoning. In the end it was deemed best if he returned to Pibor Post. But his wife really wanted to see Boma. In her role as nurse Nora agreed to accompany the accountant back to Pibor while his wife proceeded to Boma with Dick. The Murle men at Boma saw the new white woman and assumed Dick and the accountant had temporarily switched wives. They thought this was a great arrangement. There was a lot of talk and the Murle thought this was something they could learn to do. Dick had to do some serious talking to finally explain there was no wife-swapping going on and he was still committed to Nora and Nora only.

Akobo was the center of Christianity for the region. When Dick had first arrived at Akobo he had been welcomed by Don McClure, the leader of the American Presbyterian Mission. Over the following years a number of new American missionaries joined the McClures. These missionaries were dedicated and well educated. They were culturally sensitive and spent time learning the language and culture of the surrounding Anuak people. Not only did they establish a church, but over time they translated the Bible, directed a school, developed agriculture and set up a medical clinic.

Dick and Nora developed good relationships with these missionaries. It gave them contact with other people from the West. On Saturday afternoons the Lyth family would walk to the nearby mission station and play volleyball. This event would usually finish with a special American treat: cherry pie and ice cream. On Sunday mornings Dick and Nora attended the Anuak church. Dick also led a worship service with the police and other government employees based at the administrative headquarters.

When Nora became pregnant again, she opted not to follow government policy and go to Uganda to give birth to the baby. Instead she decided to have the baby at home in Akobo. She stayed fit by playing squash up until the last month of her pregnancy. Then she had the baby in her own bedroom with the help of the missionary doctor. Dick did not regard the doctor to be an expert obstetrician, but Nora was a trained nurse and had already had two babies. With Nora coaching from the top end and the doctor following her orders at the bottom end, a daughter was successfully born. She was named Jenny. The delivery system was so much more efficient than traveling all the way to Uganda that they decided to do it again. In due time another daughter was born at Akobo. They named her Susan. Their family was now balanced and complete: two sons and two daughters.

On one of its monthly trips to Akobo, the *Lady Baker* pulled up to the dock and a slight dark-haired man stepped down the gangplank. He was led to Dick's office where he introduced himself as the government anthropologist. His name was Godfrey Leinhardt and he had received his education at Oxford University. He explained, "The British government feels it can do a better job of administering the tribal people of southern Sudan if it has a good understanding of the various cultures. Therefore social scientists like myself have been hired to do anthropological research. My focus of study is the Dinka people, the largest of the ethnic groups in southern Sudan." Godfrey went on to say that as an anthropologist he was careful only to investigate and describe the Dinka culture. As an academic he tried to be neutral and not set any government policy.

Godfrey concluded his introduction by stating that he had been assigned to Akobo to do research on the Anuak people. "The Anuak speak a Nilotic language and have a traditional culture somewhat similar to that of the Dinka. That is the reason the Civil Secretary in Khartoum has asked me to make a comparison of the Anuak and the Dinka cultures."

After the introductions Dick welcomed Godfrey to Akobo and took him to the government rest house and got him settled in. Then he invited him for dinner.

That evening after a good meal featuring kori bustard, Dick and Godfrey spent time getting to know each other. Godfrey was a source of great knowledge about the Nilotic peoples. In turn Dick knew the Murle culture and language having spent a number of years in the region. Over the following days they spent many happy hours together comparing notes.

Godfrey made Akobo his base for the next two years. He frequently went out on trek by himself and spent extended time in the Anuak villages. Upon his return trips he would show up at Dick and Nora's house and Nora would always serve him a hearty meal. Godfrey was by nature a thin man and after a long trek he would look almost emaciated. Nora took it upon herself to try and fatten him up. Both Dick and Godfrey enjoyed playing chess and after dinner they would sit in silent contemplation on either side of the wooden chessboard. Godfrey usually won.

Dick was particularly interested in the Murle religion and

their belief in the God they called *Tammu*. Dick and Godfrey held long conversations on the topic of traditional religion. For Dick a strong belief in God was core to his life. Godfrey had a Roman Catholic background and was not as intense about his personal beliefs. The two men had many conversations on the topic and even though their beliefs were different, they maintained a solid friendship. Godfrey went on to write anthropological books that were considered classics. After leaving Sudan he returned to England where he taught at Oxford University for the rest of his working life.

In his role as development officer, Dick tried to introduce various economic schemes to better the lives of the local people. He came up with the idea of raising ducks. Muscovy ducks, often referred to as wattle ducks, were domesticated in various parts of the Sudan. They thrived in the heat and provided good protein in the form of eggs and meat. On the next trip to Malakal, Dick bought several pairs of ducks and brought them to Akobo. The males were large black and white birds with red wattles around their eyes. The females were half the size and the wattles were less accentuated. Dick built a pen for them in the back garden, but during the day they were free to wander around and look for food. They had an ungainly gait and waddled from side to side as they walked. Michael was intrigued by them, but also a little afraid. A big drake could easily knock him down when rushing to get food. Every night the ducks were locked in the pen to keep them away from marauding genet cats. The female ducks proved to be good layers and soon the Lyths enjoyed fresh eggs. When the females got broody, Dick made them nests out of grass. They had a good hatch and soon there were little ducklings following their mothers around the garden and splashing in the mud.

The whole project quickly got out of hand. Dick and Nora returned from a long trip to Pibor Post and upon arriving in Akobo they found themselves "up to their knees" in ducks. Dick counted over 70 of them in the flock. He hired a young Anuak man to act as "duck boy" and it became a full time job for him to care for all the ducks. Dick gave many of the ducks away to people in the neighboring villages. It worked with the Anuak since they lived in permanent villages. It did not work with the Murle since they moved constantly with their cattle and nobody was interested in carrying ducks from place to place.

Nora had heard about people in China who pickled baby ducks while they were still in the shell. She decided to try it. She took a couple of eggs that had failed to hatch and she boiled them in brine. The project utterly failed. The eggs were already rotten and they exploded, sending pieces of rotten unhatched ducklings all over Nora's dress and on the kitchen walls. The smell was terrible and it was a long time before Nora got back her appetite for duck.

During the dry season drinking water was delivered by donkey from the well to the Lyth house. In the process of unloading the donkey some water spilled on the ground and the ducks always scrambled to get a drink. The donkey did not appreciate all the ducks underfoot and one day he had enough. He lashed out with his hoof and caught a large drake full in the chest. The duck collapsed in a flurry of feathers. The "duck boy" tried to revive it, but it was already gone. That evening Dick and Nora had roasted duck for dinner. It was tasty, but they had to admit it was a bit tough.

Dick was a dog person and he kept several dogs at Akobo, offspring from his first dog Mary. One day while walking in the village Nora found a straggly back and white kitten. It was emaciated and covered with ticks. Nora cleaned it up and decided to adopt it, over the animated protests of Dick. The lonely kitten yowled all the first night keeping Dick awake. He was reinforced in his disfavor of all animals in the genus Felicidae.

But sometimes his dogs also fell out of favor. On a Sunday afternoon the family planned a picnic on an island in the Pibor River. Nora packed a hamper with food. Dick loaded up the small boat and hooked up the outboard motor. The dog Bite was eager to go with them, but there was no space so Dick locked him in the house. As they left Bite started howling, but Dick just ignored him. He put Nora and the children in the boat, pushed off from shore and started the motor. As they started upriver he saw Bite galloping along the riverbank. He had leapt through a screen window and was trying to catch up to the boat. Dick decided to outrun him. But Bite was built like a whippet and he raced along the bank until he caught up with the boat. Then he leapt into the river and started swimming as fast as he could. Again Dick chose to ignore the dog, assuming he would get tired and give up. But Bite was stubborn and kept swimming. After ten minutes his paws started going slower and slower. The boys were crying and pleading for their father to stop and rescue the dog before he drowned. Then Dick himself started worrying a crocodile would grab him. Grudgingly he turned the boat around and went back to get the dog. As he neared the exhausted animal he turned over the tiller of the motor to Nora. He moved to the front of the boat and grabbed Bite by the collar. Bite was a heavy dog and it took a big heave to get him up into the boat. In the process Dick slipped and fell under the wet muddy dog. Bite chose that moment to shake himself and he got water and mud all over Dick. Meanwhile Nora was holding a baby in one arm, stirring evaporated milk with the other hand and steering the outboard motor with her knee. She lost control of the tiller and the boat went roaring into the long grass near the shore. The tough grass got caught in the propeller and brought the motor to an abrupt stop. Bite was ecstatic to be back with his family. At this point Dick was totally fed up with the genus Canidae.

Scorpions were frequent visitors in their house. Dick worked out a technique for killing scorpions when he saw them crawling up a wall. He hit them sharply with the side of his fist, squashing them with a quick blow before they could raise their tails and sting him. One evening Dick saw a red scorpion crawling up the wall. He decided to get a pet that was less trouble than cats or dogs, so he placed a glass bottle under the arachnid and flicked it into the bottle. He named his new pet George. He fed George by catching spiders and dropping them into the bottle. George lived for many months and Dick enjoyed showing it to visitors. The red scorpion was much less trouble than the dogs, cats and ducks – but a lot less affectionate.

23

Serving God and Country

Dick took his Christian beliefs very seriously. He had originally come to Sudan to work as a missionary and he had a passion for reaching people for Christ. But he fully realized that, as District Commissioner, he was employed by the British government. He was diligent in his government responsibilities and he was careful to ensure his Christian beliefs did not impinge upon his work. However, he also firmly believed he had the right to practice his own religion. He saw no impropriety in going to church on Sunday morning. He was also convinced he had the right to preach and lead Bible studies with his employees.

Governor King was well aware of Lyth's missionary background and Christian commitment and even joked to him about it. At the same time he also realized Dick was extremely efficient and competent in his government responsibilities. He was fair, just and well liked. His knowledge of the Murle language and culture was without equal in the Political Civil Service. King knew Dick was doing a superb job in one of the toughest frontiers in all of Sudan. So the governor did not see a problem, as long as Dick only promoted Christianity during his private personal time.

But eventually King was transferred to Khartoum and a new governor was assigned to the Upper Nile. His name was Corfield and a few weeks after his installment he came on the paddle wheeler for an official inspection of Akobo. Dick led the new governor around the headquarters and then showed him the various development projects. Corfield and Dick had long conversations and it was soon obvious to the incoming governor that Dick was an excellent administrator. It was also obvious to the governor that Dick was a highly religious man. At the time he did not see it as interfering with Dick's duties as the District Commissioner. After Corfield returned to Malakal, Dick told Nora, "I am sorry to see King go, but I like the new governor and look forward to working under him."

On their vacation in 1949, Dick and Nora took a trip to visit friends in Uganda and Rwanda. They discovered there was a revival happening in that part of East Africa. It was an inspirational movement and Dick and Nora attended church meetings where they watched the spirit of God move powerfully among the local Christians. One night Dick woke up with a deep sense of conviction. He acknowledged there was sin in his life and he needed to confess it. He turned to Nora and woke her up. Then he confessed various sins to her and asked for her forgiveness. There were no flashing lights from heaven, but the confession was from the heart and it was real. He even felt guilty about his smoking. He got up, found his pipe, broke it in pieces and threw the pieces down the outhouse. He never smoked again. The next day he spoke in front of the local church, testifying and giving his confession in public. There was much rejoicing.

The following day Dick did not feel much different. In fact he was disappointed he was not immediately a new man. That night he wrote in his journal, "I have not yet had very much joy from my new start – just a feeling of resignation and duty. However, I have been faithful in performing it and perhaps joy and peace will come later." Even though Dick did not feel different, he vowed to live in closer step with God and to be more loving to others.

Upon their return to Akobo, Dick met with his missionary friends. He asked if he could speak. Quietly and humbly he confessed his sins to the missionaries. He mentioned things he had done in the war, various lies he had told and his attitude of pride. The missionaries were deeply moved. Here was the most powerful man in the district confessing his shortcomings and asking for forgiveness. It was the start of a local revival. During the following days many of the missionaries also confessed their sins. Bad relationships were dealt with and resolved. There was a new openness. One of the missionaries wrote, "The blessing had begun. Blessing followed blessing during the whole of the next seven days." Some of the missionaries initially held back because of pride, but later in the week Dick wrote in his diary, "They too came through. We were all bound together in a great oneness of love."

Dick then went on to confess his sins in front of the local Anuak church and again at the service he held for government employees. At the end of the meetings many people came forward and asked to become Christians. Others, some who had been members of the church for a long time, confessed their sins publicly. Police, clerks and messengers confessed they had stolen things and they brought these stolen items to Dick's office. Some brought back cattle and goats they had stolen. One old man even confessed to murder. Dick was in a quandary on how to deal with the murder case since there was no evidence. In the end he decided to accept the old man's confession, but not to prosecute the case.

Word traveled fast in Sudan and the British officers in Malakal soon heard there was a religious revival taking place in Akobo. More significantly it was being led by the District Commissioner. There were negative rumors and false accusations. Dick himself did not try and hide what was happening. Instead he sat down and wrote a full report to Governor Corfield. Meanwhile the revival movement continued to spread. Some of the missionaries visited another mission station at Nasir. They wired Dick and reported that "the spirit was working again" among the Nuer congregations.

During this time Dick took Nora and the children and traveled down to Pibor Post by lorry. Here Dick spoke to the small local congregation where he again confessed his sins and asked for forgiveness. The response was immediate with various government workers becoming Christians and making things right. By the time Dick needed to return to Akobo it had rained and the road was closed. Dick and Nora decided to return to

Akobo in the small metal boat. They had hardly gotten started when the propeller broke off the outboard motor. Dick did not carry a spare so they were stranded. There were only two paddles in the boat so Dick and his men took turns rowing. Then one of the paddles snapped in half. For the rest of the trip they took turns rowing with the single paddle. The trip to Akobo took five long days. The children held up remarkably well and Dick and Nora told them endless stories to keep them occupied. Dick recalled in his diary that Nora was "magnificent."

Upon arriving in Akobo, Dick received an urgent message from Governor Corfield. It demanded that Dick give more detail on the religious revival and his involvement in it. Dick wrote back in great length, giving a balanced response. The governor responded with a further set of questions.

From the tone of the questions Dick realized the governor was very concerned. He decided he had better report in person. Dick and the family boarded the medical steamer, *Lady Baker*, and sailed to Malakal. They discovered the governor was away in Khartoum, but they were invited to stay in the governor's house and await his return. Corfield had left a detailed letter for Dick and he sat down and read it carefully. The letter called into question Dick's impartiality in the treatment of Christians. It suggested Dick was in an intolerable position as magistrate, especially when confessions were made under religious pressure. It also pointed out District Commissioners must not propagate any one religious view. They must be neutral. There had to be a distinct separation of church and state. It went on to state Dick could become a major embarrassment to the British government. The northern Arabs were being trained to take over the entire government of the Sudan. These Arabs were passionate Muslims. A report of this Christian revival in the Arabic press would seriously harm the neutrality of the British government.

After reading the letter Dick penned his response, carefully answering all the allegations. His response covered several pages of closely written script. In conclusion he pointed out, "I have not neglected my official duties in any way. However, my religious views are personal and I have a right to my beliefs."

Then Dick relaxed and waited. He played squash with Nora and took rides along the Sobat River, watching the birds nesting in the tall doleib palms. When Corfield finally returned from Khartoum they had a serious conversation. Corfield was barely civil and obviously very worried. In an accusatory tone he stated, "You have compromised your position as District Commissioner."

But Dick refused to yield even an inch. "I am a competent District Commissioner! At the same time I have a right to propagate my Christian beliefs."

The governor went on to demand Dick stop speaking in churches and holding Bible studies. Dick shook his head emphatically and stated, "I will not stop! If I have to choose between serving God or the British government, I choose to serve God. If it means losing my position as District Commissioner – so be it."

Corfield realized Dick was adamant and would not capitulate. But he was not willing to dismiss Dick from government service without receiving direct orders from a higher authority. So rather than terminating Dick on the spot, he wrote a detailed report and sent it by diplomatic bag to the top government official in

Khartoum: the Civil Secretary. In order to be fair he allowed Dick to insert his own letter in which he defended his position.

That night Dick wrote in his diary, "It looks as if our days in government service are numbered." In a following entry he remarked that he and Nora had "great confidence in the fundamental rightness of all we have said and done and regret nothing."

They boarded the paddle wheeler *Tamai* and went back to Akobo. During the trip Dick wrote, "Nora and I have great assurance and peace in this situation." Upon arriving at Akobo they met with the missionaries who assured them the revival was still going on. Dick and Nora went into a waiting mode, but surprisingly were not much concerned about their future. Dick did consider the option of moving across the border into Ethiopia and working with the American missionaries on their new mission station. Nora looked around her house and wondered what to take and what to leave. Dick wrote in his diary, "Not that we have been worried about the future. We seem to know a transcendental peace in these days and feel that we shall be here as long as the Lord wants us to be."

A few weeks later Governor Corfield arrived in Akobo for an official visit. He also wanted to see both Pibor Post and Boma. He reported to Dick with a wry smile on his face. The Civil Secretary in Khartoum had responded in Dick's favor. There was to be no immediate transfer or sack. But Corfield did say, "For my sake, tone it down a little."

Dick took Governor Corfield out on tour. He was enthralled by the wild terrain and massive migrations of wild animals. After watching Dick at work with the Murle chiefs he was thoroughly convinced Dick was doing an excellent job administering the people of the region. He was ultimately pleased Dick could continue in his role as District Commissioner.

A few weeks later Dick received a letter from a Murle chief. It was addressed to "The Commissionary at Akobo." The chief had coined a new word and it was entirely accurate. Dick had ably combined the roles of Commissioner and Missionary. The term spread and soon even the British officials in Malakal were referring to Dick affectionately as "The Commissionary."

24

End of an Era

For the next four years Dick and Nora and their children continued to live at Akobo and frequently commuted to their favorite spot: Pibor Post. Dick held the position of District Commissioner until 1954. But times were changing across Africa. The British Empire was beginning to crumble and it eventually became obvious the people in the colonized countries had the right to be free and to run their own affairs. It was decided Sudan would be one of the first countries in Africa to get its freedom. The date was set for 1955. Dick's primary job for the final months was to turn over the administration of his district. Under the terms of the incoming government all parts of the Political Service were to be Sudanized – turned over to Sudanese administrators.

As the date drew near, it was obvious the next government would be made up primarily of Arabs from the north. They made up the majority of people in the country. Without doubt they would easily win the elections. The African people in the south were not happy at the prospect of being put under the authority of the Moslem northerners. When the Murle realized Dick was really going to leave, they stopped cooperating with his administration. Murle in the remote areas stopped paying the annual tribute in cattle. Raids started up again between the ethnic groups. The roads were allowed to be overgrown. Lastly the Murle chiefs stopped showing up to adjudicate court cases. Dick had to do patrols to various locations to reinforce his authority and to make a firm statement. The British government was still in control and the incoming Arab government would be in control when their time came. Gradually Dick got the district operating efficiently again.

As the day of independence neared, Dick handed over the various parts of his administration to incoming northern officials. He remarked in his diary that the new men were well qualified for their new roles. They were placed in charge of the administration, the police, the military, the jail and the justice system.

Leaving the district was a sad business for Dick and Nora. It was fairly abrupt. Once the new administrators were installed and functioning, there was no reason to stay. Dick and Nora packed up the personal belongings they wanted to take with them. These were put into several large crates and loaded on to the steamer headed for Malakal. They auctioned the things they did not want to take. The Arab merchants showed up in large numbers and they walked around the Lyth's house checking out the merchandise. Dick was not happy with them and wrote in his diary, "They acted like vultures squabbling over a bloody carcass."

The auctioneer sold every thing in the house within a few minutes. When Dick saw his precious gramophone being carried out of the house he knew the end had come. It was time to leave.

On the steamer to Malakal, Dick and Nora sat in canvas deck chairs and watched the children hanging over the rails. They talked about the past and the future. Their contract was ended and Dick needed to find a job. For fifteen years he had experienced a marvelous time in Sudan and he left knowing he had served ably: honoring both God and Country. Dick thought back over the past years. He had walked a difficult line, introducing the tribal people to the modern world and at the same time allowing them to get on with their traditional lives. Could he have done more to prepare the tribal people for the future? Perhaps. But he had done his best. The work he had done in his role as District Commissioner was largely beneficial. More importantly, the people under his administration experienced the only peace they had ever known.

It has been 59 years since Dick Lyth left Pibor District, but he is still remembered fondly by the Murle people as Kemerbong - The Red Pelican that brought them peace.

- The Commissionary

Postscript

Dick had always been interested in working with the soil and thought he would enjoy farming as a new career. While in Akobo he had planted a large garden and he regularly read magazines about animal husbandry. Now was his opportunity. After arriving back in England he applied for a job as a farm manager. But he quickly found out farming was boring. The daily ritual of milking cows, counting sheep, feeding pigs and mucking out pens quickly became mundane, especially when he compared it with his former role of District Commissioner. The cold gloomy weather in England did not help. His mind kept harkening back to the warmth and open spaces of Sudan. His body also protested against the cold weather and he suffered from severe arthritis.

Dick also wrestled with God. He had originally gone to Sudan as a missionary and he still felt the call to serve on the great continent of Africa. But he discovered farming was a full time job, leaving no time for Christian work. After a few months he talked to Nora about his disillusionment. She advised him to follow his heart. Dick called on the Bishop of Carlisle and talked to him about his dilemma. The Bishop was a wise man and he listened carefully to Dick as he poured out his heart. At the end of the discussion he advised Dick to take some college courses, be ordained and then reapply as a C.M.S. missionary to Africa.

Dick stopped working at the farm and went back to college. Upon finishing the course work, he filled out applications for the Church Missionary Society. He and Nora were quickly accepted. Dick continued to struggle with some health issues, but eventually these were dealt with and they were cleared to return to Africa. They were assigned to work in southern Uganda, close to the location where Nora had grown up. Coming back to Africa was like coming home. Dick flourished in his role as missionary and after a short time he was elevated to the position of Bishop of Kigezi, a post he held for a number of years. One of the many young men he mentored was named Festo Kivengere. Festo went on to become a noted evangelist, often referred to as the Billy Graham of Africa. Dick was well regarded by everyone in the region. Even Idi Amin, the notorious dictator, stated that the only person he trusted to stand behind him at ceremonies was Bishop Lyth.

After a long successful career in Uganda, Dick and Nora retired to England. They bought a lovely cottage in Haywards Heath in Sussex where Dick and Nora took daily walks to the nearby pond to watch the ducks and swans. Their home was frequented with visitors from Africa. Nora would make tea and Dick would pull out the photo albums and regale his guests with tales about the old days in Sudan. But Dick could not really retire. In Sussex he entered his third and final career as a country parson. It was a position he held until his death in February of 2005.

Author's Notes

I first heard of Kemerbong when I visited the Boma Plateau in 1976. The highland Murle and the Kichepo were fighting and there was serious unrest in the area. However, both sides said they would stop fighting immediately if Kemerbong came back. They still remembered the peace ceremony that had taken place in the 1940s with Kemerbong accepting the role of peacemaker.

I later discovered Kemerbong was an Englishman named Dick Lyth and he and his wife Nora were still alive, retired in Sussex, England. I arranged a visit. During that and subsequent visits, we spent many happy hours talking about life in Sudan and comparing notes about the Murle culture. Dick and Nora dug out their photo albums and the old days in Sudan came back to life in black and white. They even showed us some photos of the guesthouse designed by Nora. My wife, Barb, pointed out we had actually spent a number of months living in that very same guesthouse when we first lived at Pibor Post. The pipe trusses that Nora designed still had the strength to hold up the heavy thatch roof over our heads.

On my final visit to Sussex Dick gave me a manuscript he had written in 1946 about Lado, the first Murle Christian. I later rewrote the manuscript into the book titled *Chasing the Rain*. The book contains many of Dick's unique insights into traditional Murle culture.

After Dick's death in 2005, his son Michael kindly let me read his father's diaries. There were more than 1800 pages of notes written in his careful hand. There were of course gaps, especially during the war years, but these diaries provided valuable insights into his personal life and beliefs. In writing this book I have tried to be true to the facts. The majority of the characters are real and most of the events actually took place. Only rarely have I added material to fill gaps in the narrative. Occasionally I have used dialogue to make the characters come alive. Overall I have done my best to make the book as historically accurate as possible.

Dick lived an epic life. More importantly he lived a life dedicated to God. I was privileged to know him.

Final Footnote

The government anthropologist Godfrey Leinhardt also reentered the picture. I (Jon Arensen) completed my doctorate in Social Anthropology at Oxford University in 1991. Godfrey Leinhardt, the famous anthropologist, came out of retirement to be my examiner. Fortunately he approved of my thesis on the Murle and gave me a passing mark.

Obligatory camel ride in Egypt.

Paddle-wheel steamer arriving in Juba.

Anglican cathedral in Yambio.

Azande medicine men.

Lotuxo recruit – before training.

After training.

Learning to shoot a rifle.

Company on parade – Lyth's 120 men ready for war.

Towath – Volcanic spire on Boma plateau.

Dick's dogs – Mary and Bite.

Cape Buffalo – feeding the troops.

Murle men – Boma plateau.

Dick's house on Boma.

Fireplace in Dick's house.

Policemen at Towath Post.

Murle warriors.

Chief Keli at Maruwa Hills.

Kemerbong – the white ox sacrificed to give Dick his Murle name.

Kichepo women wearing lip plugs.

Murle men wearing elaborate mud headdresses.

Dick and Nora – married after six years of separation.

House in Akobo – built on stilts to stay above annual floods.

Dick and Nora with baby Michael on steps of Akobo house.

Michael learning to ride

Pipe scaffolding designed by Nora for guest house at Pibor.

Completed guest house – Dick and Nora's favorite retreat.

On the track to Boma.

Meeting of colonial officials at Boma.

Pibor cavalry – showing the flag.

Dick Lyth – the Comissionary.

Bibliography

Arensen, Jonathan, *Mice Are Men*, Summer Institute of Linguistics, Dallas, 1992

Austin, H. H., *Among Swamps and Giants in Equatorial Africa*, C. Arthur Pearson Limited, London, 1902

Bell, WDM, *Karamojo Safari*, Harcourt Brace and Co, NY, 1949

Boustead, Colonel Sir Hugh, *The Wind of Morning*, Craven Street Books. Fresno, California, 2006

Darley, Major Henry, *Slaves and Ivory*, Witherby, London, 1926

Henderson, K.D.D., *Set Under Authority*, Castle Press Ltd, Somerset, Great Britain, 1987

Lyth, Richard, *Personal Diaries*, 1939-1954 (Private Collection – 1800 pages)

Lyth, Richard, *Personal Communication* 1998, Taped – 60 pages typed

Orbelar, John, *Tales of the Sudan Defence Force*, Vol 1 and 2, Newport, Isle of Wight, Crossprint, 1981

Parr, Peter, *Tribal Origins*, Old Africa Books, Box 65 Kijabe, Kenya, 2011

Salvadori, Cynthia, *Slaves and Ivory Continued*, Shama Books, Addis Ababa, 2010

Swart, Morrell, *The Call of Africa*, Eerdmans Publishing Co. Grand Rapids. Mich. 1998

CPSIA information can be obtained at www.ICGtesting.com
Printed in the USA
BVOW02s0443280314

349055BV00002B/22/P